CURRICULAR CONVERSATIONS

Themes in Multilingual and Monolingual Classrooms

Stephen B. Kucer

• • • • • • • • • •

Cecilia Silva

• • • • • • • • • •

Esther L. Delgado-Larocco

• • • • • • • • • •

Stenhouse Publishers
York, Maine

Stenhouse Publishers, 226 York Street, York, Maine 03909

Library of Congress Cataloging-in-Publication Data

Kucer, Stephen B., 1950–
    Curricular conversations : themes in multilingual and monolingual classrooms /
  Stephen B. Kucer, Cecilia Silva, Esther L. Delgado-Larocco.
      p.   cm.
    Includes bibliographical references.
    ISBN 1-57110-016-4 (alk. paper)
    1. Interdisciplinary approach in education—United States. 2. Education, Bilingual—United
States. 3. Language arts (Elementary)—United States. 4. Language experience approach in
education—United States. I. Silva, Cecilia. II. Delgado-Larocco, Esther L. III. Title.
LB1570.K77 1995
372. 19—dc20   94-14599
                                                    CIP

Cover and interior design by Ron Kosciak, *Dragonfly Design*

Cover illustration by Sebastian Gallese

Typeset by TNT

Manufactured in the United States of America on acid-free paper

02 01 00 8 7 6 5 4 3 2

To our students
Who provided us with opportunities to
Discuss, reflect, and revise our
Beliefs about thematic teaching and learning

Contents

Acknowledgments

We would like to acknowledge the works of James A. Banks on multicultural education and Hilda Taba on social science education for their influence on our beliefs about curriculum and instruction.

We are grateful to the National Council of Teachers Research Foundation and the University of Southern California for funding our exploration of integrated curriculum in the classroom. We also appreciate the support of Joanne Spring and Ken Petrucelli, principals at the schools where many of the ideas presented in this book first came to light. Likewise we value the contributions made by teachers who have invited us into their classrooms and joined us in conversations about instruction.

We thank Clare Silva for reading and responding to early drafts of this manuscript. And finally, we appreciate our families, who have shared their time with this manuscript over the past years.

1

Themes?
So What's New?

• • • • • • • • • • •

Thematic Teaching as a Response to the Segmented School

We begin with two stories from real life that we believe suggest the need to reconceptualize the teaching and learning of literacy in elementary schools.

The first takes place in a third-grade bilingual classroom. It is the second month of school, and the students are working with the theme "Getting to Know About You, Me, and Others/*Tú, Yo y Otros.*" The teacher has selected this particular topic early in the school year because she wants the students to learn about and celebrate their differences and similarities. So far, the students have read and discussed a number of trade books on the topic, written and published stories and poems, and viewed and listened to videotapes, filmstrips, and records linked to this theme. But José Antonio, one of the most capable students in the class, is puzzled. He approaches the teacher one morning and asks, "Ms. Silva, it's already October. When are we going to start doing reading in here?"

The setting of our second story is a university reading and writing methods course. The class members are learning about thematic teaching and constructing a thematic curriculum they will use when they student-teach. They have gathered materials, generated instructional activities to promote the development of literacy and conceptual knowledge, and arranged the activities into a coherent curriculum. As the class shifts its attention to evaluation and assessment, one student inquires, "Dr. Kucer, when are we going to learn how to teach reading in here?"

These very similar questions by two very different students reveal a great deal about how literacy instruction and learning are conceptualized and experienced in school settings. Throughout this century, the elementary school curriculum has become progressively segmented and isolated. This segmentation and this isola-

1

Communication Systems: Skill Based				Fields of Study: Fact Based		
Literacy	Mathematics	Art	Music	Literature	Social Science	Science
|	|	|	|	|	|	|
skill	skill	skill	skill	fact	fact	fact
|	|	|	|	|	|	|
skill	skill	skill	skill	fact	fact	fact
|	|	|	|	|	|	|
skill	skill	skill	skill	fact	fact	fact
|	|	|	|	|	|	|
etc.	etc.	etc.	etc.	etc.	etc.	etc.

TABLE 1.1 A traditional view of the curriculum.

tion have had a direct effect on various school "constituents." As illustrated in Table 1.1, the curriculum—literacy instruction in particular—has been especially impacted. Breaking written language into bits and pieces divorced from meaning and scoping and sequencing reading skills are common occurrences in elementary classrooms. Literacy as a tool for generating knowledge and interacting with the world is often ignored. The disciplines of science, social science, and literature have not fared much better. All too often, these subjects receive minimal attention, especially in the lower grades, as the school seeks to improve student literacy and mathematical test scores. And when subject area knowledge is addressed, the emphasis is often on isolated facts and figures. In teaching both literacy and the disciplines, the assumption appears to be that processes and knowledge can and should be divided into discrete elements, so as to better promote student learning. As the student responses above make clear, attempts to build and implement curriculums based on alternate assumptions are frequently viewed as violations of "the way things are supposed to be."

But curriculum is not the only school constituent affected by practices that lead to segmentation and isolation; students feel the effects as well. Under the guise of attempting to meet the "instructional needs of all children," students are isolated by ability both inside and outside the classroom. Reading and mathematics ability groups and remedial programs that remove students from the classroom for defined periods of time are commonplace. Students deemed "gifted and talented" receive outside instruction, as do students with "special needs," who typically move back and forth between resource and mainstreamed classrooms. Students whose home language is other than English are equally vulnerable. At best, second language learners are placed in bilingual classrooms in which the primary and second language curriculums rarely intersect. More often, these learners experience traditional, pull-out English as a second language (ESL) programs.

The classroom teacher is also affected by these segmentation and isolation practices. With responsibility for the curriculum increasingly being appropriated by publishers and boards of education, "teachers as decision makers" have been usurped by "teacherproof materials" and faith in teachers' expertise has diminished. Implementing curriculum involves little more than following the paint-by-number lesson plans in teacher guides. Teachers are expected merely to deliver a predesigned, standardized curriculum that can be easily managed and implemented. Perhaps the most significant responsibility still left in the hands of the teacher is to decide which extension, enrichment, or supplemental activities to use with a particular set of lessons.

Although well intentioned, segmentation and isolation have had disappointing repercussions. Teachers feel disempowered by a curriculum that dictates what is to be taught when, and students experience confusion as they jump from skill to skill, from fact to fact, and from room to room. Lost is literacy as a powerful cultural tool for mediation and learning. By assuming that students must first master the "basic skills" before encountering more meaningful materials and activities, educators deny many students equal access to higher levels of knowledge, particularly students who do not reflect the cultural, linguistic, economic, or intellectual norms. These students frequently receive more than their fair share of drills on low-level skills and facts, even as their intellectual and linguistic development continues to lag behind.

One response to the failure of schools to adequately address the needs of all students has been to label those students experiencing difficulty with the established curriculum as being "at risk" and to search for more effective ways to implement the existing curriculum. Unfortunately, this many times only intensifies the segmentation and isolation that already characterize the school day. In any case, this response fails to recognize that the beliefs underlying the curriculum are a contributing factor to school failure.

A second response to the failure of the established curriculum has been to try to integrate the curriculum by using thematic units. The notion of curricular integration is not new; it has been a counterforce to the segmented curriculum since at least the time of John Dewey. However, many thematic curricular frameworks retain the segmented curriculum's teaching and learning assumptions. For example, in a first-grade classroom we visited recently, the students were in the middle of a thematic unit on bears. As part of the unit, students learned ten new spelling words a week related to bears, and the teacher used the traditional pretest-on-Monday-posttest-on-Friday instructional format. Addition and subtraction were taught by having students manipulate Gummy Bears. And students demonstrated reading comprehension by answering factual questions after reading such stories as *Brown Bear, Brown Bear, What Do You See?* (Martin 1970) and *Ira Sleeps Over* (Waber 1972). The unit topic was being used as a "cover" for the real curriculum, in which students used literacy and mathematics in very traditional ways.

This is not the only way in which thematic units can maintain the status quo. Although various materials are gathered and myriad activities are developed that relate to the topic being considered, many thematic units fail to connect the materials and activities on a deeper, more conceptual level. *Ira Sleeps Over*, for instance, is not so much about bears as it is about fear of the unknown and how a young boy uses a stuffed animal to overcome or cope with his fears. Although the stuffed animal happens to be a teddy bear, the author might have substituted any number of animals and the basic story line would have remained the same. (In fact, as the cartoon character Linus has demonstrated, a stuffed animal is not required: a blanket will do just as well.) Similarly, using Gummy Bears to add and subtract teaches the students nothing about bears.

We first noticed this lack of conceptual connection between topic, materials, and activities when we were guiding a third-grade class of bilingual immigrant students through the theme "Getting to Know About Growing and Using Plants and Seeds/*Cultivando y Utilizando Plantas y Semillas.*" We began by gathering materials and generating activities related to the topic. We carefully selected a wide variety of books (in Spanish and in English, narratives as well as exposition) and developed numerous guided discoveries and hands-on activities.

Over the course of several weeks, we began to feel uncomfortable but were unable to identify the source of our discomfort. One day, when the students were creating mosaics out of various seeds and writing stories to accompany the Mercer Mayer wordless picture book *Ah-Choo* (1976), we suddenly realized the problem: the materials and activities were linked to one another only because they involved plants and seeds. In making their seed mosaics, the students did use and expand their artistic abilities, but they learned little of significance about the theme. In writing their stories to accompany the pictures in *Ah-Choo*, the students did use and expand their writing abilities but most likely did not learn anything about plants. At best, since a central character in the book is allergic to flowers, the students may have learned that some people sneeze when they smell flowers.

The lack of meaningful connections within many thematic units was illustrated to us most recently by one of our university students. This student had developed thematic activities for *Little House on the Prairie* (Wilder 1953), which he used while he was student-teaching. A major activity was building a rather large replica of the house in which the Ingalls family lived. Over a five-week period, various students helped construct the house in the school library, and their work was impressive. However, during a debriefing at the end of the semester, the student teacher voiced his concern that the activity probably hadn't helped students understand the significant issues in the book.

Although we support efforts to integrate the curriculum and view thematic units as a primary vehicle for doing so, we have serious reservations about the way thematic curriculums are currently being developed. Assumptions from the traditional curriculum are too often simply appropriated and repackaged within a thematic framework. Instead, our curriculums must be grounded on a radically different set of assumptions.

• • • • • • • • • • •

Rethinking Themes

We're in a third-grade bilingual (Spanish and English) classroom in a large urban school. The students are exploring a theme entitled "Getting to Understand Fears/*Entendiendo Nuestros Temores*." The students have selected the topic because of fears unleashed by a recent earthquake. The teacher and students have gathered materials dealing with how people cope with their fears. Among the materials is a text set (a group of books centered on the same issue) that includes *Ira Sleeps Over* (Waber 1972), *Will You Come Back for Me?* (Tompert 1988), *There's Something in My Attic* (Mayer 1988), *What's Under My Bed?* (Stevenson 1983), *El Cururía* (Uribe and Krahn 1982), *Libby's New Glasses* (Tusa 1984), and *There's a Nightmare in My Closet/Hay Una Pesadilla en Mi Armario* (Mayer 1968).

Before introducing the books, the teacher asks the students, in groups of three, to list the things that frighten them. The groups share these fears with the whole class as the teacher lists them on a large piece of chart paper. Each student then selects a fear from the chart and draws a picture of how the fear might look if it could be seen. The students share these pictures in small groups, guessing the fear that each picture represents. Eventually, these pictures, appropriately identified, are displayed on a bulletin board labeled Looking at Our Fears.

The following day, the teacher reads *Sometimes I'm Afraid* (Tester 1979) aloud. As she reads, the students pay attention to the fears that are discussed and to how the young child in the story copes with them. After the reading, these fears and responses are listed on the board and compared with the fears the students have illustrated. At this point, the teacher introduces the text set. The students select a book to read, either independently or in "friendship groups" that they form on their own. As they read the books, they identify the fear and coping strategy used by the main character. Then the class reassembles to discuss all the fears and coping strategies. The teacher adds these fears and strategies to the chart previously developed based on *Sometimes I'm Afraid*. The students then take the fears they have previously identified and illustrated and draw a possible coping strategy they can use the next time they experience the fear.

The above example demonstrates several characteristics we believe are critical to effective thematic units. First, *Ira Sleeps Over* (Waber 1972) has a much more legitimate place here than it did in the bear unit. It is one of a group of books that center on exploring and coping with frightening things. Ira uses a teddy bear to help him deal with his fear of spending a night away from his family, one of many fears and many responses addressed in the books.

Second, the activities surrounding the reading of the books help the students search for common ideas and issues. The processes of reading, writing, drawing, comparing, and contrasting all promote a deeper understanding of the generalizable knowledge that most of us are fearful of something, that there are various ways in which we can cope with our fears, and that we may fear the unknown or what we do not understand. In contrast to the bear unit, the literacy, artistic, and thinking processes here are critical to the "coming to know" being promoted within the unit. And rather than being taught and used in isolation, these communication and thinking processes are embedded in the content of the theme.

Another significant difference between the bear unit or other more traditional thematic curriculums and the "Getting to Understand Fears/*Entendiendo Nuestros Temores*" theme is that it uses materials that vary in language (English and Spanish), in difficulty, and in perspective. Because the theme focuses on developing concepts and generalizable knowledge, no one experience is privileged over the others. Given this variety in the curriculum, students of diverse backgrounds and abilities are not barred from participation simply because a particular book, such as *Ira,* is too difficult for them to read or is not in their primary language.

Figure 1.1 shows the framework we use to think about thematic teaching and learning and captures some of the key characteristics of the way themes play out in the classroom. At the center of any unit is a core of potential generalizations and concepts. This is not to say that the teacher must decide all generalizations and concepts before developing the unit or even that all students must come to understand the same set of generalizations and concepts. Rather, what is critical is the curriculum's *intention* to move the students beyond merely acquiring topical facts and figures to investigating generalizable and conceptual knowledge.

It is through the investigation of the topic, and the resulting development of generalizations and concepts, that integration occurs within the curriculum. Students employ the various communication systems—art, music, language, mathematics, movement—to discover, learn about, and explore thematic generalizations and concepts. These communication systems engage the mind in the thinking processes involved in the various disciplines—literature, social science, science. Students use such processes as integrating and synthesizing, observing and hypothesizing, estimating, comparing and contrasting, and interpreting as they make their inquiries. Using the communication systems in conjunction with the thinking processes places the focus firmly on the thematic information and knowledge that is being generated, analyzed, and manipulated.

In contrast to the traditional curriculum depicted in Table 1.1, with its emphasis on isolated skills and facts related to separate communication systems and fields of study, this curricular framework is grounded on the symbiotic relationship

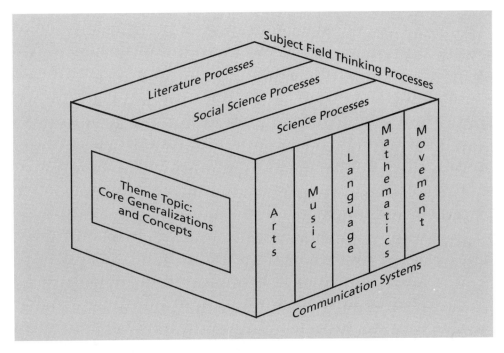

FIGURE 1.1 An integrated view of the curriculum.

between and among processes, ways of knowing, and knowledge. As illustrated in Figure 1.2, many generalizations and related concepts can potentially emerge from any thematic unit. Generalizations and concepts emerge as students explore activities using various literary, scientific, and social science materials. Similarly, these materials are explored through all the thinking processes and communication systems. At no time do students count Gummy Bears simply for the sake of learning to count. Rather, thinking processes and communication systems promote further understanding of the content at hand.

Conceptual and generalizable knowledge is developed and refined throughout the theme as students recycle and revisit key ideas and meanings in different contexts using different materials in different activities. No one experience can result in a well-formed concept or generalization; the experiences must be numerous and ongoing. Additionally, concepts and generalizations are dynamic, not static. For all of us, children and adults, knowledge evolves over time; the notion of "mastering" a concept or generalization makes little sense. In our approach to thematic units, generalizations and concepts continue to grow and change as long as the students are experiencing activities within the theme; therefore, all generalizations and concepts need not be determined before the materials and activities are selected. The arrows in Figure 1.2 show the interaction between and among generalizations, concepts, materials, activities, and processes/systems. Although the thematic topic and curriculum may lead naturally to certain generalizations

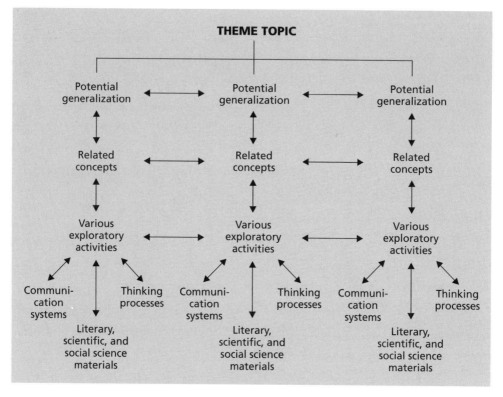

FIGURE 1.2 The interrelationship among theme topic, generalizations, concepts, activities, materials, thinking processes, and communication systems.

and concepts, the curriculum is always open to a range of ideas and meanings. This view contrasts with the traditional curriculum, which recycles predetermined skills and facts through practice ⟶ master ⟶ maintain instruction.

We believe the power of this framework is that it allows everyone to enter into meaningful and significant curricular conversations, regardless of intellectual ability or linguistic facility. All students engage in activities that allow them to make generalizations and discover concepts. This does not mean that students have *identical* experiences or encounter *identical* materials and activities. Rather, students interact with materials and activities that are appropriate to their abilities and language proficiency but that nevertheless prompt them to develop generalizations and concepts. Once again, this framework stands in opposition to the more traditional curriculum, which frequently stratifies the distribution of ideas and knowledge in the classroom in a manner similar to the social and economic stratification within the broader society. That is, the "rich get richer and the poor get poorer."

We do not deny the diversity in the intellectual and linguistic abilities of the students whom we teach. However, diversity is a wonderful part of the human condition and should not be a barrier to a more equitable distribution of knowledge. The curricular framework we propose helps ensure that diverse student populations are brought into common or shared curricular conversations, conversations that celebrate rather than deny or ignore student diversity and at the same time acknowledge the real differences that students bring to the instructional setting.

• • • • • • • • • • •

About Us and This Book

For the last twenty years, the three of us have been actively involved in thematic teaching and learning within a variety of instructional settings and with a variety of students. As elementary classroom teachers, we have used themes with primary and intermediate students, in urban, suburban, and rural environments, and with bilingual and monolingual students. As university faculty members, we have worked closely with teacher education and graduate students in developing thematic curriculums. As conference presenters and consultants, we have collaborated with classroom teachers and administrators in creating thematic curriculums. These experiences have given us the opportunity to develop our ideas about thematic curriculums more fully and, more important, the opportunity to discuss, reflect, and revise these beliefs.

In these settings, we have focused not only on generating and implementing units, but also on developing a conceptual framework for thematic teaching and learning. In developing this framework, we have drawn from relevant literacy, teaching, and curricular research. However, the time we've spent in classrooms in which teachers and students have been engaged in thematic teaching and learning has prompted our most critical insights. These teachers and students have pushed us beyond traditional curricular assumptions into uncharted waters.

The examples in this book are primarily from two classrooms. The first is an urban bilingual third grade. In a semesterlong research project funded by a University of Southern California Faculty Grant, we focused on various ways in which the curriculum might be integrated and the effects this integration had on the students. The second classroom comprises a different group of third-grade bilingual students in a different school but in the same urban setting. In a yearlong collaborative research project funded by the National Council of Teachers Research Foundation and a second University of Southern California Faculty Grant, we took what we had learned in the earlier setting and explored it further.

The primary audience for this book are classroom teachers working with diverse students in elementary settings and preservice teacher education students. Although we address a number of forms of diversity—language, culture, ability, gender—we highlight the second language learner, not only because of our own experiences with these students, but also because many teachers are desperately seeking information on how they can best work with multilingual populations. In addition, based on our work in various school settings, we know that far too often the second language learner does not experience a curriculum that is based on meaning making or receive instruction that mediates holistic learning. This is not to imply that curricular and instructional strategies that are effective with linguistically and culturally diverse students are not relevant to monolingual students. On the contrary, most curricular and instructional strategies can be used with many types of students.

Although we envision that this book will be used in teacher education programs, we also hope that it can "stand alone," that teachers can use it in their classrooms independently. With this dual audience in mind, we have avoided either a solely theoretical or a solely "how to" discussion. Unlike many other books on thematic teaching, this one does not give the teacher a series of developed themes and accompanying activities. Rather, it offers a framework, along with strategies and techniques, for developing a different kind of thematic curriculum. Supplementing the framework, strategies, and techniques are examples of how these themes play out in the real life of the classroom. Teachers are "theoreticians and researchers in action" as they go about developing, implementing, and evaluating their curriculums, and theoretical ideas are most powerful when they are contextualized in the classroom. Therefore, we have attempted a meaningful merger of theory and practice.

Along with the challenge of merging theory and practice, we faced the problem of discussing the dynamic and interactive nature of curriculum development in a linear way. Our experiences tell us that curriculum development is similar to the writing process, involving tentative plans, false starts, changes in midstream, feedback, revisions, and the like. However, because language is linear, we have been forced to structure this book that way. Throughout, however, we offer reminders of the interactive nature of curriculum development and include classroom examples that demonstrate the interactive nature of thematic teaching and learning.

The rest of the book is set up as follows: Chapter 2 is an overview of thematic teaching in a bilingual third-grade classroom in a large urban area. This overview both grounds and frames Chapter 3, which identifies potential concepts and generalizations, and Chapter 4, which addresses the selection of thematic topics and materials. The discussion in Chapter 5 of the characteristics of classroom activities that are part of the thematic curriculum generates the thinking and learning events detailed in Chapter 6. (Readers with a firm grasp of whole language and process-oriented theory may wish to skip Chapter 5 and go directly to Chapter 6.) Chapter 7 discusses how activities are to be selected and ordered within a thematic curriculum, and Chapter 8 addresses the evaluation of thinking and learning.

Each chapter within this sequence begins with a theoretical orientation that frames the curricular discussion that follows. Most chapters conclude with "a look back," a summary of all curricular activities presented thus far. Sandwiched between each chapter's introductory overview and concluding look back are various hands-on procedures for developing particular dimensions of thematic units.

In the back of the book, a bibliography itemizes twenty-nine thematic topics, points out possible generalizations and concepts to guide the exploration of each topic, and lists materials that would support such explorations. The appendix contains a number of helpful blank forms.

In the book we use the plural *we* when discussing our own experiences with thematic teaching and learning. Although some of these experiences were unique to a particular author and others were shared by two or all of us, to identify each experience that way would be cumbersome. More important, because we have collaborated in so many different settings for so many years, we are often unsure who was present for a particular experience and who was not. In other words, our thinking is very much a synthesis of our experiences and ideas, and we share them in that light.

Thematic Teaching in the Life of the Classroom

Risk Taking, Reflection, and Collaboration

How might thematic teaching look in the life of the classroom? We begin with three critical conditions to establishing a climate conducive to the kind of learning experiences we are promoting. We discuss common implementation practices developed throughout one academic year in a third-grade bilingual classroom. We conclude with a description of other, nonthematic activities that are also important in providing students with a wide range of experiences that support literacy development.

The theoretical framework for thematic teaching presented by Short and Burke (1991) postulates three conditions that support the kinds of educational experiences and inquiries we envision occurring within our community of learners: risk taking, reflection, and collaboration.

Risk taking has to do with the learner's willingness to explore learning even as he or she knows that mistakes are natural characteristics of the learning process. Reactions to mistakes involving punishment, ridicule, or deprivations inhibit the learner's ability to take risks. Moving away from a classroom where teachers not only possess but expect the right answers, we propose a classroom that supports learners—teachers as well as students—as they explore a variety of issues, responses, and ambiguities.

Providing opportunities for risk taking is important for monolingual students, but risk taking becomes even more significant in classrooms with second language learners. Learning a second language, like developing a first language, is a social process in which students construct their own hypotheses of how language functions (Freeman & Freeman 1992; McKeon 1994; Tabors & Snow 1994). These

12

hypotheses are developed from the language students hear as they interact with adults or their more capable peers. Learning environments where mistakes are viewed as a natural part of the process support second language learners in their attempts to test new hypotheses. Freed from constantly monitoring pronunciation or grammar, second language learners are more likely to attempt new communication strategies.

Reflection is the process by which learners can understand how others view the world and by which these views can be compared to the learners' own perspectives. Furthermore, reflection supports learners in risk taking; they become aware of the reasons for taking risks as they work toward solving a problem or arriving at a conclusion. Reflection allows individual learners within a community to understand that there are usually a number of logical responses to any set of questions.

Reflection is fundamental in developing the multicultural perspectives required in today's multilingual classrooms. Learning environments founded on the premise that learners have multiple perspectives validate both the monolingual and the second language learner. Furthermore, knowing that there are no right answers—and that no one culture is the right culture—students can move to identify the points at which multiple perspectives are at odds with each other, enabling them to address conflict.

Short and Burke define collaboration in terms of the formal patterns of relationships that are established in a community of learners. To develop a sense of collaboration, the learner must recognize that the knowledge created by the group surpasses the immediate abilities of any individual member. A commitment to collaborative effort within the learning community extends beyond a specific goal or objective and fosters a learning style used successfully outside school. In addition, collaboration requires that the learning community understand and value diversity; members need to view differences in perspective as natural, important, and necessary to the learning process. Learning communities that regard each member's contribution as valuable are therefore flexible. Each member contributes to the project in ways and areas that he or she sees as most appropriate. Collaboration also supports risk taking. The group shares the vulnerability that results from mistakes.

In second language learning environments it is not uncommon for teachers to develop collaboration through cooperative structures (Freeman & Freeman 1992; Johnson 1994; Kagan 1986). Students learn English most effectively as they use the language with others in order to solve problems. Research in cooperative learning indicates that in addition to supporting language and content development, cooperative learning structures promote positive cross-cultural and race relations (Kagan 1992). Kagan discusses three principles that guide the development of successful cooperative structures: simultaneous interaction, positive interdependence, and individual accountability.

Simultaneous interaction shifts the pattern of class participation away from the traditional notion of one person speaking at a time, thus providing second language learners with more opportunities to interact with other class members.

Cooperative structures, where various groups of students interact simultaneously, give these students more opportunities to take risks. To create positive interdependence, cooperative groups are set up so that each member of the group has a specific task or team recognition is based on the contributions of the group members. For second language learners this provides a structure by which to participate in the social grouping and contribute to the group's effort. Finally, by structuring cooperative groups so that there is individual accountability, the contributions of each second language learner are made known to the team.

To illustrate these principles, consider this poetry activity. Pairs of students are asked to read a particular text chorally. Since all the students, not just one or two, are reading out loud, the principle of simultaneous interaction is applied. In addition, if each pair is asked to interpret the poetry, at least half of the students in the class will be participating at any given point. Positive interdependence can then be fostered by asking each pair to create one illustration of their interpretation of the poem. This concept can be stressed by limiting the number of colors each pair can use to make their illustration. For example, if each member of the pair is given only one colored marker or crayon and the pair is told that their illustration must include both colors, the students need to negotiate how they will contribute to the final product so that both colors are represented. Individual accountability can be achieved by having each member make a journal entry in their own literature logs at the end of the activity.

When classroom teachers promote risk taking, reflection, and collaboration, the effect on their students can be quite striking. For example, the second month of school, a student named María was transferred into our third-grade classroom. We were immediately struck by the degree of hostility and aggressiveness she displayed toward other students and toward us. Physically and psychologically, María pushed away all those who came too close. Although María's transformation was gradual, the effects of a curriculum that valued risk taking, reflection, and collaboration were marked. We began to see a student more willing to participate in small-group discussions. At times, although not proficient in English, María even used her second language to participate in large-group discussions. María's writing journal comments reflected this change as she noted how she was less scared of trying new things in the classroom.

• • • • • • • • • •

Thematic Teaching in a Third-Grade Bilingual Classroom

The primary source for this book was a yearlong collaborative exploration of thematic teaching in a third-grade bilingual transitional (Spanish and English) classroom. Our school was located in a large metropolitan area and served a diverse—ethnically, linguistically, socioeconomically—population. Most of our students were Mexican American and came from working-class homes. The students had entered kindergarten speaking predominantly Spanish and were placed in bilingual classes where they had both primary language support and English as a second language (ESL) instruction. The dual purpose of the bilingual transitional program was to teach the students literacy and other subjects in Spanish and at the same time help them develop enough English to be mainstreamed into English-only programs. The third-grade students were formally making the transition to English literacy. They were grouped by language levels in the morning and then by ability for math instruction in the afternoon. Our exploration of thematic teaching took place during the morning language arts block.

Until the third grade, most of our students had experienced fairly traditional literacy programs. To a large extent, basal readers, spellers, and grammar books had "framed" their experiences with reading and writing instruction. Sound-symbol correspondence and vocabulary had been explicitly taught in isolation, as had spelling, punctuation, capitalization, and penmanship. The various disciplines had been taught as separate subjects. In addition, there was little evidence that the students had experienced such process-oriented activities as reader-response groups or writing conferences in which drafts were revised, edited, and published.

In the third grade, these students encountered a curriculum that was inquiry-based and process-oriented. It had four components: thematic units, free reading/student response, free writing/conferencing/publishing, and teacher reading/student response. During the year, students studied four themes: (a) Getting to Know About You, Me, and Others/*Tú, Yo, y Otros,* (b) Getting to Know About Amphibians and Reptiles/*Conociendo los Reptiles y los Anfibios,* (c) Getting to Understand Fears/*Entendiendo Nuestros Temores,* and (d) Getting to Know About Growing and Using Plants and Seeds/*Cultivando y Utilizando Plantas y Semillas.* Themes were selected by both the teachers and the students, and the length of each unit varied, depending on the students' interest in the topic (see Table 2.1).

Perhaps this is a good place to note the effects our thematic curriculum had on the level of participation of both limited and fluent English speakers in large-group settings. Early in the year we noticed how a thematic approach allowed all students, regardless of their linguistic, cultural, and intellectual differences, to share in the curriculum. This differed significantly from our past experiences in bilingual settings where the Spanish and the English curriculums rarely intersected: the Spanish-speaking students encountered one curriculum and the English-speaking students encountered another, and student interaction across languages and experiences was rare. We tended to limit the amount of time spent in whole-class discussions in those settings because the English- or Spanish-speaking students would disengage when the language of their particular curriculum was not being used.

Thematic units, on the other hand, expanded our use of whole-class meetings and supported students in risk taking. Because students shared some basic concepts and experiences, they were willing to focus on the meaning their classmates were attempting to convey rather than on the language forms. Students were more

Getting to Know About You, Me, and Others/Tú, Yo, y Otros	Getting to Know About Amphibians and Reptiles/Conociendo los Reptiles y los Anfibios
Topic selected by teacher in order to develop a classroom community that emphasized risk taking, reflection, and collaboration. Duration: September-November	Topic selected by the students. Investigations focused on specific reptiles and amphibians: snakes, turtles, lizards, dinosaurs, salamanders. Duration: December-March
Getting to Understand Fears/Entendiendo Nuestros Temores	Getting to Know About Growing and Using Plants and Seeds/Cultivando y Utilizando Plantas y Semillas
Topic selection sparked by the students' personal experiences with earthquakes and the school's attempt to develop a disaster preparedness plan. Duration: April-May	Topic selected by the students. Investigations focused on seeds, flowers, leaves, stems, root system, propogation. Duration: May-June

TABLE 2.1 Four themes.

at ease knowing that they could develop a general understanding even though they might not grasp all the details.

To give a sense of our classroom, we will describe some of the activities that became common events as themes were launched, moved forward, and celebrated. These "living examples" of thematic teaching and learning anchor and orient the conceptual framework for thematic curriculum development that is presented in the following chapters. These activities are not intended as a ready-made curriculum nor even as a model for how themes should be taught.

Launching a Theme

Launching activities introduce students to the theme and invite their participation. They develop background knowledge and a base of common understanding. Launching activities tend to be organized around whole-class meetings. These initial meetings are most effective when they include input from the students and provide a sense of direction for the unfolding thematic curriculum.

The theme Getting to Know About You, Me, and Others/*Tú, Yo, y Otros* was launched when the students entered the classroom for the first time in September. After the students had gathered, we directed their attention to a bulletin board labeled with the theme's name. We explained why we thought this was an appropriate theme with which to begin the year and discussed with them possible activities and materials that might be highlighted and explored.

We then initiated an activity called Getting to Know You, developed by Carolyn Burke (Harste, Short & Burke 1988). We told the class that since many of us did not know one another, we would be interviewing and introducing one of our classmates. The class brainstormed questions they would like to ask one another, and these questions were listed on the board. Once a list of possible questions had been formulated, we and the students broke into pairs and interviewed each other. Interviewers took notes on three-by-five cards and later used these notes as they introduced their partner to the entire class.

Early in the themes, new information was typically presented through group discussions, films, videos, music, books, or special articles. The book *William's Doll* (Zolotow 1972) was introduced to the students during the development of the Getting to Know About You, Me, and Others/*Tú, Yo, y Otros* theme. *William's Doll* is the story of a little boy who wants a doll. Rather than giving him the doll that he wants, his father insists on buying toys such as a basketball and a train set. At the end of the story, William's grandmother buys him a doll, explaining that by loving and caring for a doll he can practice being a father.

We selected this book as an introduction to a set of texts focusing on such potential generalizations as *Being different is okay* and *Being true to yourself may have negative as well as positive consequences* and related concepts focusing on acceptance and respect, being alike and different, and conflict and resolution. The students, who had been grouped in pairs to read *William's Doll,* were asked to assemble as a class for a large-group discussion. In the whole-class meeting, the students generally followed a reader-response format like the one outlined in Appendix 2.1.

In addition to reading the book, students were also invited to listen and respond to Marlo Thomas's musical version of *William's Doll* (*Free to Be You and Me* 1972). The students were given several opportunities to listen to and sing the musical version of the text. Then, through a Venn diagram, students compared and contrasted their previous understanding of the book with their new understanding. Listening to the musical version was particularly helpful for the second language learners, because it highlighted the key point that William was teased by others because he wanted a doll.

In launching the theme, the students engaged in a variety of other whole-class activities aimed at developing team spirit and a sense of community. Look at Me! (J. Gibbs 1987) allowed students to illustrate and share important things about themselves at four different points in their lives: as a two-year-old, as a five-year-old, now, and five years from now. Team Interview (Kagan 1992) helped students get to know one another better. Working in groups, they discussed topics like their name: the history associated with it, their nickname, the name they would have chosen had they been able to, and so on. Throughout the activity students

What We Know	What We Want to Learn
They are big and short	Why are they called reptiles?
Algunos comen zacate	Why do they haven long necks?
Algunos viven en el agua	¿Por qué no viven ya?
Some have sharp teeth	What do they eat?
Museums have their bones	Do they eat people?
Some have horns	¿Por qué tienen cuernos?
Ponen huevos	Where do they live?
Some fight	¿Por qué ponen huevos?
Some have long necks and tails	

TABLE 2.2 Things that we know and want to learn about dinosaurs.

were asked to notice how each member of the team encouraged others to participate, listen, ask questions, stay on task, and praise others for their contributions.

An activity called Uncommon Commonalities (Kagan 1992) gave groups of students a chance to reflect on similarities and differences. Each group developed a list of "uncommon commonalities" that made their team unlike any other team. For example, a group might discover that each member liked pizza with anchovies, a taste not generally shared by other students their age. In Quality Initials (Kagan 1992), the students chanted new names for themselves using their initials and adjectives.

To support students in their efforts to work cooperatively, we used a variety of self- and group-evaluation activities (Kagan 1992). For example, students were asked to reflect on behaviors such as their willingness to listen to one another, to ask questions or offer opinions, and to respect one another's point of view. Throughout these activities the teacher and students focused on "balancing the rights of participation" by controlling turn taking, discussion topics, and talk opportunities (Faltis 1993).

We launched the Getting to Know About Amphibians and Reptiles/*Conociendo los Reptiles y los Anfibios* theme using the inquiry strategy KWL (Ogle 1986; Pardo & Raphael 1991). (The initials stand for the three basic components: what we **K**now when we start the unit, what we **W**ant to learn as we move forward in the theme, and what we finally **L**earned or still need to learn about the theme at its conclusion.) An initial whole-class meeting was scheduled so that all students could share what they knew about amphibians and reptiles and frame the questions that would guide our study. Everyone took turns categorizing and recording ideas on large pieces of chart paper (see Table 2.2). Since we wanted to highlight the notion that learning communities engage in risk taking and reflection, all

	Guiding Questions				
TOPIC: Dinosaurs	Why are they called reptiles?	¿Por qué no viven ya?	Do they eat people?	Other interesting facts and figures	New questions
SOURCE: *Dinosaurios Gigantes* by Erna Rowe					
SOURCE: *Dinosaur Time* by Peggy Parish					
SOURCE: *Dinosaurios* by David Cutts					
SUMMARY					

Adapted from "Critical Reading/Thinking Across the Curriculum: Using I-Charts to Support Learning" by J. V. Hoffman, Language Arts 69 (1992), pp. 121–27.

FIGURE 2.1 Sample I-chart on dinosaurs.

students were encouraged to participate and all ideas were accepted and recorded. Questionable ideas usually generated interesting discussions as the students explored how they related to the theme and examined a variety of sources. During these meetings the students could express themselves in either English or Spanish, and contributions were recorded accordingly. As the unit progressed, we continued to use whole-class meetings to see how our knowledge was increasing and to update the group on new findings. Students took advantage of these times to challenge some of the initial comments on the What We Know charts. Questions asked in the earlier phases of the unit were answered and more questions were generated.

More recently we have participated in classrooms where the KWL strategy has been refined and personalized with individual inquiry charts, or I-charts (J. Hoffman 1992). After the class develops the initial KWL chart, students pick out the questions of particular interest to them and include them on their I-Chart (see Figure 2.1). As Hoffman states, this gives students the opportunity to become critical readers, since it encourages them to examine several sources as they consider their personal inquiries. By examining several sources of information, students also have the opportunity to reflect and to address points that might be at odds with each other.

Moving Forward

As students moved forward in a theme, they experienced a variety of support structures as concepts and generalizations emerged from the materials and activities. Most of the "moving forward" activities were organized around small groups, but these small groups were radically different from those we had traditionally formed as classroom teachers. A particularly noticeable difference was their fluidity. Groups were set up for specific, usually short-term, purposes; once the group accomplished its goals, it was disbanded and new groups were formed as needed. The notion of collaboration was central. Students were encouraged to reflect on the strategies the group used to accomplish its purpose. The following types of groups dominated our thematic teaching: (a) book groups, (b) research groups, (c) literacy support groups, and (d) writer-response groups. (Chapter 5 discusses additional grouping practices that teachers might consider when developing thematic curriculums.)

Book Groups   The majority of the thematic work groups formed on the basis of students' interests. Typically, this involved the formation of book (reader-response) groups. Reading materials for these groups were arranged into conceptually related sets of texts. In our previous discussion on *William's Doll*, we briefly mentioned how this particular book had been selected to serve as an introduction to a set of texts. Following a whole-class introduction to the book, the students were presented with four additional books that highlighted the same issues dealt with in *William's Doll: Angelita, la Ballena Pequeñita* (Rico 1975), *Oliver Button Is a Sissy* (de Paola 1979), *Oliver Button es una Nena* (de Paola 1982), and *Rosa Caramelo* (Turin & Bosnia 1976). After deciding which book they wanted to read, students formed groups with others also reading that book. As members of a book group, students read the text and engaged in small-group discussions generally patterned on the efferent and aesthetic responses (Rosenblatt 1978) used to discuss *William's Doll* (see Appendix 2.1). Students were encouraged to respond to the text by focusing on both what they were learning from it and on the feelings they experienced while reading it. Our response conferences were aimed at helping the students learn to "talk" to the author.

Book groups became one of the key structures in our implementation of thematic units. They gave students options as to materials—topic, language, and difficulty. Yet, since the reading selections in the text set were conceptually related, all students were accessing the same general meaning.

Research Groups   This type of investigative activity was also based on student interest. For example, during the Getting to Know About Amphibians and Reptiles/*Conociendo los Reptiles y los Anfibios* unit, small groups of students chose to research general characteristics of specific animals within the theme. Both the students and the teacher gathered source materials. The students acquired information and discussed ways of presenting this information to the other children in the classroom. Using the cooperative structure Jigsaw (Kagan 1992), each member of the team specialized in one aspect of the investigation (animal's habitat, eating characteristics, physical dimensions, etc.) and shared that particular aspect of the investigation with his or her teammates. In addition, each group member wrote and published an expository and a narrative text about the animal being researched.

Literacy Support Groups   The third type of grouping generally used during any theme was aimed at providing students with instructional support. These groups formed to deal with a specific issue and dissolved once the objective was accomplished. Typically, the issues addressed in these groups dealt with reading and writing difficulties. Throughout the year we identified four types of common problems: (1) the reader encounters something not recognized, known, or understood, (2) the reader has difficulty engaging with what is being read, (3) the writer has difficulty knowing what to write next or difficulty putting ideas into language, and (4) the writer has difficulty spelling particular words. Because our goal was to create independent readers and writers, we used these meetings to support students in developing various strategies for overcoming these literacy problems (Kucer 1995).

Through a series of group meetings and discussions, we developed strategies for overcoming each literacy block. In these meetings, either students were asked to share various problems they were experiencing with their reading or writing or we brought together students that were experiencing a common difficulty. We usually began each session by asking students to brainstorm all the possible solutions for the identified problem. As students collaborated in providing responses, the solutions discussed by the group were "tried out" and recorded on large pieces of chart paper. These charts came to be called "strategy wall charts" and were hung around the room for students to look at and use. Eventually, we typed the problems and solutions on eight-and-a-half-by-eleven-inch paper and gave copies to each student. Students were encouraged to use these strategies when reading and writing within the theme as well as when engaged in nonthematic activities. Table 2.3 illustrates how the charts appeared at the end of the year. These charts were good indicators of a learning community engaged in risk taking, reflection, and collaboration. Students were willing to try new ideas, compare their own literacy strategies with those applied by others, and collaborate in developing a product valuable to the entire group.

Reading Strategies	Reader-Response Strategies
When reading and you come to something that you do not recognize, know, or understand you can:	When reading and you have a hard time getting "into" or engaging with what you are reading, you can ask yourself:

Reading Strategies

When reading and you come to something that you do not recognize, know, or understand you can:

1. Stop reading ⟶ think about it ⟶ make a guess ⟶ read on to see if the guess makes sense.
2. Stop reading ⟶ reread the previous sentence(s) or paragraph(s) ⟶ make a guess ⟶ continue reading to see if the guess makes sense.
3. Skip it ⟶ read on to get more information ⟶ return and make a guess ⟶ continue reading to see if the guess makes sense.
4. Skip it ⟶ read on to see if what you do not understand is important to know ⟶ return and make a guess if it is important; do not return if it is unimportant.
5. Put something in that makes sense ⟶ read on to see if it fits with the rest of the text.
6. Stop reading ⟶ look at the pictures, charts, graphs, etc. ⟶ make a guess ⟶ read on to see if the guess makes sense.
7. Sound it out (focus on initial and final letters, consonants, known words within the word, meaningful word parts) ⟶ read on to see if the guess makes sense.
8. Stop reading ⟶ talk with a friend about what you do not understand ⟶ return and continue reading.
9. Stop reading ⟶ look in a dictionary, encyclopedia, or books related to the topic ⟶ return and continue reading.
10. Read the text with a friend.
11. Stop reading.

Reader-Response Strategies

When reading and you have a hard time getting "into" or engaging with what you are reading, you can ask yourself:

1. What is my purpose for reading this text?
2. What am I learning from reading this text?
3. Why did the author write this text? What was the author trying to teach me?
4. What parts do I like the best; what parts are my favorite? Why do I like these particular parts?
5. What parts do I like the least? Why do I dislike these parts?
6. Does this text remind me of other texts I have read? How is this text both similar and dissimilar to other texts?
7. What would I change in this text if I had written it? What might the author have done to have made this text better, more understandable, more interesting?
8. Are there things/parts in the text that I am not understanding? What can I do to better understand these things/parts?

TABLE 2.3 Strategy wall charts.

Writing Strategies	Spelling Strategies
When writing and you come to a place where you do not know what to write next or have difficulty expressing an idea, you can:	When writing and you come to a word that you do not know how to spell, you can:

Writing Strategies

1. Brainstorm possible ideas and jot them down on paper.
2. Reread what you have written so far.
3. Skip to a part where you know what you will write about. Come back to the problem later.
4. Write it as best you can and return later to make it better.
5. Write it several different ways and choose the one that you like the best.
6. Write whatever comes into your mind.
7. Talk about it/conference with a friend.
8. Read other texts to get some new ideas.
9. Stop writing for a while and come back to it later.

Spelling Strategies

1. Sound it out.
2. Think of "small words" that are in the word and write these first.
3. Write the word several different ways and choose the one that looks the best.
4. Write the letters that you know are in the word.
5. Make a line for the word.
6. Ask a friend.
7. Look in the dictionary.

TABLE 2.3 *(cont.)*

Writer-Response Groups   In writer-response groups, students reacted to their classmates' writing. After completing a draft, students met in small groups and responded to one another's texts. Initial conferences focused on ideas. Students discussed the ideas presented in the text and made suggestions for revisions. After each writer-response conference, the group briefly summarized their discussions and recorded their thoughts on a form that each author could take back to his or her desk and use in the revision process (see Appendix 2.2).

Writer-response groups were first introduced to the students during the Getting to Know About You, Me, and Others/*Tú, Yo, y Otros* theme. As an extension of the student interviews, the students wrote their own *About Me* book using many of the ideas brainstormed as possible questions to use in the interview.

Table 2.4 illustrates how "moving forward" activities were scheduled during a typical week of the Getting to Know About You, Me, and Others/*Tú, Yo, y Otros* theme. Although the greater part of the week was devoted to book-group meetings, as part of the *About Me* books the students also engaged in writer-response groups. At this point it may be important to note that students had more than one opportunity to sign up to participate in any given book group. For example, as described in Table 2.4, book groups during this particular week involved five

Theme: Getting to Know About You, Me, and Others/*Tú, Yo, y Otros*
Possible Generalizations: Being different is okay; being true to yourself may have negative consequences
Possible Concepts: being alike and different, self-acceptance and self-respect, acceptance of and respect for others, conflict and resolution

Monday	Tuesday, Wednesday, Thursday	Friday

Book: *William's Doll* (Zolotow 1972)
• Reader Response (see Appendix 2.1)
• Wall Chart Strategies (see Table 2.3)
• Song: *William's Doll* (*Free to Be You and Me* Thomas 1972)
• Response: Venn diagram, compare and contrast song and book, discuss new meanings generated by song
	Book Groups
	• Choices:
	  Angelita, la Ballena Pequeñita (Rico 1975)
	  Oliver Button Is a Sissy (de Paola 1979)
	  Oliver Button es una Nena (de Paola 1982)
	  Rosa Caramelo (Turín & Bosnia 1976)
	• Reader Response (see Appendix 2.1)
	• Wall Chart Strategies (see Table 2.3)
	Writer-Response Group:
	• *About Me* books Choices while students are waiting for their book group or writer response group to meet for discussion.
	• Statements of Appreciation [*Tribes* Boasters Activity, J. Gibbs 1987]
	• Viewing Center: *When I Grow Up* video
	• Recordings of book group choices
	• Other: Rehearse dramatization of *William's Doll*
		Dramatizations: Students' interpretations of *William's Doll*

TABLE 2.4 Sample weekly schedule.

texts. After participating in their first-choice book group, the students had an opportunity to select another book the following week.

Celebrations

The whole group also convened to celebrate the completion of a unit. These celebrations normally involved a special display of all the materials encountered and produced during the theme. Our students were usually amazed at how much they had read and done! During the celebrations, the students could revisit a book or two, talk about their favorite aspect of the theme, pay a last visit to the KWL charts to review answers to the questions they had generated earlier and add any final thoughts, and reflect on what they'd learned.

Student portfolios, discussed in Chapter 8, also became part of the celebration. Students selected pieces from their portfolio to share with one another and with their parents. Selections varied, depending on the student and the themes. Some students, for example, selected pieces that were representative of something they had learned or had enjoyed. Others selected pieces they felt demonstrated their growth.

Celebrations generally ended with a final reflection on the theme. Students evaluated the theme, shared what they had liked about it, and suggested modifications or changes for future units.

• • • • • • • • • • •

Scheduling Nonthematic Literacy Activities

In promoting thematic units as curriculums that help students make links and connections, we are aware that teaching and learning go beyond themes. At various times throughout the school day, students engage in literacy development activities that are not thematically linked. When working in elementary schools, we find the following time allotments workable:

- Thematic units: one to two and a half hours.
- Free reading and student response: a half hour to an hour.
- Free writing, conferencing, and publishing: a half hour to one and a half hours.
- Teacher reading and student response: a half hour to three quarters of an hour.

Free Reading and Student Response

We schedule a block of time when students know they can explore their own interests and read for the pleasure of reading. These blocks of free reading time are often called SSR (Sustained Silent Reading) or DEAR (Drop Everything and

Read) Time. Giving the students time to share their responses to what they have read demonstrates the value we place on self-selected reading. Although we never assign book reports or the like, we do ask students to keep daily logs in which they record what they've read and the number of pages.

For self-selected reading to be successful, there needs to be a wide range of reading materials on various topics, in different modes, and in different languages. Students' interest in reading is sparked by fresh sets of books. We relied on both school and public libraries. In addition, we encouraged students to bring reading materials from home. And we made sure there were a large number of books in Spanish.

To manage the large number of books, we moved away from traditional storing methods. Rather than lining books up on vertical shelves, we used plastic tubs coded by theme or by type. For example, all books used during Getting to Know About You, Me, and Others/*Tú, Yo, y Otros* were coded with a small red sticker and placed in buckets carrying a similar sticker. Likewise, magazines, such as *National Geographic* and *World*, had their own bucket, as did "how to" books. During self-selection time, the class librarians distributed the plastic tubs around the room. The students could then easily peruse the materials they thought they might be interested in reading.

Free Writing, Conferencing, and Publishing

Blocks of time when students can engage in self-selected writing topics, conferencing, and publishing must also be part of the daily routine. If our goal is to develop writers, we must give students time to write. Writers, as we have learned from writing teachers such as Atwell (1987, 1990), Calkins (1986), and Graves (1983), need regular and frequent time in which to grow. Students need to know that they will have time to rehearse, compose, and reflect on their writing. Although free writing and much of the writing that occurs in a thematic classroom differ as to topic, they do not differ in terms of process. Self-selected writing and thematic writing both involve a cycle in which students compose, share their work with others, revise, edit, publish, and celebrate (Harste, Short & Burke 1988).

Teacher Reading and Student Response

Finally, teachers are encouraged to read to their students. Students need to hear the sounds of language and the expression of ideas in forms they may not yet be able to read on their own. This oral reading may be related to the theme or something the students have requested; it may be chapter books, short stories, magazine or newspaper articles, or poems.

Teacher reading lets us demonstrate the various reading strategies listed on the strategy wall charts. If we read a sentence that did not make sense, we would reread it and discuss why we had done so. If we changed a word in the text without changing the author's meaning, we highlighted that behavior. If a particular idea evoked an internal response, we shared it.

• • • • • • • • • •

Final Remarks

Not all activities in the life of the classroom can or must be thematic. Teachers attempting to develop thematic units for the first time often feel that all areas of the curriculum should be integrated into any one unit of study. This misconception can lead to units that do not help students make the conceptual links and connections intended by thematic teaching. For example, a thematic curriculum may not offer elementary school students enough opportunities to develop the depth of understanding expected in the math curriculum. Consequently, although mathematics can still play a major role in thematic units, the teacher may need to provide the students with additional mathematical instruction in nonthematic settings.

Because the school in which we worked grouped students by ability for math instruction, most students left their homerooms for a specific period each day and went to another teacher for math. In other instructional settings, teachers have addressed this problem by developing two parallel themes in their classrooms. The themes taught in the morning highlight issues, content, and processes most commonly found in literature and the social sciences. The afternoon themes then focus on scientific and mathematical content and processes.

3

Focusing on the Big Picture: Facts, Concepts, and Generalizations

• • • • • • • • • •

The Tie That Binds

A thematic curriculum provides conceptual structures that support learning. These structures help children link their understanding of the new to what they already know. The distinction between and interrelationships among facts, concepts, and generalizations are particularly useful in supporting our students in their attempts to get the big picture—to make sense of their world by actively developing links between materials, activities, and their life experiences.

Our earlier attempts at thematic instruction resulted in units that meshed a large number of loosely related materials and activities around a central topic. Consequently, we developed and implemented units similar to the one on bears that we describe in Chapter 1.

Three years ago, we conducted an informal survey by asking our student teachers to identify thematic units and activities in which they had taken part or observed while they were student-teaching. Almost all the activities they identified were only loosely linked to the topic. One in particular stands out: the theme was mice and a second-grade class was learning to tell time. In keeping with the mice theme, the classroom teacher used a Mickey Mouse clock to teach students about time.

Using the Mickey Mouse clock or activities like it may be appropriate within particular instructional contexts. What we question is the assumption that such activities are thematically linked to the topic. In the examples just mentioned, the materials failed to help students broaden their knowledge or understanding of bears or mice. The activities failed to build on one another, and students were not offered opportunities to make connections between the materials, activities, and their previous life experiences. In fact, the activities may have decreased the students' disposition to explore these topics.

In considering how materials and activities can help students arrive at the big picture, we must be sure that they do more than develop isolated facts. Students need a curriculum that supports them in making links and connections. This is particularly true for culturally diverse students who are simultaneously trying to make sense of a new language, a new culture, and the curriculum. A "tie that binds" across the various instructional experiences is essential, a curricular framework that will keep students wanting to learn.

Even though thematic units place teachers at the center of curricular decisions, students also need to be part of the process—not in a tug-of-war between student-centered or teacher-centered instruction, but as partners in a curriculum centered on learning. With learning as its focus, the curriculum becomes a reflection of both students' and teachers' voices. The insights of experts outside the classroom become "part of the knowledge that the experts inside the classroom use as they think and work together" (Short & Burke 1991, 5).

With this in mind, we struggled to conceptualize an alternate framework for organizing the curriculum. Like Short and Burke, we first reflected on our beliefs about learning. A curricular framework had to be consistent with the beliefs we had acquired through our own teaching and learning experiences. Our beliefs are based predominantly on the work of Dewey (1916, 1938), Smith (1975, 1981), and Vygotsky (1978, 1986).

We believe that learning is a continuous, natural, and social process. When students are able to choose from a range of activities and/or topics in which they are interested, their curiosity will provoke learning. This process is enhanced through the interactions and contributions of the various disciplines, which are drawn upon in a holistic fashion rather than as separate, compartmentalized subject areas. The guiding question becomes, What contributions can the disciplines make to the topic being explored? Finally, learning is facilitated through collaboration with other learners. This collaboration provides opportunities to share varied perspectives and to negotiate meaning. Collaboration also fosters learning as students (and teachers) scaffold for each other. Scaffolding enables us to perform at higher levels than we could attain individually. Mindful of these aspects of learning, we wanted the curricular framework to furnish opportunities for students to make connections between the things they were learning and also to link them to previous and possible future experiences.

Our struggle led us to reconsider the conceptual frameworks suggested by social science educators (Banks 1991, 1994; Taba et al. 1971). We find their distinction between facts, concepts, and generalizations particularly useful in supporting our students as they attempt to integrate their learning, because it helps students organize information and make sense of the world and supports their inquiry.

A thematic curriculum that focuses on concepts and generalizations is of particular benefit to second language learners, who are especially hard hit by the segmentation and isolation that has dominated educational practices. A conceptually linked curriculum allows language-minority students to engage in meaningful experiences while continuing to develop their language skills. Rather than offering a watered-down curriculum that emphasizes language drills and the memorization of facts, the framework we advocate provides the "conceptual hangers" students need to link the language functions, structures, and meanings that they are developing (Snow, Met, & Genesee 1992). This approach helps second language learners identify significant patterns across materials and activities instead of forcing them to concentrate on individual entities. The primary language of these children can be validated by using conceptually linked primary language materials. Furthermore, since the collaborative environment facilitated by this framework enables students to share their perspectives, all students are able to draw from their own experiences even if they have occurred in different cultural contexts. Students have a forum in which to mediate culture as well as language.

• • • • • • • • • • •

Hierarchy of Knowledge

Recent work by Banks (1991, 1994), as well as earlier writings by Taba et al. (1971), suggests that one of the most important goals of the schools is to help students learn to construct generalizations from the concepts and facts developed across various learning experiences. To help us define the different levels in the hierarchy of knowledge, we will use examples from a teacher-initiated thematic unit—Getting to Understand Fears/*Entendiendo Nuestros Temores*—that was prompted by a recent earthquake and the fears this disaster caused. Figure 3.1 illustrates the hierarchy of knowledge and the relationship among facts, concepts, and generalizations as they might relate to *Ira Sleeps Over* (Waber 1972), *Will You Come Back for Me?* (Tompert 1988), and *Libby's New Glasses* (Tusa 1984). In the figure, each level of generality or specificity in the hierarchy is represented by the size of the print. As we have already indicated, *Ira* is a story about a young boy who is fearful about spending the night at a friend's without taking along his teddy bear. In *Will You Come Back for Me?* a young girl named Suki is left in day care for the first time and worries that her mother may not come back for her. In *Libby's New Glasses*, Libby, afraid that her new glasses will make her friends reject her, runs away from home.

Facts

Facts, as traditionally defined, are items at the lowest level of abstraction, are situationally grounded, and provide very specific information. Although necessary

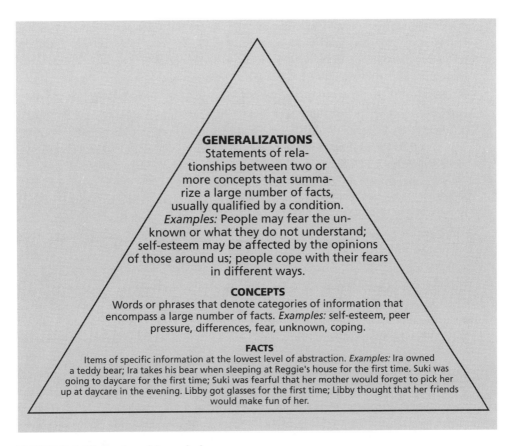

GENERALIZATIONS
Statements of relationships between two or more concepts that summarize a large number of facts, usually qualified by a condition. *Examples:* People may fear the unknown or what they do not understand; self-esteem may be affected by the opinions of those around us; people cope with their fears in different ways.

CONCEPTS
Words or phrases that denote categories of information that encompass a large number of facts. *Examples:* self-esteem, peer pressure, differences, fear, unknown, coping.

FACTS
Items of specific information at the lowest level of abstraction. *Examples:* Ira owned a teddy bear; Ira takes his bear when sleeping at Reggie's house for the first time. Suki was going to daycare for the first time; Suki was fearful that her mother would forget to pick her up at daycare in the evening. Libby got glasses for the first time; Libby thought that her friends would make fun of her.

FIGURE 3.1 Hierarchy of knowledge.

to the development of generalizations and concepts, facts have little or no transfer or predictive value. Factual information can be easily verified within the context of a story. In *Ira Sleeps Over*, it is a fact that Ira owns a teddy bear and that Ira takes the bear with him when sleeping at a friend's house. Similarly, in *Will You Come Back For Me?* it is a fact that Suki is going to day care for the first time, and in *Libby's New Glasses* it is a fact that Libby thinks that her friends will make fun of her. However, these facts are context-specific, may be quickly forgotten by the students, and provide students with little understanding of the central concepts related to the stories' plots, such as self-esteem, fear, or coping. Nor do facts, alone, enable students to reach in-depth understanding of a theme.

Concepts

As large amounts of factual information are classified or categorized, concepts emerge. They become the building blocks of analytic frameworks (Hansen 1979) and are instrumental in formulating generalizations. For example, in the Ira, Suki, and Libby stories, prominent concepts may be fear of the unknown, self-esteem, and coping. The fact that Ira sleeps with a teddy bear or that Suki does not want to attend day care or that Libby runs away from home is meaningful only as it relates to these concepts. Furthermore, concepts allow students to interrelate facts found in other books within the theme. Libby does not have a bear, but she does cope with her fears by running away. This fear of the unknown, manifested differently in each book, contributes to students' conceptual knowledge. Because concepts may be addressed differently in different materials, their definition must remain flexible in order to guide students' understanding by allowing them to identify the commonalties in distinctive instances. As the context in which a particular concept is found changes, new features are noted and incorporated into the general understanding of the concept. However, we must keep in mind that some concepts are more definitive than others. For example, in a thematic unit on plants we may have a series of definitive concepts such as roots, vegetables, and cuttings, as well as broader concepts such as germination and growth. In the social sciences, concepts tend to be inherently more flexible.

As students interact with the various texts, they will not only discover new conceptual features but may also identify additional concepts that are relevant to them. For example, while reading *Ira Sleeps Over,* one of the third-grade students in our classroom questioned Ira's gender. These native-Spanish-speaking students had not previously encountered the name Ira. Because Ira ends in *a,* a feminine marker in Spanish, some of the students thought that Ira had to be a girl. The illustrations were not explicit enough to reveal Ira's gender. With a passion, students related various incidents in the story to substantiate their position, experiencing firsthand how the same facts could be turned around to support the opposing position. There was no satisfaction until one of the students referred to the text and identified the pronoun *he* used to refer to Ira. But by that time they had a sense of a new concept: gender stereotypes.

This confusion over gender and the ensuing discussion by the students led us to ask the students what would have happened if Ira had been a girl. Many of the students felt it would have changed the story. If Ira had been a girl, would her sister have made fun of her for taking her teddy bear to her friend's house? For a girl, this probably would have been "no big thing." Through the discussion, the students were coming to the conclusion that taking a security object to a sleep-over might not have been a point of conflict had Ira been a girl. The students then debated why there were different expectations for girls and boys, why Ira's gender made a difference, and whether it should or should not make a difference. As the students compared and contrasted these ideas to their own experiences, they explored their understanding of gender stereotypes.

This gender discussion was not planned. Nevertheless, the students raised valid issues and their point-counterpoint debate enhanced their understanding not only of the story, but of the concepts it dealt with. They came to a fuller appreciation of how norms develop in a society, how they differ across cultures, how not everyone agrees with every norm, and how societal norms can be questioned and can change over time. This unanticipated shift in the students' focus allowed us to revisit two books, *William's Doll* (Zolotow 1972) and *Oliver Button Is a Sissy/Oliver Button es una Nena* (de Paola 1979, 1982), which had been read in an earlier theme, Getting to Know About You, Me, and Others/*Tú, Yo, y Otros*. The conflicts depicted in these two books enhanced the students' conceptual development of gender stereotypes.

Generalizations

An asserted relationship between and among concepts is a generalization. Generalizations summarize a large number of facts and are sometimes qualified by a condition. Generalizations that we had anticipated emerging from *Ira Sleeps Over, Will You Come Back For Me?*, and *Libby's New Glasses* were *People may fear the unknown or what they do not understand*, *Self-esteem may be affected by the opinions of those around us*, and *People cope with their fears in different ways*. However, as we've just seen, our students also helped us discover the gender-based generalization *Society may have different expectations for males and females*.

As with conceptual knowledge, in order to develop generalizable knowledge students must be provided with varied materials and experiences involving the same concepts. No one book or activity can provide the base needed to develop generalizations. Well-formed concepts and generalizations require numerous and ongoing experiences. We must keep in mind that concepts and generalizations are dynamic rather than static structures of knowledge. In fact, failure to provide students with adequate experiences frequently results in stereotypic knowledge. Often students are asked to generalize before they have been given enough opportunities to develop a knowledge base from which generalizations can emerge.

• • • • • • • • • • •

The Development Process

A visual representation of a general model for developing conceptually linked thematic units of study is depicted in Figure 3.2 (adapted from Silva & Delgado-Larocco 1993). In the development process, tentative initial concepts and generalizations are identified by classroom teachers, who bring to the process a clear understanding of their community of learners and an understanding of the curricular expectations for the grade levels that they teach. These concepts and generalizations are always tentative in that they may grow and change as the students engage in the learning process. The curriculum is always open to discovering a range of ideas and meanings. However, formulating tentative concepts and generalizations is important in that it forestalls the use of materials and the development of activities that lack a clear focus, such as using *Ira Sleeps Over* in a study of bears.

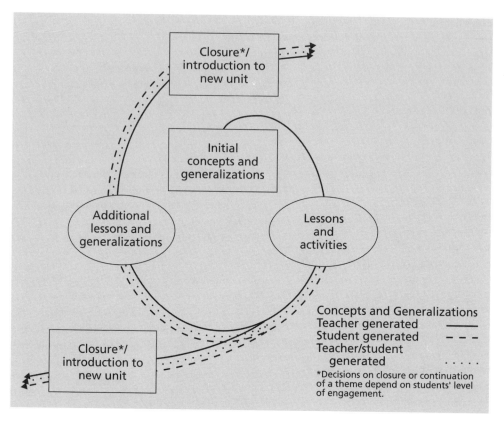

FIGURE 3.2 Development of concepts and generalizations.

There is no special recipe for identifying concepts and generalizations. In delineating the organizational framework, the process may appear linear and lockstep when in reality it is interactive and fluid. One way to identify concepts and generalizations is to start with a topic, one that reflects both students' interests and teachers' expertise. Then start gathering related materials, identifying potential concepts and generalizations as you make the selections.

This is how we first developed thematic units with our third-grade bilingual students. We knew that Getting to Know About You, Me, and Others/*Tú, Yo, y Otros* was going to begin the school year. This topic guided us as we perused materials in our local bookstore and library. As we came across possible materials, we put them in piles that "seemed to go together." As these piles grew, we then attempted to articulate how and why the materials were linked. Through this articulation, we modified the piles, created new piles, moved materials from one pile to another, deleted material, and came to a fuller understanding of the topic.

Another possibility is to start out with concepts identified in curriculum guidelines, state frameworks, and/or available textbooks, then look for additional materials to support them. As these initial concepts and generalizations are generated, however, the process must remain fluid so that the curriculum continues to be representative of the students' voice. (We return to this issue in Chapter 4, where we discuss selecting thematic topics and materials.)

In stressing that the intention to move students beyond the acquisition of mere facts is critical to the development of thematic units, we emphasize the role of both the teacher and the students in identifying concepts and generalizations. The curricular framework proposed in this chapter is built on the premise that the student must be able to relate to and interact with the concepts being studied. The recurrence or recycling of the concepts in different contexts is essential in enabling students to identify significant patterns and, therefore, generalizable knowledge. As the concepts recur, the students increase the breadth and depth of their knowledge. Since the interaction allows students to make their own connections between the concepts they identify and their own life experiences, it facilitates curriculum access for culturally and linguistically diverse students. Furthermore, students establish relationships among the concepts as they interpret them. Those generalizations initially identified by the teacher at the beginning stages of unit development become secondary as students become involved and as they interact with one another and with the available materials. When students collaborate in the creation of knowledge, the classroom environment is transformed into one that fosters risk taking and reflection. It is precisely this type of environment in which culturally and linguistically diverse students will flourish. The emphasis on meaning rather than on form allows them the freedom to experiment with language, to share their ideas, and to ask questions to further their understanding, thereby enriching the educational process for all students in the classroom.

Given this interaction between the students and the materials, the teacher is constantly evaluating the curriculum to ensure that the focus remains on the most significant aspects of the theme. Concepts and generalizations, whether student- or teacher-identified, become the sieve through which all activities and materials are filtered. Lessons and activities are designed to help students understand the concepts and generalizations already identified and to encourage students to identify additional concepts and arrive at new generalizations. Moreover, we need to emphasize that this is not necessarily a linear process—that is, learning does not always start with facts, advance to concepts, and culminate in generalizations. Sometimes the generalizations may emerge first, then facts are identified to support the generalizations, and finally, as facts are discussed, analyzed, and organized, the concepts may be developed.

As the students engage in lessons and activities, the teacher monitors and evaluates the overall progress of the thematic unit. This monitoring is essential in deciding whether to (a) support students in bringing the unit to an end or (b) explore additional concepts and generalizations. Closure involves developing lessons and activities that synthesize the understanding developed throughout the unit and that celebrate and reflect on the newly acquired knowledge. Further

	Getting to Know About You, Me, and Others/*Tú, Yo, y Otros*	Getting to Know About Amphibians and Reptiles/*Conociendo los Reptiles y los Anfibios*	Getting to Understand Fears/*Entendiendo Nuestros Temores*	Getting to Know About Growing and Using Plants and Seeds/*Cultivando y Utilizando Plantas y Semillas*
Generalizations	• Being true to yourself may have negative as well as positive consequences. • People need to accept and respect themselves as well as others for who and what they are. • People are oftentimes more than they appear. • People are both similar and different in nature. • Self-esteem may be affected by those around us.	• Ancient amphibians and reptiles have been part of the literature of many cultures for centuries. • Amphibians and reptiles are both similar and different. • Amphibians and reptiles are "friends" of humankind.	• People may fear the unknown or what they do not understand. • People cope with their fears in different ways. • Facing our fears can lead to personal growth.	• A region's vegetation can influence the local culture and its folklore. • The use of pesticides can have negative as well as positive consequences. • Plants and seeds can be started and grown in many different ways. • All plants have certain common requirements. • Plants and seeds "travel" in various ways with the help of "others."
Concepts	Peer pressure; Acceptance; Respect; Similarities; Differences; Conflict resolution; Feelings; Appearance/Image; True self; Self-esteem	Amphibians; Reptiles; "Friends"; Cold-blooded; Skin; Life cycle; Hibernation	Fear; Unknown; Coping; Growth; Facing fears	Cuttings; Growth; Requirements; Roots; Culture; Folklore; Fruits; Vegetables; Germination; Seeds; Organic/inorganic pesticides

TABLE 3.1 Four theme topics, generalizations, and concepts.

exploration means identifying additional conceptually related material and designing new lessons and activities.

Table 3.1 contains the generalizations and concepts that ultimately framed the four thematic units we developed with our third-grade bilingual students. In our early attempts at developing themes, the materials tended to be the dominant source for generalizations and concepts. As we became more experienced in working with thematic curriculums, there was more of an interplay among previously identified generalizations and concepts, the materials collected, and our students' interactions with the materials. Additional examples of theme topics, generalizations, and materials can be found in the theme bibliography.

4

Getting Started: Selecting Themes and Materials

. . . .

Putting the Learner at the Center

Our selection of themes and materials is built on the assumption that learning must be meaningful and purposeful for the learner. Moving away from the notion that students are empty vessels waiting to be filled, we view learning as a process by which students deliberately engage in problem-solving experiences in order to understand the world around them (Dewey 1929; Smith 1975; Vygotsky 1986). The belief that learning at its core is a process of inquiry, of asking and seeking answers to one's questions, brings the student to the forefront of the learning process.

In selecting topics and materials for thematic instruction that is meaningful and purposeful, we keep in mind the relationship between the learner's prior experiences and classroom materials. Drawing from Rosenblatt's (1978) notion of transaction, we consider that in the learning process the characteristics of the student are as important as those of the materials selected for instruction. What the student is able to learn depends on what is already known. Consequently, various students may engage in the same activity, view the same film, or read the same poem, but what they get out of these experiences will vary based on their prior knowledge. Although we stress that the development of concepts and generalizations must be at the core of thematic teaching, we know that different meanings or perspectives can and will emerge as students engage in the curriculum.

By the time students enter school they have developed a wide range of knowledge and tools that have allowed them to explore their world and to solve new problems. Thematic teaching enables students to continue their exploration of personal interests and to make connections between new information and prior knowledge. Consequently, teachers take into consideration the interests of their students when selecting themes.

When deciding the likelihood that selected themes will generate authentic, engaging problem-solving experiences, teachers consider how a particular topic may facilitate the students' understanding of the world in which they live. For example, recently we had the opportunity to observe the implementation of a thematic unit entitled The Color Red. This unit, developed in a combination kindergarten–first-grade classroom with a large number of second language learners, was intended to offer students the opportunity to learn color words and focused on the acquisition of a series of facts related to the color red. Few opportunities for problem solving were presented within the unit. Although the learning of this type of factual information naturally occurs within a thematic curriculum, it does not warrant the development of an entire unit of study. If learning is to be meaningful and purposeful, then we must move beyond the development of "cute" themes that might result in meaningless learning experiences.

● ● ● ● ● ● ● ● ● ● ●

The Interactive Nature of Topics, Generalizations, and Materials

When we reflect on our earlier experiences as classroom teachers involved in thematic teaching and learning, we now recognize how often we took curriculum development for granted. Developing thematic units was an intuitive enterprise in which we moved through what seemed to be a rather linear and easy-to-follow series of steps. A truer as well as a more complex understanding of the nature of this process emerged as we started to present workshops and courses for preservice and inservice teachers. As we looked at the various ways in which we developed our themes, we began to understand the interactive nature among the selection of topics, generalizations, and materials (see Figure 4.1), as well as the various starting points involved.

Thematic topics may be student- or teacher-initiated. Key to the unit development process, however, is the early identification of tentative or potential concepts and generalizations that will guide the learning process. Although these concepts and generalizations may change as the unit progresses, an early concern allows the teacher and students to sustain a meaningful focus throughout the unit.

The topic and generalizations, however, are not identified in isolation from the materials. Each element influences and is influenced by the others. Some teachers begin developing thematic units by first locating materials related to a tentative topic. Then, from pursuing the available materials, tentative generalizations and

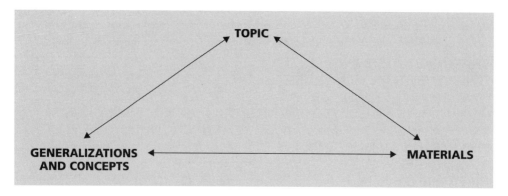

FIGURE 4.1 The relationship among topic, generalizations/concepts, and materials.

concepts begin to emerge. In turn, these generalizations and concepts provide a framework for deciding which materials are most appropriate to the topic and may even lead to modification of the topic. As this process of reviewing potential materials continues, the initially identified concepts and generalizations may also be modified. Or, after an initial review of the materials available, the teacher may even decide that a unit is not worth teaching because there is little substance to it.

The development of our unit Getting to Know About You, Me, and Others/*Tú, Yo, y Otros,* began with a topic. We wanted to start the school year with a unit that would develop a classroom community where students felt comfortable with one another. As we examined the materials, we began to clarify the concepts and generalizations on which we wanted to focus. Books such as *William's Doll* (Zolotow 1972) influenced our decision to highlight concepts such as acceptance and respect and to formulate generalizations such as *People need to accept and respect themselves as well as others for who and what they are.* These concepts and generalizations, we felt, were critical in developing the community of learners we wanted our classroom to become. As we continued to look through our materials, we were able to identify additional concepts and generalizations that might be significant in the unit. Formulating these tentative concepts and generalizations prevented us from developing a thematic unit in which students were asked to focus on a number of facts only tangentially related to the topic, without the necessary supporting structure to help them organize this body of knowledge.

Other teachers, either because of their experience in developing thematic units or because they are relying on existing curricular guidelines, begin their search for thematic materials with a fairly clear idea of the general issues that will ground the theme. In California, for example, a fifth-grade teacher interested in a social studies unit on immigration can identify from the state framework (History–Social Science Curriculum Framework and Criteria Committee 1987) the key issues to be explored within the unit. In many instances, the teacher can also develop tentative concepts and generalizations before looking for materials. In this instance, the fifth-grade teacher might generate a list similar to this:

Theme Topic: Immigration: Strangers in a Strange Land

Possible Generalizations:

To a large extent, the United States is a land of immigrants.

There are many reasons why people immigrate to one country from another.

Immigrant groups have made significant contributions to society in the United States.

Immigration can lead to conflict and change among various groups within a society.

Possible Concepts:

Immigration, migration, economics, religion, demographics, ethnicity, culture, acculturation, assimilation, prejudice, contributions, democracy, pluralism.

When one is identifying topics based on existing curricular guidelines, we again stress the need to brainstorm possible concepts and generalizations. External curricular frameworks may mandate that teachers cover particular topics, yet these frameworks typically do not specify the concepts and generalizations that support the units of study. Consequently, such frameworks too often lead to units that focus on numerous topical facts but do not help the students understand the interrelationship among these facts and why these facts are being studied. In an immigration unit, for example, students might learn about the successive waves of immigration to arrive in the United States without exploring concepts that would help them understand the reasons for immigration.

A recent experience we had with a student teacher illustrates this point. When we visited the school, the student teacher was presenting a unit on "the farm." All students were to study farm animals, and the unit was to culminate with a visit to the local university farm. Aside from mandating that all kindergarten students study "the farm," the school curriculum guide did not support the students or teacher in gaining a deeper understanding of this topic. In order to help students conceptually link activities, the student teacher brainstormed a list of tentative concepts (animals, plants, agriculture, responsibility, dependence, supply and demand, resources, food chain) and generalizations (urban environments depend on farms for food supplies, running a farm requires responsibility and collaboration, agriculture can impact the local economy) that helped her develop a more cohesive unit.

• • • • • • • • • • •

Selecting Topics

The Student as a Theme Source

Classroom teachers involved in thematic teaching find that when students are interested in a particular theme—that is, when they have asked real questions to guide the unit of study—students tend to push the learning experience beyond the teacher's expectations. This was the case in our third-grade bilingual classroom when the students proposed a thematic unit focusing on snakes, turtles, and frogs. The students' interest resulted in the twelve-week curriculum Getting to Know About Reptiles and Amphibians/*Conociendo los Reptiles y los Anfibios*, a thematic unit that went on much longer than we had ever imagined. Much to our surprise, students continued to generate new questions long after we had personally lost interest in the theme. Taking advantage of the teachable moment, however, we continued to support the students' inquiries.

Because gathering materials and arranging learning events for a thematic unit involves a considerable amount of planning, it is useful to involve students in brainstorming possible themes early in the academic year. A word of caution, however: don't ask the students to brainstorm like this until they have actually engaged in a thematic unit. As students become comfortable with the thematic learning process they can better understand and anticipate how their questions might be addressed. Consequently, consider opening the year with a teacher-generated topic, such as Getting to Know About You, Me, and Others/*Tú, Yo, y Otros*, and then invite the students to help select a few tentative themes to be developed later in the year.

We have seen teachers use a variety of strategies to get students involved in proposing thematic topics. Students can reflect on their interests and explore possible questions in their journals. As students develop these ideas, the class generates a brainstorming chart listing all possible topics. Using the class chart as a departure point, students then determine priorities. For example, they might place a red sticker by their first choice, a blue sticker by the second choice, and so on.

In a classroom with linguistically and culturally diverse students, student collaboration in topic selection is crucial, particularly when the students' culture differs from the teacher's. It is a way of ensuring that their interests and perspectives are incorporated into the curriculum. Given that many of the experiences of culturally and linguistically diverse students may be significantly different from those of the teacher and other students in the class, their choices may provide unique experiences for all. They may also enable culturally diverse students to lead the class inquiries and become resources for others.

The Teacher as a Theme Source

We believe that teachers need to consider their own knowledge and experience as professionals, as well as their own personal interests, when selecting classroom themes. As professionals, classroom teachers understand their particular community of learners and know the curricular expectations for the specific grade level(s) they teach and are therefore well qualified to mediate the curriculum. For example, a third-grade teacher we know, aware that the district's social science curriculum calls for the study of the local community's history, takes this into account when considering possible topics for thematic teaching. Or again, teachers of culturally diverse students know they should identify topics that reflect the students' cultures. This type of unit promotes better cross-cultural understanding and appreciation for all class members. It also places the second language learners in the role of expert and boosts their self esteem and cultural pride.

Teachers involved in thematic instruction often discover that their personal interests are an excellent source for topics. Recently, we met a teacher from a school in an agricultural community located two hours inland from the Northern California coast. The teacher, an avid deep-sea diver, successfully created an environment in which her fourth-grade bilingual students became very interested in studying oceanography, a topic far removed from their personal experiences. Another teacher we know is an amateur photographer and shared this interest with his sixth-grade students in a unit on pinhole photography. Using the teacher as a source for topics not only allows the teacher to bring a wealth of experience and knowledge to the theme, but also introduces students to issues they may never have considered.

Although many teachers rely on themes that focus on what some have termed the cognitive domain, thematic topics don't need to be this limited. Thematic units can and should support the students' affective development as well. Precisely because we wanted to develop a community of learners that worked together effectively and accepted one another on the basis of individual worth, we began the academic year with our Getting to Know About You, Me, and Others/*Tú, Yo, y Otros* theme, in which the students explored concepts such as self-esteem, peer pressure, feelings, conflict, and resolution.

As Eisner (1982) notes, however, this distinction between cognition and affect can result in "practical mischief." That is, schools too often value the cognitive over the affective and focus on what students know over what students feel. In reality, there can be no affect without cognition, nor can there be cognition without affect. To have feelings is to have a reaction to something that is known, to an idea. Similarly, to know something always entails accompanying feelings. Even the lack of feelings is, in fact, an affective response to something known.

Topic Significance as a Theme Source

Significance is often overlooked when a theme is being selected. What topics or issues are important for the students to explore? What ideas are worthy of inquiry? What ideas warrant the time and effort spent by both teachers and students within the thematic curriculum? Although there are no easy answers to these questions, we believe they need to be asked.

Several years ago we, along with a number of our colleagues, were questioning the use of a social studies curriculum that had students learn a myriad of facts and figures about Latin America. Although we found the topic significant, especially because we were teaching in Southern California, we wondered what and how much students would "carry away" with them. One colleague, a look of shock on his face, responded, "What would we teach if we didn't teach this?!"—precisely the question that should be asked when various theme topics are considered.

We have found the ideas of Dewey (1938) and Eisner (1982) to be particularly valuable as we seek worthy thematic topics. Dewey suggests that all genuine education comes about through quality experiences. In order for a theme to promote quality experiences, it must first speak to and be connected with the life experiences of the students. It must affirm, build on, and *extend* what the students bring to the classroom. A quality experience must also lead to—and live on in—future quality experiences. The theme must generate activities that encourage students to seek other worthwhile experiences.

Building on Dewey, Eisner proposes that quality experiences must expand the student's ability to construct diverse forms of meaning through a range of communication systems. Not only must the theme topic generate knowledge through oral and written language, it must also promote experiences that involve other forms of representation, such as art, music, and movement. This expanded view of communication systems is critical because the kinds of meanings constructed directly depend on the communication system engaged. Eisner says it best: "The kinds of nets we know how to weave determine the kinds of nets we cast. These nets, in turn, determine the kinds of fish we catch" (49). Thematic topics should generate experiences in which students learn to weave various kinds of nets and catch various kinds of fish.

Topics that incorporate various communication systems are especially important for bilingual students because access to the generalizations and concepts within the theme are not limited to the written word. Rather, students also engage the critical issues in the curriculum through art, music, and movement and through formats such as videos and records, which use additional communication systems along with language.

• • • • • • • • • • •

Selecting Texts and Materials

Gathering thematic materials is one of the most time-consuming aspects of thematic teaching. This is especially true for teachers who have little experience in developing curriculum beyond that provided by a textbook. We encourage teachers to draw from a number of sources as they begin their search for materials. School and public librarians are experts on books and are invaluable guides. Directors of curriculum and trade book publishers can also provide assistance. Perhaps most important, students can help in the search. Student involvement is critical, since they will experience the curriculum that is ultimately constructed. Often, material brought into the classroom by the students proves the most useful and best received. In addition, involving the students in the process of searching for themes-related material from home engages the parents, thus creating another link between school and the community.

Here are a number of guidelines that can be helpful as teachers and students consider materials for the curriculum:

- Materials should focus on the same set of generalizations and concepts.
- Materials should be grouped into text sets that focus on specific generalizations and concepts.
- Materials should integrate the disciplines: sciences, social sciences, and literature.
- Materials should integrate the modes of discourse: narratives, expositions, dramas, poems.
- Materials should integrate various resources: books, magazines, newspapers, filmstrips, records/audiotapes, movies/videotapes.
- Materials should integrate a range of literacy and thinking abilities.
- Materials should integrate the home and the school culture and language.
- Materials should represent multiple perspectives toward the generalizations and concepts.

Because of individual differences among students, thematic units work best when a wide range of materials are used in the classroom, thus providing equal access to all students regardless of their ability and language background. Given that all thematic materials focus on a core of potential generalizations and concepts, different students can experience different materials and activities and still come to know. Access to the critical ideas within the theme and involvement in the curricular conversations centering on these ideas are guaranteed for all students.

Focus on Common Generalizations and Concepts

Regardless of when in the process of curriculum development potential generalizations and concepts are identified, ultimately, the materials selected must focus on common or shared ideas and issues. This is not to say that each piece of material must address all generalizations and concepts. However, in total, the materials must adequately cover the range and depth of the core meanings to be explored. Materials that are only tangentially related to key ideas usually result in activities that lack meaningful links to other activities and materials within the curriculum. Students may become confused as they attempt to make sense of such material in light of what they have previously experienced.

Text Sets

In order to maintain our focus on the initial concepts and generalizations, we often group our materials into text sets (Harste, Short & Burke 1988). These sets are groupings of two or more texts or other materials that are conceptually linked to a specific generalization or issue. For example, in our theme Getting to Understand Fears/*Entendiendo Nuestros Temores,* although we had dozens of books that focused on a number of generalizations, we were able to group these materials into various text sets, each set addressing a particular generalization. For the generalization *People oftentimes fear what they do not understand,* the text set comprised *Got Me a Story to Tell* (Yee and Kokin 1977), *The Hundred Dresses* (Estes 1971), and *Angel Child, Dragon Child* (Surat 1983). Each book addresses the fear of differences from a different vantage point and has a different degree of reading difficulty. Using such sets within a theme gives students a deeper understanding of the generalization and allows students to read at their own ability level.

Integrated Disciplines

Well-conceived thematic units draw on various fields of study in order to provide students with a wealth of information and multiple views of the topic. Even when the theme focuses on a particular discipline, materials from other fields should at least be considered. For example, in our third-grade unit Getting to Know About Growing and Using Plants and Seeds/*Cultivando y Utilizando Plantas y Semillas,* our materials were not limited to the natural sciences. We also used the predictable stories *Jack and the Beanstalk* (Paulson 1992) and *The Great Big Enormous Turnip* (Tolstoy 1971) to reveal the role plants play in a culture's literature. Social science articles, such as those found in *National Geographic* and *World* magazines, were also incorporated into the unit as the students explored the influence of a region's vegetation on the local culture.

Because topics invariably cut across the disciplines, incorporating materials from various fields of study into the unit encourages students to develop a fuller and multidimensional understanding of the topic and related generalizations and concepts. As Harste (1993) points out, the disciplines provide perspective and each perspective necessarily involves asking different questions and providing different answers. Therefore, both what professionals in different fields have to say about a topic and how they say it will vary. The botanist's understanding of seeds and plants is different from the geographer's, and both differ from that of a writer of short stories. Students need to interact with materials from different fields.

Integrated Modes of Discourse

When selecting materials for thematic teaching, we also consider ways of integrating various modes of discourse: narrative, poetry, drama, and exposition. Because each field of study views the same topic from various perspectives, the written materials in each field often use different organizational patterns. Science materials are often informational, while social science materials are frequently time-ordered. Literary materials may reflect narrative as well as poetic and dramatic patterns. If students are to learn to use these patterns effectively in their own writing, the patterns must be encountered in the thematic unit.

Another purpose for including various modes of discourse within a unit is the variety of responses that these modes may elicit from the reader. As Rosenblatt (1978) suggests, narratives, poetry, and drama typically engage students in aesthetic reading, where the focus is on enjoyment, on the lived-through experience. Encounters with these texts focus on the feelings and attitudes that the ideas in these texts arouse in the reader. Expository texts, on the other hand, provide students with efferent reading. Students focus on what remains after the reading, on the ideas and meanings they carry away. Expository text, or text written to convey factual information, is generally connected with social studies, the natural sciences, or other disciplines.

However, it is important to remember that response always depends on the interaction among the reader, context, and purpose. A student of ours, Elvis, did not engage aesthetically with our thematic unit Getting to Know About You, Me, and Others/*Tú, Yo, y Otros*. Although the unit included numerous narrative texts, songs, and movies, the topic did not appear to "speak" to Elvis in any meaningful way. Nevertheless, when the topic changed to Getting to Know About Reptiles and Amphibians/*Conociendo los Reptiles y los Anfibios*, a theme that relied more heavily on expository material, Elvis responded with great enthusiasm. For Elvis, not only was the entire theme a lived-through experience, it was also one in which he learned a great deal of new information.

Integrated Resources

The more successful units we have planned and implemented were not limited to textbooks. A wide range of language materials—magazines, newspapers, encyclopedias, trade books, movies—and nonlanguage materials—maps, globes, cartoons, pictures, music—were also included. When we go beyond the classroom textbook, we begin to help students see connections between what we do in schools and the real world.

In addition, students who have access to a wide variety of resources focusing on the same concepts or generalizations develop a better understanding of the theme being studied. Important for all students, this is especially so for the second language learner, whose home culture may be different from that of the school community. A variety of resources helps the teacher provide a context for concepts that might otherwise be difficult for these students to learn. Table 4.1 categorizes some of the resources available to most classroom teachers that go beyond the traditional text.

An Integrated Range of Thinking and Literacy Abilities

Focusing learning around thematic units offers students numerous opportunities to develop a rich source of knowledge that promotes their reading, writing, and thinking abilities. Because most classrooms contain students with varying abili-

	ACADEMIC DISCIPLINES		
Resources	Natural Sciences	Social Sciences	Literature
Newscasts **Newspapers** **Magazines**	Weather reports Science news Scientific reports and magazines Essays	Current events Feature articles Political news	Reviews Television guides Narratives in magazines Essays
Research **Materials**	Encyclopedias Journals Logs Magazines Computer bulletin boards Databases	Encyclopedias Biographies Autobiographies Histories Speeches Court decisions Research reports Community members Computer bulletin boards Databases	Biographies Autobiographies
Symbolic **Materials**	Graphs Chemical symbols Films Thermometers Scales Equipment Photographs Maps Recordings Collections Models Museums	Globes Maps Morse code Photographs Fine art Music Cartoons Ballots Dance Films Blueprints Recordings Collections Museums	Book illustrations Wordless picture books Films Dance Plays Music Television Art Recordings Collections

TABLE 4.1 Grid of thematic resources.

ties, materials that reflect a wide range of difficulty are critical to the success of any thematic unit.

Far too often we have observed teachers working with the entire class on a quality piece of literature that is far beyond the abilities of some students, especially the second language learners. In California, for example, all grade levels have identified core works of literature that all students must encounter. Typically, these core works are read aloud, the teacher calling on students one at a time.

Problem-Solving Materials	Experiments	Building models	Mysteries
	Recipes	Clothes patterns	Theme and plot
	Cookbooks	Reconstructing cultures	analysis
	"How to" books	from artifacts	*Choose Your Own*
	Science kits	Bus, airline, train	*Adventure* books
	Simulations	schedules	"How to" books
	Calculators	"How to" books	Computers
	Computers	Simulations	
	Databases	Calculators	
		Computers	
		Databases	
Trade Books	Biographies	Biographies	Biographies
	Autobiographies	Autobiographies	Autobiographies
	Fiction	Fiction	Fiction
	Nonfiction	Nonfiction	Nonfiction
	Poetry	Poetry	Poetry
		Plays	Plays
Primary Sources	Conservation records	Family documents	Student creative
	Research notes	Letters	writing
	Scientists	Government	Performances
		documents	Storytelling
		Interviews	Authors
		Experts	
		Specialists	

Text Books/Basals

TABLE 4.1 *(cont.)*

Essentially, the class becomes one large reading group. One reason teachers use this instructional framework is because they realize that some students are unable to read the literature on their own. By having the text read aloud, they hope that these students will be able to "follow along."

Unfortunately, what often happens is either these students listen to the story being read without monitoring the print or they disengage altogether. Although listening to stories being read is a valid classroom activity, our concern is that less proficient readers not be deprived of meaningful print experiences. It is only through such experiences that students will be able to expand their literacy abilities.

A wide range of materials all focused on a common core of generalizations and concepts ensures that students will have access to both the central issues within the thematic curriculum as well as meaningful encounters with print.

For example, concepts and generalizations related to a unit focusing on the underground railroad can be accessed through books such as *Freedom Train* (Sterling 1954), *Wanted Dead or Alive* (McGovern 1965), *Go Free or Die* (Ferris 1988), and *Steal Away* (Armstrong 1992). Common to these four books is the story of a woman running away from slavery. *Freedom Train, Wanted Dead or Alive,* and *Go Free or Die* all deal with how Harriet Tubman led other slaves to freedom. *Freedom Train* is written with a more proficient reader in mind, but *Wanted Dead or Alive* and *Go Free or Die* can be read by less proficient students. *Steal Away,* on the other hand, is the story of two girls who run away from the South. Written in two voices, the book lets a more proficient reader gain new insights into the theme.

Integrated Culture and Language

If understanding requires that the learner tap into his or her knowledge of the world, then teachers need to keep in mind differences in culture and language between home and school. When students cannot make connections between the new information being presented in the classroom and their prior knowledge, comprehension will, at best, be very limited. In addition, teachers working with students from various cultural backgrounds understand that the students' interpretations of a text differ from their own and from one another's.

Bilingual classrooms traditionally offer two distinct and separate curriculums. Primary language materials seldom, if ever, correspond to those being used by students in English. Thematic teaching offers classroom teachers and students the opportunity to focus on the same core of meaning, thus simplifying what many teachers view as a struggle to maintain two different programs. As concepts are presented, the students can choose both the difficulty of the materials they use and the language in which those materials are written. In our unit Getting to Know About You, Me, and Others/*Tú, Yo, y Otros*, we dealt with the concepts *conflict* and *resolution* by providing texts in English and Spanish. Children could choose between *Oliver Button Is a Sissy* (de Paola 1979) and its Spanish translation, *Oliver Button es una Nena* (de Paola 1982). An additional Spanish text dealing with these concepts, *Rosa Caramelo* (Turín & Bosnia 1976) was also available.

Themes and materials should also foster and affirm cultural diversity. Rather than ignoring cultural differences, teachers and students need to address issues of pluralism and diversity. For example, in Chapter 3 we discussed how third-grade bilingual students read and responded to *Ira Sleeps Over* (Waber 1972), *William's Doll* (Zolotow 1972), *Oliver Button Is a Sissy* (de Paola 1979), *Oliver Button es una Nena* (de Paola 1982), and *Rosa Caramelo* (Turín & Bosnia 1976). The discussion went beyond the teacher-identified concepts. As the third graders discussed Ira's experience in light of William's and Oliver's conflicts and their own experiences, they posed new questions: Was Ira a boy or a girl? Should boys play with dolls? Would Ira have felt differently about taking his teddy bear to Reggie's house had the character been a girl? As students compared and contrasted these texts with their own experiences, they explored their understanding of gender stereotypes as they appear not only in the literature but in their everyday lives. These unexpected questions allowed us to introduce additional books, like *My Dad Takes Care of Me* (Quinlan 1987), that we used to investigate other dimensions of gender stereotypes.

Similarly, in an immigration unit students can examine the concepts related to ethnicity, immigration patterns, and prejudice through materials like *Wilfredo* (Oropeda 1986), *Angel Island Prisoner, 1922* (Chetin 1982), and *Angel Child, Dragon Child* (Surat 1983). A different text set, one that includes *I Speak English for My Mom* (Stanek 1989) and *I Hate English* (Levine 1989), might provide students the opportunity to explore how various individuals deal with the acquisition of a second language as part of the acculturation process. Again, the intent of these text sets is to allow students to focus on the same core meaning while using a range of materials.

Multiple Perspectives

One way students, as well as adults, come to a fuller understanding of a topic or issue is by "trying on" multiple perspectives or stances. As demonstrated by our students' discussion about whether or not boys should play with dolls, it is important that students encounter more than one view of the issues being presented within the thematic materials. Although at times these perspectives may be culturally based, they can also reflect conflicting views within a culture. As we were beginning our unit Getting to Know About Growing and Using Plants and Seeds/*Cultivando y Utilizando Plantas y Semillas,* issues related to organic versus inorganic gardening and the use of pesticides emerged. The local orange groves were being infested by fruit flies and aerial chemical spraying was being considered as a way to eradicate the pests. The appropriateness of this response was hotly debated in the local newspapers and on radio and television. We brought these perspectives and resources into our theme discussions.

• • • • • • • • • • •

A Look Back

At this point in the development of the thematic curriculum—after thematic topics and materials have been selected—the teacher, with student collaboration, will have

1. Identified a significant thematic topic,
2. Gathered a variety of materials, and
3. Identified a set of potential generalizations and corresponding concepts on which the thematic curriculum can begin to be built.

5

Demonstrations, Mediations, and Engagements Within the Thematic Curriculum

· · · · · · · · · · ·

Supporting the Learner Through Holistic Instruction

We see teaching and learning within the thematic curriculum as involving a series of demonstrations, mediations, and engagements. Frank Smith (1981) has defined demonstrations as events that tell the student, "This is how something is done." Demonstrations highlight or display the key elements in an activity. By their nature, demonstrations are holistic and operate within authentic, purposeful contexts. Teaching, according to Smith, is a cluster of demonstrations experienced by students over time. As demonstrations relate to thematic instruction, they are instructional events that tell the student, 'This is how particular communication systems, thinking processes, or ideas operate.'

Watching demonstrations, although an important dimension of thematic teaching, is not usually sufficient for learning to occur. Mediation on the part of the teacher and engagement on the part of the learner are also required. Mediations are pedagogic structures by which the teacher supports the students as they encounter and move through a demonstration. Engagement, on the other hand, represents the learner's involvement with a demonstration: it is an active transaction between the student and the event.

Before discussing in greater detail the kind of instructional support we are advocating, let's look at an experience in which such support is demonstrated, mediated, and engaged. The original activity was developed by a close friend and colleague, Mitzi Lewison, and we have adapted and modified it over the years. It involves activities that support the reading of William Shakespeare's "Sonnet

60," a text most people find difficult to read and comprehend. Our example therefore uses experiences similar to the kind we propose for elementary students, especially students who are learning English as a second language or whose culture varies from that of the school. We have used this example with quite a few teachers over the years and share some of their responses at pertinent points.

Because we believe learning is inherently social, we encourage you to find collaborators when trying out the "Sonnet 60" activities for yourself—it will give you a fuller understanding of and deeper appreciation for them. But whether you do these activities with others or alone, pay attention to their characteristics.

• • • • • • • • • • •

Moving Into, Through, and Beyond "Sonnet 60"

Before reading Shakespeare's "Sonnet 60," consider what *time* means to you. Don't discuss it, just think about it, then jot down your ideas in the left-hand column of Appendix 5.1 and illustrate these ideas in Appendix 5.2. (You may write first or illustrate first, whichever you prefer.)

If you are collaborating with others, share your illustration of time and have your colleagues interpret what time means to you from your illustration. After listening to their interpretations, read aloud what you have written and discuss its relationship to your illustration. Give each person with whom you are working the opportunity to share in the same way. Then discuss the similarities and differences among your writings and illustrations. The left-hand column in Figure 5.1 and upper-left segment of Figure 5.2 represent one teacher's interpretation of time. How does your concept of time compare with this teacher's?

Now that you have reflected about time, read the poem below (1966). Because poetry is usually intended to be read aloud, you may want to do so. As you read, think about how this poet's understanding of time is both similar to and different from your own.

"What Is Time?"
Phyllis McGinley

Is it something to touch like a tree,
A table, a boulder?
Can you see,
From the tail of your eye,
Time strolling by?

Can you hear Time?
Blowing like the wind past your shoulder,
Or smell it like leather
Or taste it, perhaps, on your tongue

What do you think time is?	What does Phyllis McGinley think time is?	What does William Shakespeare think time is?
Time is the learning and growing process of what is around you. At first it is small and as you grow it becomes larger and you become more knowledgable. As time passes, you should be seeing more and with this comes wisdom—finally throughout time you should have made a mark. You are now worldly, etc.	That time is a part of us all, but we cannot touch it, or see it, but we can be part of it. It is a part of us—as time changes, so do we. With each second our heart beats so does time.	Night and day time passes, but there can be major differences between the two. One can be full and the other bare—but it can still be the same. Differences can come and go, but time will always be.

FIGURE 5.1 Written interpretation of time.

Like rolls from a pan?
No, nobody can,
Not the old, not the young.

Yet all of us share
Invisible Time like the air.
It is real as the boulder,
The table, the tree.
It moves and you with it (like Me),
Growing up growing older;
Each of us borne like a boat on
A river of Time which we float on
All our lives long.

And what's most exciting and strange is
That hour by hour it changes
As hour by hour do we.
Although we can't touch it or taste it,
We can save it or use it
Or waste it,
But chiefly we measure it out.

And that is what Clocks are about.

Now go back to Appendix 5.1 and 5.2 and jot down and illustrate what McGinley thinks time is.

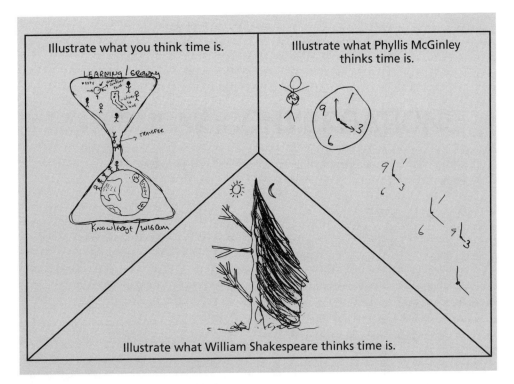

FIGURE 5.2 Illustrative interpretation of time.

Once again, if working with others, give each person in the group the opportunity to share his or her ideas and illustration about the McGinley poem. Compare and contrast McGinley's view of time with your own. Then look at Figures 5.1 and 5.2 to see how that teacher understood the McGinley poem.

You are now ready to read "Sonnet 60." As with the McGinley poem, you may want to read orally, and you will want to think about Shakespeare's view of time.

"Sonnet 60"
William Shakespeare

Like as the waves make towards the pebbled shore,
So do our minutes hasten to their end;
Each changing place with that which goes before,
In sequent toil all forwards do contend.
Nativity, once in the main of light,
Crawls to maturity, wherewith being crown'd,
Crooked eclipses 'gainst his glory fight,
And Time, that gave, doth now his gift confound.
Time doth transfix the flourish set on youth,

And delves the parallels in beauty's brow;
Feeds on the rarities of nature's truth,
And nothing stands but for his scythe to mow,
And yet, to times in hope, my verse shall stand,
Praising thy worth, despite his cruel hand.

Jot down and illustrate in Appendix 5.1 and 5.2 what Shakespeare seems to think about time. If you are working with others, share what you have written and drawn. Discuss the relationship between Shakespeare's view of time and your own as well as the relationship between Shakespeare's view of time and McGinley's. Return to Figures 5.1 and 5.2 to see how that teacher interpreted Shakespeare's sonnet.

Now, read "Sonnet 60" a second time, underlining your favorite phrases and circling those phrases you find confusing or difficult to understand. Share your favorite lines with a friend.

In the top box of Appendix 5.3, write one phrase that you identified as confusing or difficult to understand. Below the phrase, write your best guess as to what you think the phrase might mean. Have two or three colleagues write down other possible interpretations. Read them all and select the one that makes most sense to you. Reread the sonnet a final time to determine how well the interpretation works.

Figure 5.3 shows the phrase identified by the teacher whose comments and drawings are shown in Figures 5.1 and 5.2 and various interpretations for the phrase. Before continuing with this chapter, reflect on the activities you have just engaged in and discuss how they supported you in mediating "Sonnet 60."

• • • • • • • • • •

Characteristics of Thematic Activities

Our "Sonnet 60" example highlights some of the key characteristics we believe should be reflected in thematic activities:

- Thematic activities are linguistically, cognitively, socioculturally, and developmentally authentic.
- Thematic activities provide students with opportunities to use various communication systems—language, mathematics, art, music, movement—to learn about the generalizations and concepts within the theme.
- Thematic activities provide students with opportunities to use thinking processes from various disciplines—literature, natural sciences, social sciences—to learn about the generalizations and concepts within the theme.
- Thematic activities provide students with opportunities to use communication systems for various purposes or functions.

"SONNET 60"
William Shakespeare

A phrase that I am unclear about is:
    "And nothing stands but for his scythe to mow."

My interpretation is:
    Nothing stands in his way.

Another possible interpretation is:
    The scythe is the Grim Reaper's tool—he, Death, mowes our lives down like the farmer mowes his field.

Another possible interpretation is:
    Time ends for individuals at death and "cuts down" the person's life experiences. They no longer matter to anyone.

Another possible interpretation is:
    Nothing can stand the effects of time. Eventually all people die (or are mowed down).

FIGURE 5.3 Various interpretations of Shakespeare.

- Thematic activities integrate the language and culture of the home with the language and culture of the school.
- Thematic activities represent a range of literacy and thinking abilities.
- Thematic activities engage students in both independent and collaborative experiences.
- Thematic activities provide students with opportunities for problem solving, divergent thinking, and risk taking.
- Thematic activities encourage students to take multiple perspectives.
- Thematic activities engage students in the generation of new meaning as well as in revisiting prior meaning.
- Thematic activities encourage students to integrate and synthesize current and prior meanings.

Authenticity

An unfortunate aspect of teaching and learning in schools is that students are often asked to perform certain tasks—what Edelsky and Smith (1984) refer to as tricks—that they will never encounter or experience in the world at large. Filling in blanks on worksheets, answering literal comprehension questions, and responding to vocabulary or phonic flash cards—even if done in connection with thematic materials—belong to the schools and the schools alone.

As we evaluate the value of existing lessons and generate new thematic learning, the concept of authenticity is a useful criterion to help us avoid such activities (Edelsky & Smith 1984; Kucer 1991, 1994). Authenticity is a powerful concept because it provides a framework in which other characteristics of teaching and learning can be embedded. It is also a filter to ensure that thematic lessons reflect the ways and means in which literacy is used in the home, culture, and workplace, thereby unifying school and real-world literacy events. This classroom-world link is particularly important for students whose language, culture, and/or socioeconomic status varies from that of the school. These students need to see the relevance of instructional activities to their home experiences; if they don't, they may choose one over the other or, possibly, become alienated from both.

There are four dimensions to thematic authenticity: linguistic, cognitive, sociocultural, and developmental (see Figure 5.4). First, literacy events within thematic units as we envision them are authentic linguistically. As in life, reading and writing activities engage the students in whole, unadulterated pieces of discourse. The language in the lessons is not basalized or divided into bits and pieces, nor are parts of language taught in isolation. Simply stated, students read and write whole, natural texts.

In our Shakespeare exercise, language remained intact as you interacted with the two poems. Although you were asked to identify favorite and difficult phrases in the sonnet, you did so within the context of the entire text. You were not given vocabulary lists before reading, nor were you asked to answer a series of comprehension questions. Instead, your responses involved comparing and contrasting various conceptualizations of time as you have experienced it and as it was expressed through two poems.

Linguistically authentic thematic activities are especially important for second language learners. Teachers who work with second language learners know they need to give their students what Krashen (1982) has labeled "comprehensible input." Comprehension involves making and confirming predictions. When attempting to make predictions, both first and second language learners use all the linguistic cuing systems—textual, semantic, syntactic, graphophonic—to reduce uncertainty (Goodman 1985; Goodman, Goodman & Flores 1979; Rumelhart 1985). The more linguistic cues available, the more comprehensible the language and the more meaningful the text. For example, it is easier for a second language learner to understand a word within the context of a story than in isolation. As students see the whole, they can better understand how the parts make sense.

Thematic lessons are also cognitively authentic; they engage students in those thinking processes and strategies that are involved in the various communication systems and disciplines. Table 5.1 (communication systems) and Table 5.2 (subject

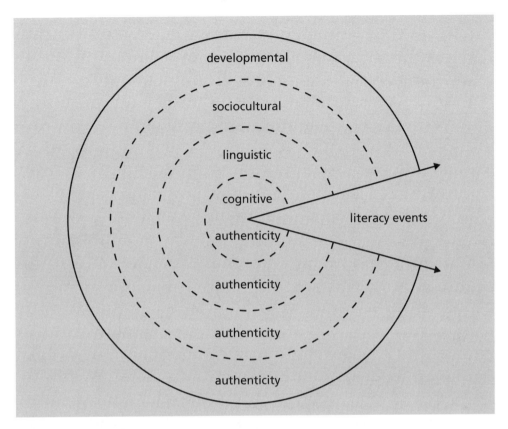

FIGURE 5.4 Dimensions of authenticity.

area thinking processes) identify many of those processes used when individuals communicate within and across the disciplines. Cognitively authentic thematic lessons provide students with opportunities to interact with these processes by using whole texts in meaningful ways.

The Shakespeare exercise involved a range of cognitive processes. In order to compare and contrast the various perspectives on time, you had to read for the major ideas expressed in the two poems and integrate the ideas in each into a coherent whole. You were explicitly asked to use your background knowledge before, during, and after each reading and used various linguistic cues as you read. As ideas were expressed artistically, elements and principles of design were used to form a coordinated whole. Similarly involved were such literary thinking processes as analyzing information, making associations among the two poems, and interpreting the writing of the two poets. You used all of these processes to interact with whole texts, either written or illustrated.

Socioculturally authentic lessons reflect the ways in which we use literacy to mediate our interactions with their world. We engage cognitively with whole texts

Literacy: Reading

1. Generates and organizes major ideas or concepts.
2. Develops and supports major ideas and concepts with details and particulars.
3. Integrates meaning into a logical and coherent whole.
4. Uses a variety of linguistic cues: textual, semantic, syntactic, graphophonic.
5. Uses a variety of text aids: pictures, charts, graphs, subheadings.
6. Uses relevant conceptual and linguistic background knowledge.
7. Makes meaningful predictions based on what has been previously read.
8. Revises—rereads, reads on, or rethinks—when meaning is lost or purposes are not met.
9. Generates inferences or goes beyond the information given.
10. Reflects on, and responds to, what is being read.
11. Uses reading for various purposes or functions: instrumental, regulatory, interactional, personal, heuristic, imaginative, informative, diversionary, perpetuatory.
12. Varies the manner in which texts are read based on different purposes and audiences.
13. Takes risks.
14. Sentences are meaningful as read.

Literacy: Writing

1. Generates and organizes major ideas or concepts.
2. Expands, extends, and elaborates on major ideas or concepts.
3. Integrates meaning into a logical and coherent whole.
4. Uses a variety of linguistic cues: textual, semantic, syntactic, graphophonic.
5. Uses a variety of text aids: pictures, charts, graphs, subheadings.
6. Uses relevant conceptual and linguistic background knowledge.
7. Predicts/plans future meanings based on what has been written.
8. Revises when meaning is lost or purposes and needs of the audience are not met.
9. Uses writing to explore ideas and to discover new meanings.
10. Reflects on and responds to what is being written.
11. Uses writing for various purposes or functions: instrumental, regulatory, interactional, personal, heuristic, imaginative, informative, diversionary, perpetuatory.
12. Varies the manner in which texts are written based on different purposes and audiences.
13. Takes risks.
14. Sentences are meaningful as written.
15. Revises conventions—spelling, punctuation, capitalization, penmanship—after meaning and purposes are met.

Mathematics

1. Uses various mathematical functions—adding, subtracting, multiplying, dividing—to solve problems and to investigate the world.
2. Estimates to solve problems and to investigate the world.
3. Uses mathematical knowledge to explain events.
4. Interprets events using mathematical knowledge.
5. Summarizes mathematical information.
6. Predicts events using mathematical knowledge.
7. Integrates and connects mathematical functions and information to solve problems and to investigate the world.
8. Organizes mathematical information to solve problems and to investigate the world.

TABLE 5.1 Communication systems.

9. Draws conclusions using mathematical knowledge.
10. Categorizes information using mathematical knowledge.
11. Seeks and forms patterns using mathematical knowledge.

Movement
1. Uses body parts for various actions—jumping, skipping, tumbling, stretching, clapping—to express ideas and feelings.
2. Varies how actions are done—quickly, smoothly, slowly, lightly—to express ideas and feelings.
3. Varies actions in space—up, down, forward, sideways, to the left, to the right—to express ideas and feelings.
4. Varies the actions in relationship to a partner, group, object, to express ideas and feelings.
5. Uses going and stopping contrast—running and stopping, bouncing and crouching, striding and stopping—to express ideas and feelings.
6. Uses body-part contrasts—hands clap/ feet jump/arms swing/ feet stamp/feet slide—to express ideas and feelings.
7. Uses qualitative contrasts—glide/ explode/rush/pounce—to express ideas and feelings.
8. Uses spatial contrasts—traveling movements (leaping, rolling) with in-place movements (rising, sinking)—to express ideas and feelings.
9. Integrates various elements of movement to form a coordinated whole and to express ideas and feelings.
10. Reflects on and responds to the movement of others using knowledge of various elements of movement.
11. Evaluates the quality or value of the movement of others.

Music
1. Uses pitch—high, low, melody, scale—to express ideas and feelings.
2. Use rhythm—meter, tones—to express ideas and feelings.
3. Uses harmony—tones, cords—to express ideas and feelings.
4. Uses form—repetition, variation, patterns—to express ideas and feelings.
5. Uses texture—thick, thin, opaque, legato, staccato—to express ideas and feelings.
6. Uses tempo—speed, variation—to express ideas and feelings.
7. Uses dynamics—volume, variation—to express ideas and feelings.
8. Uses timbre—tonal qualities—to express ideas and feelings.
9. Integrates various elements of music to form a coordinated whole and to express ideas and feelings.
10. Reflects on and responds to the music of others using knowledge of various musical elements.
11. Evaluates the quality of value of the musical expression of others.

Art
1. Uses elements of design—color, line, value, shape, form, texture, mass, space, volume—to express ideas and feelings.
2. Uses principles of design—balance, symmetry, asymmetry, contrast, dominance, repetition, rhythm, theme and variation, unity—to express ideas and feelings.
3. Integrates design elements and principles to form a coordinated whole and to express ideas and feelings.
4. Reflects and responds to the artistic expression of others using knowledge of design elements and principles.
5. Evaluates the quality or value of the artistic expression of others.

TABLE 5.1 *(cont.)*

Literature	Social Science	Science
1. Analyzes information. 2. Interprets. 3. Establishes interpretations supported by textual information and background knowledge. 4. Makes associations between and among texts. 5. Forms mental images. 6. Engages in vicarious experiences. 7. Fantasizes. 8. Adopts an efferent or aesthetic stance. 9. Reflects on and responds to the meanings being generated. 10. Evaluates the quality or value of the text. 11. Develops concepts and generalizations.	1. Analyzes information. 2. Develops concepts and generalizations. 3. Generates hypotheses. 4. Formulates decisions. 5. Formulates values. 6. Compares and contrasts. 7. Offers alternatives. 8. Observes. 9. Describes. 10. Differentiates. 11. Explains.	1. Observes and gathers data. 2. Generates hypotheses or predictions. 3. Tests hypotheses. 4. Modifies hypotheses. 5. Compares and contrasts. 6. Orders and classifies. 7. Measures. 8. Describes. 9. Infers or draws conclusions. 10. Develops concepts and generalizations.

TABLE 5.2 Subject area thinking processes.

for purposeful, functional reasons, not simply to practice reading and writing. In the world, literacy is always a tool to accomplish "acts" in the user's life. Within the thematic curriculum, thinking and learning attempt to reflect the functional nature of these acts. For example, rather than just practice letter writing, students can write and send letters to various organizations requesting information they might need for a particular investigation. Similarly, the activities related to time in the Shakespeare exercise were intended to help you become more aware of your personal understanding and feelings about time. In addition, by comparing and contrasting your understanding and feelings with those of McGinley, Shakespeare, and your colleagues, you also came to appreciate the understanding and feelings of others.

Although important for all students, the sociocultural dimension of literacy impacts language minority students in unique ways. As documented by Ferdman

(1990), Gee (1990), Heath (1983), and the California Bilingual Education Department (1986), literacy is always culturally framed and defined. Literacy practices and norms vary across groups—cultural, ethnic, class, occupational—and individual acts of literacy reflect the values of the group in which the literacy act is embedded. Typically, the manner in which literacy is used in the schools reflects middle-class, Eurocentric norms. Students from minority cultures may perceive these school practices as a rejection of their home experiences and may feel that becoming literate requires a similar rejection on their part. In order to avoid this either-or situation, thematic activities should reflect and build on the literacy practices of the students' communities. Furthermore, thematic activities that build on home literacy practices foster positive self-concepts by valuing home language and culture.

There are a number of ways in which literacy practices can be characterized. We have found the framework developed by Halliday (1973) and Smith (1977) to be especially powerful. Below, we list and describe nine functions for literacy and give several thematic activities for each function, many of which we used with third graders in connection with the theme Getting to Know About Growing and Using Plants and Seeds/*Cultivando y Utilizando Plantas y Semillas*. It is important to note, however, that activities frequently address more than one purpose and that we have simply classified each activity as to its most prominent function.

1. Instrumental: "I want"—a means for getting something, satisfying material needs.
   - Listing materials needed to plant a garden.
   - Ordering seeds from a seed catalog.
2. Regulatory: "Do as I tell you" "This is how it must be"—a means to control the behavior, feelings, or attitudes of others.
   - Reading and writing directions for planting a garden, conducting experiments with plants and seeds, or cooking with plants and seeds.
   - Reading and writing directions for caring for plants.
3. Interactional: "Me and you" "Me against you"—a way to interact with others, form and maintain relationships, establish separateness.
   - Comparing and contrasting the plants and seeds class members eat at home.
   - Writing thank-you notes after a visit to a nursery, greenhouse, farm, etc.
4. Personal: "Here I come"—a way to express individuality and uniqueness, awareness of self, pride.
   - Listing favorite and least favorite foods.
   - Describing plants and seeds grown/eaten by the student's family.
5. Heuristic: "Tell me why"—a way to explore the environment, to ask questions, to seek and test knowledge.
   - Conducting plant and seed experiments.
   - Reading "how to" books on growing plants and seeds.
   - Researching plants and seeds.

- Listing "What I know," "What I want to learn," and "What I have learned" about growing and using plants and seeds.
- Investigating what household items are made from plants and seeds.

6. Imaginative: "Let's pretend"—a way to create new worlds, to make up stories, poems, and fantasies.
   - Reading and writing imaginative stories, poems, and plays involving plants and seeds.

7. Informative: "I've got something to tell you"—a means of communicating information to someone who does not possess that information.
   - Sharing information about plants and seeds from experiments and research projects.

8. Diversionary: "Enjoy this"—a means of entertainment.
   - Reading or creating jokes, riddles, and puns dealing with plants and seeds.
   - Singing or composing songs about plants and seeds.

9. Perpetuating: "How it was"—a means of documentation.
   - Keeping records/journals of observations of plant and seed experiments.
   - Researching what plants grew in our environment before the arrival of the Europeans.
   - Researching what new plants were introduced to the Americas by the Europeans and what new plants were taken to Europe from the Americas.
   - Investigating how the introduction of new plants to the Americas and Europe changed the lives of the Native Americans and the Europeans.
   - Researching how the Native Americans used plants and seeds.

The last characteristic of authenticity is developmental. A developmentally authentic activity captures the way in which literacy is learned. Decades of language and learning research (e.g., Halliday 1975; Vygotsky 1978; Smith 1981; Harste, Woodward & Burke 1984; Wertsch 1985; Freeman & Freeman 1994) have shown that children learn to read, write, and think in both their first and second language through mediation with and demonstrations by more capable peers and adults. Initially, the child observes literacy being used by significant others; these uses demonstrate the role of reading and writing in everyday living. The child encounters these demonstrations in collaborative, socially supported situations before using literacy in individual, independent contexts. Through such collaborative experiences, the child comes to a general, holistic understanding of literacy. Over time the child's sensitivity to acts of literacy increase and he or she develops the particulars and details of reading and writing.

The child, whether a native or a second language speaker, accomplishes this whole-to-part learning much as a scientist discovers new knowledge: by gathering data (engaging in socially supported encounters with print), generating hypotheses (formulating guesses as to how literacy operates), testing hypotheses (trying out guesses during reading and writing and receiving feedback), and modifying hypotheses (changing guesses when they fail to work). Such a developmental process stands in stark contrast to a behavioristic position that views learning as a part-to-whole process involving imitation, practice, and mastery.

Because literacy is encountered and learned in social contexts, lessons within a thematic curriculum engage first and second language learners in collaborative and socially supported situations. These initial lessons allow students to learn the general aspects of literacy before moving to the details. In addition, the lessons allow students to construct rather than imitate the processes of reading, writing, and thinking.

Although students receive social support throughout the year, in our Shakespeare example, we attempted to illustrate how such support might look by encouraging you to engage in the activities with others, sharing your interpretations, ideas, and illustrations, and by providing you with the responses of a fifth-grade teacher for comparative purposes.

Multiple Communication Systems

A second characteristic of learning and thinking within a thematic unit is using varied communication systems in connection with the concepts and generalization within the theme. Figure 1.1, the Shakespeare demonstration, and Table 5.1 all show that students use not only language but also art, music, movement, and mathematics to communicate and learn. Just as each field of study has its unique way of looking at a particular topic, each communication system has its unique way of expressing ideas. When planning activities for our units, we seek ways to have students reflect on what they have learned and to recast this learning through alternative systems of communication. As students cross—transmediate—the systems, they learn how the systems operate and at the same time discover insights into the meaning that they are trying to express. In a thematic unit, there are a variety of perspectives from which the students will come to understand the topic and multiple ways in which they will learn to express these understandings (Eisner 1982; Suhor 1984).

Being able to access meaning through a variety of communications systems is particularly useful to second language learners. Transmediation promotes language development by providing these students with context cues other than language to make sense of both the oral and written language used in the classroom (Freeman and Freeman 1992, 1994). Understanding the intimate and symbiotic relationship between alternate communication systems and language, second language teachers give their students the opportunity to use various communication systems in order to convey meaning. For example, students may use art or movement, rather than discussion, to express their understanding and feelings about a story.

In our thematic unit Getting to Know About Growing and Using Plants and Seeds/*Cultivando y Utilizando Plantas y Semillas*, the students explored the role that plants and seeds play in the literature of various cultures. As part of this exploration, we read *The Great Big Enormous Turnip* (Tolstoy 1971). After the story was read and discussed, we asked the students to draw a diagram of the meaning in the story. They used lines, shapes, and color to express their ideas, but no language. In the days following this activity, the students were allowed to choose additional activities: they wrote poems and songs about the story, grew and measured the growth of turnip seeds, illustrated key parts of the story with music, and compared and contrasted the story with other plant stories we had read, like *Jack and the Beanstalk* (Paulson 1992) or its Spanish version, *Juanito y las Habas* (EdiNorma n.d.). Second language learners especially enjoyed using body movement to represent the growth cycle of a seed. In these activities, the students created and recreated meaning through language, mathematics, arts, music, and movement. In the process, not only did they come to understand the story more fully, they also learned about various mathematical functions and their uses, they experimented with expressing meaning artistically through the integration of elements and principles of design, and they applied their knowledge of such musical elements as pitch, rhythm, and harmony in the songs they sang.

Multiple Thinking Processes

Table 5.2 identifies the thinking processes used in the subject areas of literature, the natural sciences, and the social sciences. For example, in our Shakespeare demonstration you supported your interpretation of the text by first applying your background knowledge about time. Furthermore you expressed your ideas and feelings by drawing a picture. Finally, you reflected on and responded to the meaning being generated by yourself and others.

As activities are selected or generated, the teacher must consider how to incorporate these processes into various lessons. The disciplines not only present different perspectives, they also engage the mind in different manipulations of information. Because the mind is not divided into separate, isolated compartments for each field of study, many of the thinking processes quite naturally cross the disciplines. What varies as one crosses the disciplines is the content being manipulated, not the processes being used. As opposed to some curriculums that teach "critical thinking" as a separate subject, we consider thinking processes an integral part of the curriculum—they are how students explore content and formulate concepts and generalizations.

Our students read a number of books about various types of reptiles (lizards, snakes, dinosaurs, turtles, alligators, crocodiles) and amphibians (salamanders, frogs, toads) in the theme Getting to Know About Reptiles and Amphibians/ *Conociendo los Reptiles y los Anfibios: The Book of Reptiles and Amphibians* (Bevans 1956), *Como Descubrimos los Dinosaurios* (Asimov 1986), *Reptiles* (Ballard 1982), and *Reptiles and Amphibians* (Sabin 1985). When we read *Let's Look at Reptiles* (Huntington 1973) to the class, Alma asked about the difference between a reptile and an amphibian. Her question prompted a series of activities to help the students discover the differences. First, the students created two research forms that they used to discover the common characteristics of a number of amphibians and reptiles. (The research form for amphibians is included as Appendix 5.4.)

The students formed five-member research groups. Each group revisited the books they had read about salamanders, frogs, and toads and listed the characteristics of each. A spokesperson from each group then shared with the whole class what the group had learned. As each group shared, the characteristics of salamanders, frogs, and toads were listed on the board. Common characteristics were then determined and recorded, and students listed them in the "common characteristics" column of their research form. After the activity was repeated for reptiles, the common characteristics of amphibians and the common characteristics of reptiles were compared, contrasted, and discussed—and Alma's question was answered.

If we look at the various thinking processes listed in Table 5.2, it is readily apparent that the students engaged in a number of them as they attempted to answer Alma's question. They analyzed information as they reread various books and searched for the characteristics of each amphibian and reptile. They compared and contrasted the characteristics they discovered for various amphibians, for various reptiles, and between amphibians and reptiles. And they developed conceptual and generalizable knowledge about amphibians and reptiles.

Multiple Purposes

Students should use communication systems and thinking processes for a number of different purposes. Too often, because schools view themselves as transmitters of a well-defined body of knowledge, the primary function of classroom communication is informative. In such instructional contexts, students share or recall information to prove that it has been mastered. However, as suggested by Smith (1977) and Halliday (1973), communication in the real world is used for other reasons as well, and students need opportunities to explore these functions.

The list on pages 63–64 includes activities used in the theme Getting to Know About Growing and Using Plants and Seeds/*Cultivando y Utilizando Plantas y Semillas* that reflect the various functions of literacy. We stress again, however, that all thematic activities need to be authentic. As you brainstorm activities that provide your students with opportunities to explore language functions, always assess whether these activities are authentic.

Home and School Language and Culture

Thematic units as we conceptualize them not only integrate the disciplines and the systems of communication, they also integrate the culture and language of the home with that of the school. Dewey (1938) termed this home-school link the "continuity of experience." He suggested that while the school was responsible for extending the experiences of the student, the experiences the student brought to the school were the foundation for this extension. For second language learners the affirmation of home experiences is especially critical. Many minority students find that the school language or dialect, as well as its cultural norms, varies from that of their community. If we conceive of learning as a process in which new information is understood in light of the old, many minority students quite naturally have difficulty linking school and home. Activities within the thematic unit should attempt to build bridges between what the student brings to the school and what the school brings to the student.

As part of our Getting to Know About Growing and Using Plants and Seeds/ *Cultivando y Utilizando Plantas y Semillas* theme, we wanted our students to explore how cultural background and locale influences the foods eaten in the home. Among other books, the students read *Growing Plants from Fruits and Vegetables* (Sholinsky 1974). In this book, various fruits and vegetables are identified that contain seeds or parts that can be propagated. As they read the book, the students identified the fruits and vegetables that were eaten in their homes. As homework, the students then explored their kitchens to find other fruits and vegetables their families ate. When possible, they brought seeds or parts from these plants to school and grew them in the classroom. For example, students brought in *mango* and *tamarindo* seeds, two fruits common in Latin America. Seeds from plants discussed in *Growing Plants from Fruits and Vegetables* that were unfamiliar to these second language learners were also grown. Since many of the students were recent immigrants from Latin America, we were able to compare the local vegetation in Southern California with that of their homelands. In addition, the class investigated immigration patterns of several common food items. They discovered that cocoa was used by the Aztecs long before the Europeans arrived in Mexico and that corn was a staple food throughout the American continent. As a final activity, each student made and illustrated a book of the fruits and vegetables eaten in his or her home, and many took seeds home to start gardens of their own.

Range of Abilities

Thematic units invite all students into the curricular conversations taking place in the classroom, regardless of ability. Because the focus of the curriculum is always on the development of generalizations and concepts, rather than on any particular piece of material or activity, students of varying abilities have equal access to the significant ideas within the theme. Students of different backgrounds and abilities can engage in those activities most appropriate to their abilities, yet still encounter the same basic ideas. Far too often students whose abilities, culture, or language differs from that of the school experience separate, unequal, and usually less demanding curriculums. When they *are* included within the "regular" curriculum, few attempts are made to vary the lessons to meet their needs. Activities in your thematic units should vary in the demands they place on the learners but should lead to the same content, generalizations, and concepts. In this way, all students can be involved in activities appropriate to their abilities, yet still have access to the thematic content.

In our theme Getting to Know About You, Me, and Others/*Tú, Yo, y Otros*, the students explored the concepts of differences and similarities between and among people and the generalization that people are both similar and different. In one activity, the students read about a number of characters who were different in some way and how others reacted to these differences. Because of the range of both English and Spanish literacy abilities in the class, we selected stories of varying difficulty, written in both languages, but addressing the same basic concepts:

Crow Boy, by Taro Yashima (1983).
Ferdinand the Bull/Ferdinando el Toro, by Munro Leaf (1977).
The Gold Cadillac, by Mildred Taylor (1987).
Got Me a Story to Tell, by Sylvia Yee and Lisa Kokin (1977).
How My Parents Learned to Eat, by Ina Friedman (1984).
The Hundred Dresses, by Eleanor Estes (1971).
My Dad Takes Care of Me, by Patricia Quinlan (1987).
Oliver Button Is a Sissy /Oliver Button es una Nena, by Tomie de Paola
   (1979/1982).
Tight Times, by Barbara Hazen (1983).

These books range from relatively easy to read with numerous pictures supporting the print (*Oliver Button Is a Sissy /Oliver Button es una Nena*) to more demanding chapter books with few supporting pictures (*The Hundred Dresses* and *Got Me a Story to Tell*). Several have both Spanish and English versions. Because these materials all addressed the same concepts and generalizations within the theme, we and the students were able to generate various activities that gave all students access to the same concepts.

In one activity, the students selected at least two books to read—more capable students were asked to select more—and to keep a list of how the main characters of the two books were both similar and different. Although different students read different books, they all encountered the concepts of similarities and differences and the generalization that people are both similar and different.

Independent and Collaborative Experiences

Learning in general and literacy learning in particular involve interaction and communication with others (Dewey 1938, Vygotsky 1978). There would be little need for a student to be proficient in the various systems of communication in a nonsocial environment. Therefore, thematic activities need to provide a rich social environment in which students work together, exchange ideas, and mutually construct meaning.

That's why, in the Shakespeare exercise, we encouraged you to collaborate with others on the various activities related to time. That's also why we included the perspectives of a fifth-grade teacher who had completed the same activities. By "hearing the voices of others," your conceptualization of time was expanded, modified, and enriched.

Although individual and whole-class activities are part of any thematically based curriculum, small-group work is one of the best ways to encourage social interaction in the classroom, especially for second language learners (Faltis 1993; Johnson 1994). Many second language learners are reluctant to speak or share their work in front of the entire class: they are much more comfortable in small, supportive groups. Grouping peers of varying levels of second language proficiency fosters second language development. Working with others allows the student to accomplish tasks that could not be done independently. With the support of others, the student becomes "a head taller than him/[her]self" (Vygotsky 1978, 102).

Another important grouping consideration for bilingual settings is providing opportunities for students to develop their primary language as well. Grouping students in primary language groups will support second language and academic development and will enhance the second language learners' self-esteem by validating their home language and culture (Faltis 1993; Johnson 1994).

We need to go beyond the traditional reading ability groups to which students are assigned for the entire year. Rather, groups should be formed and re-formed around the needs and interests of the students.

As we discussed in Chapter 2, research groups are common in the thematic curriculum. In the Getting to Know About Growing and Using Plants and Seeds/ *Cultivando y Utilizando Plantas y Semillas*, students formed groups to investigate the parts of a seed; the differences between fruits and vegetables; the role sunlight, water, fertilizer, and temperature play in growing seeds; and the items in society that are produced from plants and seeds. Materials in both Spanish and English were available for these investigations. Before the groups were formed, the students brainstormed questions they had about plants and seeds. These questions were listed on the board and each student identified one question to investigate. Students then formed groups around the question being investigated. Each group selected a team leader, someone to monitor the group and make sure that all its members had the opportunity to participate and that they were doing so. Another group member became the recorder/librarian, the person who kept track of the information that was being gathered by the group. And a third student was the presenter, the one responsible for sharing the information with the entire class. (The teacher or a student may assign these roles, depending on the class make-up or the activity.)

A related way in which interest groups can be formed is to initiate book groups. A number of books and/or articles related to the generalization(s) or concept(s) being studied are identified and briefly shared with the students. The students are then asked to form a book group with students who want to read the same book they do. The teacher meets with each group and they decide when the group will next meet, how much will be read for the meeting, the format for the meeting, and possible activities to go along with the portion to be read.

In our bilingual third-grade class, book groups were formed during all the themes we explored. Since our limited funds made it impossible to buy twenty-six copies of every theme book, book groups allowed us to buy a few copies of each book, gave the students some choice in what they read, and guaranteed that a range of materials would be included within the curriculum. As part of the theme Getting to Know About Reptiles and Amphibians/*Conociendo los Reptiles y los Anfibios,* we examined how dinosaurs have been portrayed in literature. The class was arranged in groups of five, and each group was given four books to peruse: *Brontosaurus Moves In* (Austin 1984), *The Tyrannosaurus Game* (Kroll 1976), *Dinosaur Bob* (Joyce 1988), and *Patrick's Dinosaurs* (Carrick 1983). Each student decided which book he or she wanted to read, then formed a book group with the other students who were reading that book, meeting later to discuss it.

Literacy support groups can be based on the reading and writing needs of students. Using the literacy processes listed in Table 5.1, a teacher can develop lessons that highlight certain processes for various groups of students. This same type of grouping can also be used when students are experiencing difficulty understanding key concepts or generalizations. Writing conferences were a common form of this kind of grouping with our third-grade bilingual students. A number of students in the class were finding it hard to elaborate or extend their ideas as they wrote. We brought them together frequently and taught various brainstorming strategies they could use to discover things to add to their writing. The strategy wall charts discussed in Chapter 2 and illustrated in Table 2.3 are another example of literacy support groups. We should emphasize once again, however, that although this type of grouping is most common in elementary schools, these groups should not be static. They must be formed, disbanded, and formed again as needs change throughout the year.

Friendship groups are another way in which students can be brought together. In this type of grouping, students work with their friends (a tactic sure to encourage social interaction) but within a structured environment. When you use this type of group, take care that the instructional activity is well defined and the interaction is directed toward the goal of the lesson.

Finally, students can do the same activity in small heterogeneous groups and then share and discuss their varied results as a class. This type of grouping works especially well when the teacher is trying to help students understand a concept or generalization from a number of perspectives. Most recently, James Hoffman

(1992) has extended this idea through the development of what he calls inquiry charts (I-charts) (see Chapter 2). A blank I-chart is included in Appendix 5.5. Although I-charts can be used in various ways and with various types of groups, they are especially powerful when the students are heterogeneously grouped.

I-charts are developed by having the students brainstorm various questions about a particular topic. (These are similar to the "What we want to know" questions in the KWL strategy.) These questions are then explored in groups using a multitude of resources. As the students find "answers" to their questions, they record them under the appropriate question and note the source of the information (see Figure 2.1). Once the questions have been answered by all groups, the students share their information as a class, considering different viewpoints and talking about why their answers vary.

Although we have discussed a number of ways in which groups can be formed within the thematic curriculum, here are some other criteria by which groups can be formed:

- *Paired Reading:* Each student is paired with a partner to read a particular book or story. Only one copy of the text is available to the pair, and students are encouraged to read the piece chorally and to support each other's reading as required.
- *Reader-Response Groups:* After reading a particular text, small groups of students are brought together to discuss what they have read, considering: (1) What was the purpose for reading the text? (2) What was learned from reading the text? (3) Why did the author write the text? (4) What parts were liked best and why? (5) What parts were liked least and why? (6) How was the text similar and dissimilar to other texts? (7) What might the author have done to improve the text? (8) What parts/things were difficult to understand? What can be done to understand these parts/things?
- *Compare/Contrast Groups:* After reading several pieces related to the same thematic issue, students in small groups analyze and discuss how the texts are both similar and different.
- *Expert Groups:* Groups of students identify, investigate, and report on issues related to the theme being studied.
- *Learning Logs:* Students review activities in which they have been engaged during the previous week and record what they have learned from these activities.
- *Writing Conferences:* In small groups, students share drafts of their writing, receive feedback that focuses on meaning and organization, and revise their texts accordingly. Revised texts are edited by the students and/or the teacher and published. These conferences are an integral part of the thematic units as well as of free writing.

For additional grouping suggestions please refer to Rhodes (1983), Berghoff and Egawa (1991), Kagan (1992), Faltis (1993), Johnson (1994), and Pardo and Raphael (1991).

Problem Solving, Divergent Thinking, and Risk Taking

A major goal of all thematic activities is to develop students who are able to continue learning without constant teacher attention. We want students to pose as well as solve their own inquiries, to solve problems in new and different ways. Basic to such independent learning is the student's ability and willingness to take risks—to try something new, to make mistakes, and then to be willing to try again. Without the making of mistakes, there is no growth.

If independence is to be fostered within the unit, activities must allow, even encourage, students to make mistakes and to learn from them. This requires an environment in which errors are not penalized but are rather understood for what they are: attempts on the part of the student to stretch beyond what he or she is currently capable of doing.

Activities can encourage this cognitive stretching in a number of ways. First, students can engage in discovery-type activities in which they monitor and regulate their own behavior. Telling students how something is done is not usually as effective as allowing them to figure it out for themselves. Activities like this are a natural part of the thematic curriculum, since students are invited to generate and carry out their own inquiries. The strategy wall charts in Chapter 2 are just one example.

Independent learning is also promoted by open-ended activities. Allowing students to generate and share a number of solutions or responses gives them new insights into the problem and promotes continued risk taking. At one point during the theme Getting to Know About You, Me, and Others/*Tú, Yo, y Otros*, the students had read at least one of the following books:

Amazing Grace, by Mary Hoffman (1991).
The Carrot Seed/La Semilla de Zanahoria, by Ruth Kraus (1945).
The Gold Cadillac, by Mildred Taylor (1987).
Oliver Button Is a Sissy/Oliver Button es una Nena, by Tomie de Paola (1979/1982).
William's Doll, by Charlotte Zolotow (1972).

We asked each student to return to one of these books and analyze the story using the chart in Appendix 5.6. Afterward they paired with someone who had read a different book. After each summarized the book he or she had read, the pair used the chart in Appendix 5.7 to list all the ways the two books were alike. These similarities across books were then shared and discussed with the entire class. Similarities across books included (a) characters had to negotiate their personal and social realities, (b) prejudice was shown toward the characters, (c) characters demonstrated the willingness to keep trying, (d) acceptance and change was experienced by the characters, and (e) characters challenged the stereotypic boundaries and expectations set for them by others. The similarities gave students new insights and perspectives into the books and validated the divergent thinking that had occurred.

Multiple Perspectives

In Chapter 4, we suggested that the materials gathered for a thematic unit should reflect multiple perspectives, various points of view on the key issues being explored. Similarly, the activities generated should build on these multiple perspectives and encourage students to take various stances.

In our unit Getting to Know About You, Me, and Others/*Tú, Yo, y Otros*, we asked our students to consider how Emily, her classmates, and her teacher felt about the constant teasing of Emily in the book *Emily Umily* (Corrigan 1987), a story about a young girl who says *um* continually as she talks. Students drew pictures of the feelings of Emily, the students who did the teasing, and the teacher. Students also role-played possible responses by Emily and the teacher to the teasing. In our Getting to Know About Growing and Using Plants and Seeds/*Cultivando y Utilizando Plantas y Semillas* unit we recycled the topic through the disciplines (Harste 1993). We asked the students to consider the cultivation of vegetation from the perspective of a biologist, an economist, and a literary critic. In both units, the students came to a deeper understanding of the topic, generalizations, and concepts as they shifted their stances and therefore their perspectives. Inquiry charts are another excellent way in which students can be helped to see an issue through various lenses.

Revisiting Prior Experiences

As we are all aware, comprehension involves a process of integration. The learner must link new meanings and ideas to what is already known about a topic. In a sense, this involves a "marriage" between old and new information. Because materials and activities in a thematic unit are conceptually related, students have the opportunity to build the background knowledge that is necessary for comprehension. It is not enough for background knowledge to be available, however; students must be willing to use it. Throughout the theme, students must experience activities that encourage them to integrate the current experiences with past experiences. More traditional thematic units frequently assume that the students will make the link or connection across and among activities without mediation simply because the activities are thematically related.

Requiring students to use previous experiences when engaged in current activities not only promotes learning in the present, it also enhances understanding of the past. Returning to past experiences helps students rethink what was learned and develop a clearer understanding of the past in light of the present. Just this kind of thinking occurred when, in answering Alma's question "What is the difference between reptiles and amphibians?" the students returned to books and articles they had previously read. This kind of thinking was also encouraged during the theme Getting to Know About You, Me, and Others/*Tú, Yo, y Otros* when students analyzed books they had already read and searched for similarities among them.

• • • • • • • • • • •

A Look Back

At this point in the development of the thematic curriculum, the teacher, with student collaboration, has:

1. Identified a significant thematic topic,
2. Gathered a variety of thematic materials,
3. Identified a set of potential generalizations and corresponding concepts on which the thematic curriculum can begin to be built, and
4. Considered the characteristics of the activities to be generated from the thematic materials.

6

Generating Thematic Thinking and Learning Events

• • • • • • • • • • •

Moving Students Into, Through, and Beyond the Thematic Curriculum

A powerful dimension of thematic teaching is that it reprofessionalizes the class-room teacher. Rather than letting a basal reading series, workbooks, and activity sheets determine the curriculum, the teacher and the students take control. Many teachers initially feel uncomfortable with this mediating role and the responsibility it entails. Even teachers who are familiar with generic activities that can be easily embedded within a theme, such as reader-response groups, writing conferences, and other collaborative learning techniques, often do not feel they have the expertise to develop authentic learning experiences.

Webbing and brainstorming strategies can provide the necessary guidance. We have experimented with numerous strategies and have found the "into, through, and beyond" procedure to be the most useful. In contrast to other brainstorming techniques, it not only supports the generation of activities, but also considers how such activities might be potentially arranged within the curriculum.

In generating "into," "through," and "beyond" activities, it is important to remember the characteristics of thematic thinking and learning discussed in Chapter 5. These activities need to focus on developing generalizations, concepts, communication systems, and thinking processes. A thematic curriculum integrates content and processes into a unified whole.

It is also important that the students whom we teach be involved in the process. Once the students are familiar with the way in which knowledge is being investigated and generated within the theme, they should become co-constructors of the evolving curriculum. This does not mean that the curriculum must spontaneously evolve from minute to minute or from day to day. Rather, curriculum is predicted in pencil. The teacher and the students plan various thinking and learning units, yet are always open to revision.

To brainstorm "into," "through," and "beyond" activities, you and your students need to have assembled all the significant pieces of material that will be used in the theme. In addition to printed materials, these include movies, songs, simulations, works of art, games, and the like (see Table 4.1). It is important to withhold judgment about the appropriateness of the activities being generated. Brainstorming is most effective when the mind is allowed to wander without too many constraints. Later in the process you and your students will be able to select and order those activities that appear to be the most appropriate.

Many "into," "through," and "beyond" activities for one piece of material can serve as "into," "through," and "beyond" activities for other materials as well. For example, having students predict the content of a book by looking at the pictures is an activity that can be used with a range of reading materials. Writing conferences in which work is revised, edited, and published can be held in connection with various writing experiences. Given the generic nature of some activities, it helps to keep a list of those that can be used across materials and themes. Generic thinking and learning activities are discussed in such professional books as *Whole Language for Second Language Learners* (Freeman & Freeman 1992), *Talking About Books* (Short & Pierce 1990), *Readers and Writers with a Difference* (Rhodes & Dudley-Marling 1988), *When They Don't All Speak English* (Rigg & Allen 1989), *Creating Classrooms for Authors* (Harste, Short & Burke 1988), and *In the Middle* (Atwell 1987).

• • • • • • • • • •

Grouping Material

Developing "into," "through," and "beyond" activities is easier if the materials are grouped by their common or shared focus. (For example, the materials listed in Table 2.4 deal with acceptance and respect.) This grouping is fairly easy if you consider potential generalizations and concepts as materials are being gathered. This common focus ensures that the group of materials and corresponding activities will help students develop generalizable knowledge. Because some material will naturally have more than a single focus, particular materials may become part of several groups. If students have been helping gather materials, they will have a general sense of the content and can be part of the grouping procedure.

After materials have been grouped, either a single piece or a subset of conceptually related materials—a text set—from one group is selected to begin the brainstorming process. For the examples below, we use a single text from our theme Getting to Know About Growing and Using Plants and Seeds/*Cultivando y Utilizando Plantas y Semillas* and a conceptually linked set of texts from the theme Getting to Know About You, Me, and Others/*Tú, Yo, y Otros*.

• • • • • • • • • •

"Into" Activities

"Into" activities have two characteristics. First, they give students the conceptual and linguistic foundation they need to understand the new piece of material— "into" activities precede the students' engagement with the material and support future understanding and learning. Second, they are a link between the selected piece of material and previous learning activities. Within a thematic curriculum, each learning experience builds on and extends previous instructional experiences.

"Into" activities are *not* so-called readiness activities that prepare the learner for the "real thing." "Into" activities are meaningful and significant in their own right, not simply fillers. They are the mortar that binds together previous and future thematic activities.

In the Shakespeare demonstration in the previous chapter, "into" activities included (1) writing and illustrating your conceptualization of time, (2) sharing and encountering other conceptualizations of time, and (3) reading, writing about, illustrating, and discussing the poem "What Is Time?" by Phyllis McGinley (1966). All of these activities helped you examine your own view of time, supported the exploration of time from a number of perspectives, and provided a framework for reading "Sonnet 60" by William Shakespeare.

Keeping in mind the piece of material and potential generalizations and concepts, you can brainstorm some "into" activities by listing all the activities that will facilitate student understanding for that piece of material. For example, in the theme Getting to Know About Growing and Using Plants and Seeds/*Cultivando y Utilizando Plantas y Semillas*, we were interested in helping our third-grade bilingual students explore such generalizations as *New plants can be started in different ways* and the supporting concepts of germination, seeds, roots, cuttings, and growth requirements. Therefore, we selected the nonfiction paperback *Growing Plants from Fruits and Vegetables*, by Jane Sholinsky (1974), to begin the inquiry. Because we knew this book would generate a great deal of student interest, we decided that everyone would read it. The first section of Table 6.1 lists experiences that might serve as appropriate "into" activities.

This particular book was also part of another set of materials that focused on how culture and locale influence the foods eaten in the home (see Chapter 5). Traditionally, materials are not used more than once, because "the students have already read that." A comment like this assumes that the students have already gleaned as much information from the material as possible, that they will be bored if they encounter the material a second time, or both. We believe that reusing materials in other contexts and for other purposes supports and encourages students to revisit and link past experiences and meaning with current learning. It also allows students to "try on" different stances or perspectives at different points in the curriculum, and the multiple perspectives that result facilitate a deeper understanding of the concepts being addressed.

Our third-grade students taught us the acceptability of using materials several times within a thematic curriculum. At the beginning of the year, we gave the students specific material as the theme unfolded. Materials we planned to use later in the unit were usually kept on a shelf in the back of the room. However, because our classroom did not have areas that were "off limits," students soon discovered the set-aside materials and read them during free reading or as part of the inquiries they were pursuing. We wondered whether students would be interested in using the material during another part of the curriculum. To our surprise, we found that if the material was interesting and spoke to the students, using it again prompted little notice or concern.

For our second theme, Getting to Know About You, Me, and Others/*Tú, Yo, y Otros*, rather than brainstorm "into" activities for a single book, we used a text set: *Big Al*, by Andrew Clements (1988), *Earl's Too Cool for Me*, by Leah Komaiko (1988), and *Arnie and the New Kid*, by Nancy Carlson (1990). Big Al is a big, scary-looking fish with no friends. Inside, Al is a warmhearted fellow, and one day he is given the opportunity to show that he is more than he appears. Earl, on the other hand, is the coolest kid in town and the envy of a fellow classmate who would do anything to be his friend. However, the classmate is afraid to approach Earl because he is so cool. Eventually, the two boys become friends when the classmate discovers that Earl is just a regular guy. Arnie, somewhat of a bully, teases Philip, the new boy in school, because he is confined to a wheelchair. When Arnie breaks his leg and has to use crutches, he discovers that Philip is really not so different.

The first section in Table 6.2 illustrates "into" activities that might be done with this set of books. It is important to note that all these activities are general enough to apply to all the books. Therefore, whatever book or books students select to read, they will receive the necessary support as they move into the material. The advantages of generating activities with a set of books are that it allows students to select different "into" activities for different materials and that it allows the teacher to engage students in a common or shared "into" experience even though they are reading different books.

• • • • • • • • • • •

"Through" Activities

"Through" activities support or guide the students as they work with the material, focusing the students' attention and highlighting what is of significance. Because

Theme Topic: Getting to Know About Growing and Using Plants and Seeds/*Cultivando y Utilizando Plantas y Semillas*
Generalization: Plants can be grown in many different ways
Concepts: Fruits, Vegetables, Germination, Seeds, Roots, Cuttings, Growth requirements
Text: Growing Plants from Fruits and Vegetables, by Jane Sholinsky

Into
- Students bring seeds from food they eat at home. Graph the various kinds of seeds the students bring.
- Students share how the foods from which the seeds come are prepared to eat.
- Discuss what seeds the students like to eat. Graph the various kinds discussed. Follow the discussion and graphing by reading *The Popcorn Book* (1978), by Tomie de Paola, to the students.
- Students share their experiences with starting new plants. In what different ways can new plants be started? Are seeds the only way by which new plants can be started?
- Brainstorm what is needed to start new plants.
- Begin an inquiry chart. Students use the three columns on the chart to record (1) what they already know about growing plants, (2) what they want to learn or find out about growing plants, and (3) what they have learned about growing plants from reading and study.
- Students discuss what they think the differences are between fruits and vegetables. Record differences on an I-chart.

Through
- Students read the book, identify a plant they want to grow, and list the procedures and materials necessary for growing the plant.
- As the book is read, the students identify all those plants they have and have not eaten at home.
- Students read the book in pairs, supporting each other when they encounter something not known or understood.
- Students identify additional plants they eat at home not found in the book that also could be grown.
- When reading the book, the students apply the following strategies when encountering something not known or understood:
  1. Stop reading, think about it, make a guess, read on to see if the guess makes sense.
  2. Stop reading, reread the previous sentence(s) or paragraph(s), make a guess, read on to see if the guess makes sense.
  3. Skip it, read on to get more information, return and make a guess, continue reading to see if the guess makes sense.
  4. Skip it, read on to see if what you do not understand is important to know, return and make a guess if it is important, do not return if it is unimportant.
  5. Put something in that makes sense and read on to see if it fits with the rest of the text.
  6. Stop reading, look at the pictures, charts, graphs, etc., make a guess, read on to see if the guess makes sense.

TABLE 6.1 Sample "into," "through," and "beyond" activities.

7. Sound it out, read on to see if the guess makes sense.
8. Stop reading, talk with a friend about what you do not know or understand, return and continue reading.
9. Stop reading, look in a dictionary, encyclopedia, or books related to the topic, return and continue reading.
10. Read the text with a friend.
- When reading the text, the students "think about" the following things:
  1. What is my purpose for reading this text?
  2. What am I learning from reading this text? Am I learning what I want or need to learn?
  3. What parts do I like the best? What parts are my favorite? Why do I like these particular parts?
  4. What parts do I like the least? Why do I dislike these parts?
  5. Why did the author write this story? What was the author trying to teach me?
  6. Does this text remind me of other texts I have read? How is this text similar and dissimilar to other texts?
  7. What would I change in this text if I had written it? What might the author have done to have made this text better, more understandable, more interesting?
  8. Are there things/parts in the text that I am not understanding? What can I do to better understand these things/parts?
- Students add new learning to their inquiry charts.

Beyond
- In reader-response groups, discuss the "think about" questions.
- Bring to class all of those plants mentioned in the book that the students have never eaten for a "taste test."
- Students grow one of the plants dicussed in the book.
- Students chart and graph the growth of various seeds and plants. Which seed grows first? last? Which plant grows fastest? slowest? Which plant grows the largest? smallest?
- Students form "expert groups" and research a fruit or vegetable that they find interesting.
- In small groups, students share things not understood and try various strategies to make sense of these things.
- Examine various fruits and vegetables. What are the similarities and differences between the two?
- Grow various plants and seeds and vary the water, light, soil, warmth, that they receive. What conditions are best for each plant or seed?
- Students share the new learning that they have added to their inquiry charts.
- Start various seeds and cuttings on wet paper towels that are put into baggies. Students write and draw their observations in a journal.
- Return to the I-chart on differences between fruits and vegetables. Evaluate what was written and add new insights to the chart based on reading the book.
- Students develop an inquiry focusing on heredity as it relates to plant propagation.
- Students identify various ecosystems. Students research how plant growth is affected by interactions with other organisms within each ecosystem.
- Students share new learning using the visual arts.

TABLE 6.1 *(cont.)*

Theme Topic: Getting to Know About You, Me, and Others/*Tú, Yo, y Otros*
Generalization: People are oftentimes more than they appear
Concepts: Appearance/Image, True self
Texts: Big Al, by Andrew Clements; *Earl's Too Cool for Me,* by Leah Komaiko; *Arnie and the New Kid,* by Nancy Carlson

Into

- Have students share experiences in which they were judged as being "different." How did it make them feel?
- Have students share experiences in which others misjudged them. How did it make them feel?
- Have students share experiences in which they have misjudged someone else.
- Ask students if they have ever heard of the saying "You can't judge a book by its cover." Discuss what it means to them.
- Have students write poems in which each line is constructed, "I seem to be . . ., but really am . . ." Student poems can be shared and the class guesses which student belongs to which poem.
- In pairs, students trace each other's head profile. Students cut out their profiles and make a collage on each side. One side illustrates "I seem to be"; the other side illustrates "I really am." Student silhouettes can be shared and the class guesses which silhouette belongs to which student. Silhouettes can then be hung as mobiles over the students' desks.
- Read the book *Angel Child, Dragon Child,* by Michelle Maria Surat (1983). Children brainstorm the two sides of the story's main character.
- Through visual arts or movement, students depict the feelings they have experienced when they have been judged as being different.
- Students predict what the book will be about from looking at all of the pictures.

Through

- Students read to the point in the book where the protagonist's problem is identified. Students write a solution.
- Throughout the reading of the book, stop occasionally and have students predict what will happen next. Read on to see how accurate the predictions were.
- As students read the book, they consider the question, Why was the protagonist misunderstood?
- Students read the book in pairs, discussing the ideas and helping each other through the "rough spots."
- As the book is read, students think about how the saying "You can't judge a book by its cover" applies to the characters in their book.
- On an I-chart, students keep a list of how the main character appears to be and how he really is.
- Students monitor their predictions of story content based on looking at the pictures.

TABLE 6.2 Sample "into," "through," and "beyond" activities.

Beyond
- Students compare their predictions with what actually happened in the book.
- Students share how the main character appeared to be and really was.
- Students compare and contrast the three books, noting how each character was misjudged.
- Students discuss what "You can't judge a book by its cover" means to them now.
- Discuss how the experiences of the main character in *Angel Child, Dragon Child* were similar to the main characters in these three books.
- In a learning log, have students write what *People are oftentimes more than they appear* means to them.
- Using a Venn diagram, illustrate the similarities and differences among the three books.
- In book groups, have students discuss the story from the point of view of various characters in the story.
- In book groups, students make a storyboard to share with the other groups. (A storyboard is a graphic depiction of the major events in the story.)
- Students in each group decide which events are the most important to them and sketch six to eight key scenes in sequence on a storyboard. Students share their storyboard with other groups. Students who read the same book may form smaller groups, make their storyboards, and then compare and contrast storyboards for the same story.
- For one of the main characters in one of the books, students make a silhouette collage similar to the one they made for themselves as an "into" activity. Students compare and contrast their own silhouette collage with the main character's.
- Students discuss why the protagonist was misunderstood.

TABLE 6.2 *(cont.)*

we believe that one goal of any literacy curriculum is to create independent thinkers, we also tend to think of "through" activities as learning events that focus on the processes listed in Tables 5.1 and 5.2. By engaging in these processes under supportive conditions, students are able to develop independent communication and thinking abilities.

In the "through" portion of the Shakespeare demonstration, you were asked to consider Shakespeare's view of time—to be written about and illustrated in future activities—as you read his "Sonnet 60." This general pattern of reflect ⟶ write ⟶ illustrate ⟶ share had been established in the previous "into" activities, and a portion of the pattern was incorporated as part of the "through" experience. "Through" experiences for *Growing Plants from Fruits and Vegetables* and for the text set—*Big Al, Earl's Too Cool for Me, Arnie and the New Kid*—are described in the middle sections of Tables 6.1 and 6.2. Many of the "through" activities in Table 6.1 have been taken from the literacy strategy wall charts in Table 2.3. These charts were developed to help students "work through" particular reading, comprehending, writing, or spelling problems, and are activities that support student independence.

• • • • • • • • • • •

"Beyond" Activities

"Beyond" activities support, extend, or integrate student understanding after the material has been encountered. These activities help students reflect on and respond to what they have learned. "Beyond" activities may also provide a base for—and a link to—the next piece of material or activity to be experienced. Finally, "beyond" activities may help students link the current experience to previous activities within the theme.

Once again returning to the Shakespeare demonstration, you engaged in the following "beyond" activities: (1) writing about and illustrating Shakespeare's view of time, (2) comparing and contrasting Shakespeare's view of time with McGinley's and your own, (3) underlining and sharing your favorite phrases in the sonnet, (4) circling, sharing, and getting alternate views for phrases you found confusing, and (5) rereading the sonnet a final time. The third sections of Tables 6.1 and 6.2 contain "beyond" activities for *Growing Plants from Fruits and Vegetables* and for the text set comprising *Big Al, Earl's Too Cool for Me,* and *Arnie and the New Kid.*

• • • • • • • • • • •

Crossing the Lines

We have discussed activities as being "into," "through," or "beyond." Often, however, the distinctions become blurred, and an activity serves many purposes.

An activity might begin as an "into" or "through" activity and conclude as a "beyond" activity. In one activity in the "into" section of Table 6.1, the students generate an inquiry chart, recording what they currently know about growing plants and what they want to learn. As they move through *Growing Plants from Fruits and Vegetables,* the students record their new learning and later share what they have learned in a "beyond" activity.

Similarly, some activities may be classified as "into" or "beyond" or both. In one "into" activity in Table 6.2, the students write "I seem to be . . ., but really am . . ." poems. We classified this as "into" because we wanted the students to draw on their experiences related to the generalization *People are oftentimes more than they appear* before encountering the issue in the books they were going to read. But the students might also write such poetry after the books have been read and discussed.

• • • • • • • • • •

Student Involvement

Just as students need to help select thematic topics and materials, they need to help generate activities. The challenge is that brainstorming "into," "through," and "beyond" activities often requires an intimate understanding of the material. This is especially problematic with "into" activities: it is difficult for students to brainstorm activities for material they have not yet experienced. To a certain extent, giving students choices when they engage in "into," "through," and "beyond" activities promotes student involvement. Providing these choices will be addressed in Chapter 7.

Another way to ensure student involvement is to ask students to brainstorm "through" activities after they have experienced the "into" activities. After this introduction, a general presentation of the material to be dealt with should give students enough of an idea of the content to be able to generate "through" activities. It is even easier for students to generate "beyond" activities, since they've already experienced the material.

Our class of third graders were especially effective at generating "through" and "beyond" activities during book or reader-response groups. Typically, before they selected a book group to join, students had had common experiences with a series of "into" activities, had examined a number of reading materials, and had selected one to read.

The generating process becomes easier as thematic units are carried out throughout the year. The students are able to draw ideas from activities they enjoyed in previous units and/or suggest adaptations to former activities.

• • • • • • • • • •

A Look Back

At this point in the development of the thematic curriculum, after all significant materials have been grouped, the teacher, with student collaboration, has:

1. Identified a significant thematic topic,
2. Gathered a variety of thematic materials,

3. Identified a set of potential generalizations and corresponding concepts on which the thematic curriculum can begin to be built,
4. Considered the characteristics of the activities to be generated from the thematic materials,
5. Grouped materials by generalizations, and
6. Brainstormed "into," "through," and "beyond" activities for all significant materials.

7

Selecting and Arranging Thematic Thinking and Learning Events

· · · · · · · · · · ·

Principles for Selecting and Ordering Materials and Activities

Selecting and arranging thinking and learning activities within a theme is like writing a novel. The novelist decides not only which events to include but also how these events will be juxtaposed. These two activities—selecting and arranging—form a single symbiotic process. The events in a novel need to be able to be logically ordered into a coherent whole. Which events to include depends on how they are to be arranged, on what is to come before and what is to follow. No particular event stands alone; each event is more or less probable depending on previous episodes and leads to predictable subsequent episodes. Arrangement always depends on the events available.

So it is with thematic units. Besides deciding which thinking and learning activities to select, the teacher and students must also consider how these activities are to be ordered to promote effective teaching and learning. Each activity and its placement within the curriculum depend on the selection and arrangement of all other activities.

As we noted in the previous chapter, curriculum development is a tentative process in which plans are written in pencil. The teacher predicts the thinking and learning activities he or she will use, attempts to represent these predictions in print, and frequently revises the planned approach as new ideas are discovered through the teaching processes. This kind of interaction between predictions and revisions can produce tension within the penciled curriculum. The teacher, in collaboration with the students, must plan upcoming instruction yet still be open to a change in the direction of the curriculum.

Teachers often have little experience with selecting and ordering curricular activities. Basal readers, language arts series, and mathematics, social studies, and science textbooks have appropriated this responsibility and "tell" teachers not only what to teach, but also when. Although teachers frequently supplement textbook-driven curriculums with their own activities, the modifications are usually additive. The basic substance and arrangement presented in the curriculum's scope and sequence guide are usually left intact.

We believe that selecting and arranging thinking and learning within a curriculum is the proper domain of the classroom teacher. Selection and arrangement are worthy of discussion and reflection because they have a direct impact on student learning. As John Dewey (1938) noted over fifty years ago, "the problem of selection and organization of subject-matter for study and learning is fundamental" (78).

During the last twenty years, we have struggled with the selecting and organizing issue with classroom teachers, with our students, and among ourselves. We know firsthand that although webbing techniques are useful in generating activities, they provide little guidance in determining which activities should be selected and how they should be ordered. Teachers can spend a great deal of time selecting and generating materials and activities only to find, as one of them put it, that they "don't know what to do with it all!"

Although we discuss this fundamental problem by first addressing selection, then arrangement, selection and arrangement are interrelated processes and a number of issues overlap. There is also the danger that by addressing these issues linearly, we will produce a scope and sequence guide very similar to ones we currently find in many textbooks. The process of selection and arrangement is dynamic, interactive, and tentative, and we attempt to capture these characteristics at the same time that we attempt to present a workable framework within which a curriculum can evolve.

• • • • • • • • • • •

Selecting Materials and Activities

The "into," "through," and "beyond" brainstorming procedure discussed in Chapter 6 generates activities that precede, guide, and extend each significant piece of material. In many cases, however, there will be too many to use with one piece of material or in one thematic unit. Teachers therefore need to sort through and identify the activities that will best promote student thinking and learning.

This winnowing process is important: we don't want to overburden students with too many activities, and at the same time we need to provide the support necessary for meaningful student engagement with the curriculum.

Here are a number of useful selection principles:

- Select activities that support the students in moving into, through, and beyond the material to be encountered.
- Select varied activities. Even the most worthy ones can dull the senses if encountered too frequently.
- Select activities in which students are interested. They will engage more deeply and more meaningfully if the activities touch their lives in some significant way.
- Select activities that permit the students to make choices. They have many interests and abilities and should have options about the materials and activities in which they will engage.
- Consider the amount of time required for each activity and the amount of time allotted to the thematic unit as a whole. Maintain a balance between short-term and long-term activities.
- Consider what activities must precede or follow a particular activity to make the activity meaningful. Activities within a thematic unit never stand alone; they are linked conceptually to what has come before and what is to follow.
- Select activities that encourage students to reflect on and integrate past experiences with current experiences.

Into, Through, and Beyond

To foster student interaction and curriculum access, consider using at least one "into," one "through," and one "beyond" activity for each significant piece of material. The number of activities selected should be determined by (1) the difficulty of the material, (2) student familiarity with the concepts and generalizations addressed in the material, (3) the literacy and thinking abilities of the students, and (4) connections to home and community experiences.

When second language learners are formally encountering English literacy, you'll want to select quite a few "into" activities—activities that draw on or build relevant background knowledge so that the ideas expressed in the readings become predictable and easily understood. Many of these activities will probably involve oral language (in the first and second language), art, and music, since these communication systems are frequently more developed than the students' English literacy abilities. The following activities from Table 6.2 draw on the students' background:

- Students share experiences in which they were judged as being "different." How did it make them feel?

- Students share experiences in which others misjudged them. How did it make them feel?
- In pairs, students trace each other's head profile. Students cut out their profiles and make a collage on each side. One side illustrates "I seem to be"; the other side illustrates "I really am." The class guesses which silhouette belongs to which student.

It's also good to select collaborative activities that are recycled throughout the into-through-beyond process. Students experience more success if they are able to pool their resources as they interact with the material. Repeating an "into" activity as a "through" or "beyond" activity lets students examine and reexamine an issue using the same material. The following activities illustrate recycling characteristics:

- (Through) Students read the book, identify a plant they want to grow, and list the procedures and materials necessary for growing the plant. ⟶ (Beyond) Students grow one of the plants discussed in the book.
- (Through) Students read the book in pairs, supporting each other when they encounter something not known or understood. ⟶ (Beyond) In small groups, students share things not understood and try various strategies to make sense of these things.
- (Into) Students discuss what they think the differences are between fruits and vegetables and record differences on an I-chart. ⟶ (Beyond) Return to the I-chart on differences between fruits and vegetables. Evaluate what was written and add new insights to the chart based on reading the book.
- (Into) Students share their experiences with starting new plants. In what different ways can new plants be started? Are seeds the only way in which new plants can be started? ⟶ (Through) As the book is read, list all of the new ways that you discover plants can be started. ⟶ (Beyond) Students share all of the new ways in which plants can be started.

Variety

Although literacy activities will probably take place daily in any theme, the students should also experience activities that involve such communication systems as art, music, movement, and mathematics. Variety is, after all, the spice of life.

We rediscovered variety while teaching the thematic unit Getting to Know About Reptiles and Amphibians/*Conociendo los Reptiles y los Anfibios*. Initially, the exploration of each reptile or amphibian began with a KWL chart (Ogles 1986; Pardo & Raphael 1991). We wanted to use this particular inquiry chart to assess what the students knew, what they wanted to investigate, and what was being learned. Although this strategy is a powerful learning device, the students soon tired of it. Considering alternative thinking and learning activities helped us reconceptualize how we were presenting the material to our students.

Student Interest

A powerful dimension of thematic teaching and learning is that it taps into the interests and curiosities of the students. Students are provided with opportunities to explore topics and issues that touch their lives. Not only can students be involved in generating "into," "through," and "beyond" activities, they can also help select the activities and materials in which they are most interested.

Two of our bilingual students, Elvis and Evelia, were very disengaged from the curriculum at the beginning of the year. They rarely participated in class discussions and remained distant from most activities. When we began our theme Getting to Know About Amphibians and Reptiles/*Conociendo los Reptiles y Los Anfibios,* a topic of great interest to them, they suddenly became the most active students in the class. On the first day of the unit, when we asked the class to brainstorm what they knew about the topic, Elvis and Evelia took the lead. They not only contributed the majority of ideas, but also challenged ideas of other students that they felt were incorrect or not fully developed. Throughout the entire unit, Elvis and Evelia led the way, sharing ideas, materials, and books with the class as well as with us.

Student Choice

Student choice is related to student interest. Students have many interests and abilities and need to learn to assume responsibility for their own learning. The development of this responsibility can be promoted by empowering students to make choices. Rather than all students always engaging with the same materials and in the same activities, they should be able to choose from a variety of materials and activities that focus on common generalizations and related concepts. This works particularly well in bilingual classrooms, because it allows students to pursue their interests, work in either the first or second language, and still share a common curriculum.

There are a number of ways in which choice can easily become an integral part of the thematic curriculum. It may be accomplished individually or in collaborative pairs or small groups of students who agree on what is to be done. The number of activities selected can vary depending on each student's needs, abilities, and interests. Here are a number of ways in which students can be given choices (teachers will undoubtedly discover others as they develop thematic curriculums):

- If "into," "through," and "beyond" activities have been generated from a set of materials, as in Table 6.2, students can select the piece of material from the set that they find the most engaging. Book groups can form around the selections.
- If all students are to encounter the same piece of material, each can choose the activity he or she will pursue.

- After encountering a particular piece of material, students can brainstorm and select their own "into," "through," and/or "beyond" activity.
- After generating a list of "what I want to know" questions with the KWL strategy, students can select the questions they wish to investigate.

Time

Time is a constraint under which we all work. Although thematic units, because they integrate a number of curricular areas, afford teachers greater flexibility in scheduling and using time, the school day and year determine what is and is not possible within the curriculum. Some activities will be completed in one class period; others may continue over several days or weeks. A balance between long-term and short-term activities works best.

Research activities and process writing are two instructional strategies that typically involve large amounts of time. As our students investigated questions of interest in research groups, they had to decide which questions were to be investigated and by whom. They had to locate and read materials to answer their questions. And they had to find a format in which the information could be presented to the class—writing, art, song, drama. Similarly, process writing involved drafting a piece, receiving feedback on its content, making revisions, taking part in an editing conference, making editorial changes, and producing and binding a final version. All of these activities took a number of days or weeks to complete. When we scheduled these activities, we attempted to select shorter-term teaching and learning events to accompany them.

Before and After

Activities cannot be selected within a vacuum. The activities that come before and after influence what students learn from any particular activity. Teachers therefore need to consider where and when in the curriculum the activity will be taught as well as how each activity might relate to the other activities within the unit.

Revisiting

The traditional curriculum often focuses on "looking ahead": the curriculum's scope and sequence are concerned with what new pieces of information are to be added to what has already been presented and learned. *Don't look back unless there are problems* is the guiding principle. We usually "look back" only when certain students need additional practice to maintain the facts or skills they've learned or have failed to master what has already been taught. In either case, "looking back" is perceived as a glitch.

In thematic teaching, looking back is valued as much as, if not more than, looking ahead. Woven throughout the curriculum are instances in which students are asked to reflect on and integrate past experiences with current activities. This ebb and flow is essential if students are to develop a rich, elaborated understanding of the content they are studying. It is important for students to recycle concepts through different contexts in order to identify significant patterns throughout the unit. Across thematic activities, students encounter particular concepts repeatedly in order to understand the critical issues more fully and generate their own generalizations more easily. This is particularly crucial for second language learners. As we conceptualize thematic units, adding up facts is always secondary to developing concepts and generalizations. In the selection process, teachers will want to include activities that ask students to revisit their past instructional experiences.

We've already mentioned how one of our students, Alma, initiated a revisiting activity by asking, "What is the difference between reptiles and amphibians?" A less spontaneous revisiting activity occurred in a fifth-grade unit on bridges developed by two of our university students, Sherrie Frank and Matthew Youngberg. At one point in the curriculum, the students were asked to review the materials and activities in which they had engaged. As they looked back, they were to list how physical bridges between two geographical points are similar to and different from emotional bridges between people. This revisiting activity helped the students develop such generalizations as *Friendships are built on many bridges, Bridges transcend physical, emotional, and cultural boundaries,* and *Bridges ease movement between or across barriers.*

Keeping in mind the seven principles for selecting materials and activities we have just discussed, those activities to be (potentially) included in the thematic curriculum now need to be selected. This can be handled in a number of ways. If you are new to the process of curriculum development and need to "see" the entire unit before you teach it, you can use all the activities from the into-through-beyond charts already generated. Or, to allow for student input and still provide a curriculum overview, you can select only major or significant activities from these charts as an evolving framework in which activities and materials will be added based on student choice and interest.

● ● ● ● ● ● ● ● ● ● ●

Principles for Arranging Materials and Activities

Just as the into-through-beyond procedure provides an initial framework from which to select activities for a particular piece of material, it provides an initial framework for ordering the thematic thinking and learning related to that piece of material. However, this framework needs to be expanded to consider how *all* the potential generalizations and concepts as well as *all* the materials and activities within the thematic unit will be organized. A number of principles guide this process:

- Group materials and activities around common generalizations and concepts.
- Order generalizations and concepts so that each builds on and extends the others.
- Arrange materials and activities based on student familiarity with the generalizations and concepts to be encountered, from most to least familiar.
- Arrange activities to take students into, through, and beyond the material so that each activity builds on and extends past experiences and advances student thinking.
- Arrange materials and activities based on conceptual density and the development and elaboration of ideas, from most general and global to most specific, detailed, and elaborated.
- Arrange materials and activities from the most concrete to the most abstract, from hands on to hands off. Learning is promoted when students initially have experiences that they can relate to their own lives and experiences. Experiences that students can "touch" and "feel" provide the basis for significant learning.
- Arrange materials and activities from socially supported (group) experiences to independent (individual) experiences. Collaborative learning and cooperative groups give students the cognitive support necessary to learn new principles, concepts, and processes.
- Throughout the thematic unit, incorporate activities that require students to revisit and integrate prior experiences and meaning with current experiences and meaning.
- Begin the unit with activities that introduce students to the theme and culminate the unit with activities that draw together and celebrate what has been learned and accomplished.

Grouping Common Generalizations and Concepts

Once the materials and their corresponding "into," "through," and "beyond" activities have been selected, they need to be grouped by their shared generalization and concepts. Because these materials and activities focus on a set of common issues, this is usually fairly easy to do. Just write the name of each material and activity on a note card, then sort the cards into piles that address a common issue. Often, there will be materials and activities that address more than one issue; these can become part of several groups. In Chapter 6, for example, *Growing Plants from Fruits and Vegetables*, by Jane Sholinsky (1974), was used to help students explore the generalization *New plants can be started in different ways* in the theme Growing and Using Plants and Seeds/*Cultivando y Utilizando Plan-*

tas y Semillas. This book, however, can also support the generalization *All plants need food, water, light, and air in order to survive.*

The top segment of Figure 7.1 illustrates the grouping of note cards (materials and activities) based on common generalizations and concepts, with each line in each group representing a note card.

Ordering Generalizations and Corresponding Concepts

After the materials and activities note cards have been grouped by common generalizations and concepts, the groups can be tentatively ordered. Some concepts and generalizations need to be understood before others can be fully appreciated. The second grouping in Figure 7.1 illustrates this ordering of the groups.

Although several concepts and generalizations may be embedded in an activity, it's best to highlight a limited number of them. Otherwise, the activity will lack focus, and students may become confused about the purpose of the lesson. A focus will enable students to build a coherent understanding and compare and contrast fully developed generalizations and concepts. In addition, when teachers focus on a limited number of concepts and generalizations, they provide students with opportunities to generate ones that are meaningful to them.

After the generalizations and concepts have been ordered, you have a general curricular framework, even though the activities within each group have yet to be arranged. To keep the curriculum fluid and open to change, some teachers do this only for the first group of activities. This allows them to initiate the thematic unit without committing themselves to a rigid scope and sequence for the entire curriculum. As the first group of activities are taught, the teacher, in collaboration with the students, makes adjustments to subsequent groups of activities as required. Regardless of whether you order activities and materials in only the first group or in all of the groups, you will want to consider the following issues.

Student Familiarity

Comprehension and understanding are facilitated when the learner has prior knowledge to which the new information can be attached. Learning is promoted when links are made between the known and the unknown, the familiar and the unfamiliar. After the learning materials and activities have been grouped by common generalization, those within each group are arranged by familiarity, from most to least familiar. Students initially encounter those materials and activities to which they can most easily make cognitive links, followed by those that are less familiar.

The concept of familiarity is particularly important for students who are using English as a second language. We know that well-developed background knowl-

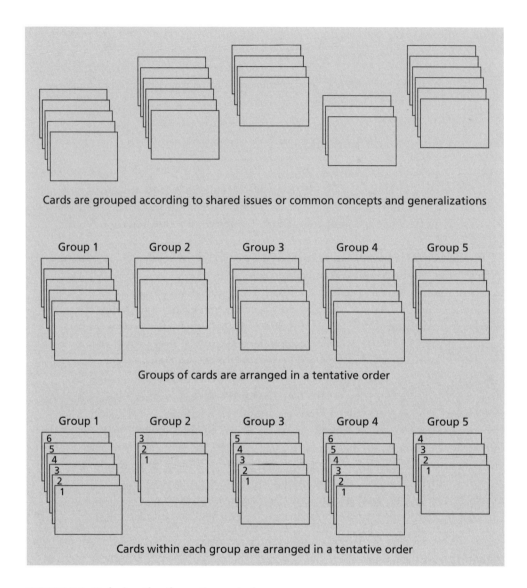

Cards are grouped according to shared issues or common concepts and generalizations

Groups of cards are arranged in a tentative order

Cards within each group are arranged in a tentative order

FIGURE 7.1 Ordering the thematic curriculum.

edge supports efficient and effective literacy. The reading and writing processes become more predictable, more easily managed, when the topic is familiar to the student. For students first developing English literacy, being able to draw on prior knowledge can help them make meaning from and through written language. This was the case with Elvis and Evelia and their interest in and knowledge of amphibians and reptiles. Although both students were less than proficient in oral and written English, their facility markedly improved when engaged in activities related to this topic.

Into, Through, Beyond

Thinking and learning are arranged so that each event builds on and extends past events. New activities within the thematic unit should add new meaning to what has already been learned. Previous meaning is the foundation or framework on which new meaning can be constructed. Activities are arranged so that each moves students forward in their understanding of the thematic generalizations and concepts.

Because each activity generated was conceived as being "into," "through," or "beyond," you can use this framework to order the learning events around each piece of material, making additional decisions when there are several activities that precede, support, or extend the material.

Conceptual Density

Within thematic units, students often encounter expository or informational texts. In contrast to narratives, which usually follow a predictable and time-ordered sequence that reflects normative human behavior and experience, informational texts present and develop facts, concepts, and generalizations. The extent to which such facts, concepts, and generalizations are developed and elaborated varies greatly from text to text. Materials should be arranged so that students initially encounter texts that address the critical issues in general ways. A general presentation of ideas gives students the greatest chance to link the information to their prior knowledge. It also keeps the students from being so overwhelmed with facts and details that they miss the big picture. Once students have developed a general familiarity with the facts, concepts, and generalizations, they will be better able to interact successfully with the materials that are more specific, detailed, and elaborated.

In our unit Growing and Using Plants and Seeds/*Cultivando y Utilizando Plantas y Semillas* we had the following group of books that focused on seeds, their common characteristics, the various types, and how they travel: *Plants Do Amazing Things* (Nussbaum 1977), *The Life of Plants* (Macdonald Educational 1977), *What Is a Seed?* (National Geographic Society 1983), and *Travelers All* (Webber 1944). As we considered which one to use to introduce this part of the unit, we analyzed both the breadth and depth of the information presented in each. We selected *What Is a Seed?* because it gives a general overview of all the issues to be addressed—common characteristics of seeds, various types of seeds, and how seeds travel—and includes numerous pictures and illustrations. *Travelers All* and *Plants Do Amazing Things* focused too much on a single issue, and *The*

Life of Plants was too detailed and conceptually dense to be used as an introductory book.

Concrete/Hands-On and Abstract/ Hands-Off Experiences

There is a common misconception that the degree of concreteness or abstractness demanded by a particular learning experience is related to the age of the student. That is, elementary students require many concrete, hands-on experiences if learning is to occur. Adults, on the other hand, are capable of dealing with abstract issues. Our experiences, however, indicate that the degree of concreteness or abstractness required for learning to take place depends not so much on developmental level as it does on previous experiences with any particular topic.

The arrangement of materials and activities within a theme should take into account the degree of concreteness or abstractness. When concepts or generalizations are new to the students, especially second language learners, more hands-on or experiential learning will be necessary. For instance, reading an expository chapter from a science book about what various plants and seeds require to grow may not be as effective as experiments that guide students to discover these requirements. After experiencing such activities, the science chapter will be more comprehensible to students and even allow them to compare and contrast their own discoveries with the ideas presented in the chapter.

As another example, before encountering *What Is a Seed?*, even though it was an introductory piece of print material, our students had conducted a series of hands-on experiments in which they dissected different kinds of seeds and grew seeds in water glasses with damp paper towels.

Collaborative and Independent Learning

As the materials and activities are ordered, teachers need to consider whether activities should be undertaken independently or collaboratively. Learning is inherently social, and students actively construct their knowledge through interaction with, and mediation by, more capable others. Collaborative activities should be viewed as a natural part of the ongoing curriculum, not as a special event. The social nature of learning is especially critical when new concepts and generalizations are involved because students lack the prior experiences to which this new meaning can be attached. For second language learners, collaborative activities provide the cognitive support necessary for content as well as linguistic learning to occur.

Although there are a number of ways in which collaborative experiences can be embedded within the thematic curriculum, we have found the following pattern particularly useful: class or large-group demonstrations ⟶ small-group or paired interactions $\longrightarrow$ independent interactions. Typically, when we were introducing students to new ideas, strategies, or linguistic forms, the entire class or a large group engaged in several demonstrations. For instance, we introduced our third-grade bilingual students to reader-response strategies through teacher reading. Each day we read aloud a story, article, or poem that was related to the theme we were studying. During the reading, we would occasionally stop and comment on the meaning being presented—new ideas; things liked, disliked, or not understood; links to other things we'd read; and so on. After each comment, we invited the students to share their responses. Once students were comfortable with this strategy, we asked groups of students to generate similar responses in their book groups or during paired reading. Eventually, we asked each student to share his or her responses to what he or she had read during free reading.

Revisiting the Old

Although the ongoing development of knowledge is certainly one aspect of thematic teaching and learning, a significant opportunity for learning is missed when previous meaning and experience are not revisited. Thematic teaching attempts to help students see the interrelationship among all activities within the curriculum. The concept of revisiting involves both reflection and synthesis. At critical points in the curriculum, students are engaged in thinking and learning that require them to synthesize and reflect on a number of individual activities previously experienced.

Students might be asked, for example, to compare and contrast a number of different books that have been read on a particular topic. Different perspectives offered by various authors might be analyzed. Students can review the thematic activities of the previous week and list all the significant things they have learned. Or they can keep ongoing learning journals in which they record the activities they have engaged in and what they learned.

In our third-grade bilingual classroom, we put the name of the theme above the chalkboard in the front of the room. As we reviewed the thematic activities at the end of each week, we asked the students how each activity related to the topic we were studying. Not only did this help the students link the activities, it also let us know how the students were interpreting events within the curriculum. These revisiting activities can help students view and review the curriculum globally.

Initiating and Culminating Activities

The teacher will want to open the unit with several activities that introduce students to the theme and potential generalizations and concepts and close the unit with activities that draw together and celebrate what has been learned and accomplished. These activities usually cannot be found on the list of "into," "through," and "beyond" activities generated for specific materials. In fact, initiating and culminating events are usually best considered after the tentative outline for the unit has been developed.

Some teachers with whom we have worked like to begin and end their themes by asking students to quickwrite. In a quickwrite, students write continuously for a brief period (three to five minutes) anything that comes into their minds about the topic. These quickwrites are then shared with other students in the class. When quickwrites have been used as an initiating activity and are then used again as a culminating activity, students can look back at their quickwrites from the beginning of the theme and see how much they have learned about the topic. Here are Bob's pre- and post-quickwrites from the thematic unit Getting to Know About Making and Flying Kites:

> Pre-Quickwrite
> Kites are fun to play with. They are made of plastic. You fly kites. Sometimes you have to run to get them up. You can only fly kites on windy days, but not too windy. I like to fly kites, don't you?
> Post-Quickwrite
> You can do more with kites than fly them for fun. There are different kinds of kites and kites can be used to do a lot of different things. Kites played a very important part in wars, such as the Boer War in Africa. Buford designed a chart for wind speeds by using kites. The first radio signal was sent by a kite. A bridge was built across Niagra Falls with a kite. Benjamin Franklin showed that there was electricity in lightning and he did it by tying a key to the end of the string on a kite and stood in a shack.

It is obvious that Bob not only increased his knowledge of the topic, but that this knowledge was more elaborate and specific.

Another frequently used initiating and culminating activity is the KWL inquiry chart. The teacher begins the unit by having students brainstorm and record ideas about what they know or would like to know. As the theme progresses, students continue to add areas of interest or questions and record the new things they are learning. At the end of the unit, students reflect on what they knew before they began the theme, the questions that evolved during the theme, and what new learning occurred because of their engagement with the theme.

Culminating activities provide both the students and the teacher with valuable evaluative information. Students and teacher can judge the effectiveness of the curriculum in promoting knowledge of the various communication systems and the disciplines. With this in mind, many teachers end their units by having students present to the class and invited guests special projects, works of art, plays, songs, and published writing that represent what has been accomplished. We typically ended our themes by displaying all of the activities and student work that the theme generated. We then asked students to comment on their favorite and least favorite activities and for ways in which the theme might have been improved.

• • • • • • • • • •

Putting It All Together

Earlier in this chapter, we suggested that each material and activity selected from the "into," "through," and "beyond" webs be written on a three-by-five card, that these cards be grouped by common generalizations, and that the groups be ordered. Using the guidelines for arranging thematic materials and activities as a framework, the cards within each group are tentatively ordered in the sequence in which the students will experience the activities. Laying the cards out on a table or on the floor helps you see the big picture of the curriculum. The advantage of using cards rather than listing the activities in order on a sheet of paper is that the cards can be easily arranged and rearranged and activities deleted and added. The bottom portion of Figure 7.1 represents the final step in this process.

Appendix 7.1 contains cards for the "into," "through," and "beyond" activities generated from the books *Big Al* (Clements 1988), *Earl's Too Cool for Me* (Komaiko 1988), and *Arnie and the New Kid* (Carlson 1990). Using the guidelines presented in this chapter, select at least twelve activities to accompany the three books. As always, collaborating with others in this process can be beneficial. After selecting the activities, experiment with various ways in which the activities might be arranged by (1) grouping cards by shared issues or common concepts and generalizations, (2) arranging the groups of cards into a tentative order, and (3) arranging the cards within each group into an order (see Figure 7.1). The thought processes, insights, and discussions generated by this activity should help you better select and arrange activities with your students in your classroom's own thematic units.

• • • • • • • • • •

A Look Back

At this point in the development of the thematic curriculum, after all activities have been selected and arranged, the teacher, with student collaboration, has:

1. Identified a significant thematic topic,
2. Gathered a variety of thematic materials,
3. Identified a set of potential generalizations and corresponding concepts on which the thematic curriculum can begin to be built,

4. Considered the characteristics of the activities to be generated from the thematic materials,
5. Grouped materials by generalizations,
6. Brainstormed "into," "through," and "beyond" activities for all significant materials,
7. Selected activities to include in the curriculum, and
8. Arranged activities into a tentative order.

8

Evaluating Thematic Thinking and Learning Events

Evaluation as a System of Values

Evaluation always reflects the value systems of those doing the evaluation or assessment. What the evaluator holds to be of importance determines both *what* is selected for evaluation and *how* what is selected is ultimately interpreted. Therefore, evaluation within the thematic curriculum highlights and examines those aspects of teaching and learning that are most valued. Within the curricular framework proposed in Chapter 1 (see Figure 1.1), and expanded on in Chapter 5 (see Table 5.1), what we value are the communication processes (language, mathematics, music, art, movement), subject fields (literature, social science, natural science), and core concepts and generalizations with which students engage throughout the thematic unit. Consequently, the ultimate purpose of evaluation within the thematic curriculum is always threefold:

1. To document student growth in using the communication systems and thinking processes in various contexts.
2. To document student growth in understanding the concepts and generalizations explored within the theme.
3. To determine the effectiveness of the thematic curriculum in developing students' process and content knowledge.

As Anthony et al. (1991) have noted, authentic evaluation occurs within authentic situations. Processes and products should emerge from student participation in the activities designed for the study unit rather than in testing situations that are separated from the curriculum. In a sense, the curriculum creates these "observable moments" for evaluation. For example, in Tables 6.1 and 6.2 we shared various "into," "through," and "beyond" activities that might be used with two theme topics. One activity suggested to introduce *Arnie and the New Kid* (Carlson 1990) in the theme Getting to Know About You, Me, and Others/*Tú, Yo, y Otros* was to ask the students to predict the content of the story by looking at the pictures. As the students predict, the teacher can see how effectively they are able to use their relevant background knowledge and the pictures. Relevant background knowledge and text aids are important strategies in the reading process (see Table 5.1). Student engagement with such thematic activities is the source for evaluation.

● ● ● ● ● ● ● ● ● ● ●

Who Evaluates Within a Thematic Curriculum?

The stakeholders in an evaluation program range from state and national education programs, members of the local community, the school board, and school administrators to the parents, teachers, and students. Not all of these stakeholders evaluate students' work, but they have an interest in the evaluation of educational programs.

Throughout this book we have emphasized the collaborative nature of curriculum development. We believe curriculum should emerge from the collaborative efforts of students and teachers, not be prescribed by publishers or other outsiders. Evaluation within a thematic curriculum also requires the collaboration of teachers, students, and a third stakeholder, parents.

Each of these three stakeholders brings a different perspective to the evaluation process, and therefore can potentially provide a more detailed holistic picture of the students' abilities and learning process. Parents are often left out of educational programs, although they can provide pertinent insights otherwise completely disregarded. Parent participation takes some planning by teachers. Time must be spent inviting and preparing parents to collaborate in the evaluation of their children's education—perhaps during "back to school" nights or other parent meetings. Guidelines and goals for the process can be jointly developed. Sensitivity to parents' educational, cultural, and linguistic background is essential in designing ways for parents to communicate, observe, record, and share their information with teachers and students. When appropriate, observation forms with cover letters including questions to focus parents' observations can be sent home, and this information can be included in cumulative evaluations made at the end of the unit or marking period. Parent-teacher conferences are an opportunity for both these stakeholders to partake equally in sharing new information with each other and together identifying patterns in a student's learning process. During teacher-parent-student conferences, student goals for the following unit or marking period can be jointly identified.

Whether teachers hold three-way conferences with students and parents or have separate conferences with them is not as important as ensuring the collaboration of all. Students have the most to gain or loose in the evaluation process. When students become participants in the evaluation process, they provide teachers with another perspective. For example, they may select some of the pieces to be included in their portfolio and provide their rationale for the selection. Teachers can also support students as they engage in self-reflection and set goals. These two outcomes are pivotal in the students' lifelong journey as learners. Including students and parents in the evaluation process makes the teacher's role fivefold:

1. Make instructional and curricular decisions based on ongoing assessment.
2. Assess student progress in:
   - Using communication systems and thinking processes in various contexts.
   - Developing thematic concepts and generalizations.
3. Evaluate the effectiveness of the thematic curriculum in developing students' process and content knowledge.
4. Design a framework to include parents as evaluative and interpretive collaborators.
5. Scaffold learning for students in order to engage them in self-reflection and goal setting.

• • • • • • • • • • •

What Do We Look At and When?

Because the thematic curriculum as we have conceptualized it is always process- as well as product-focused, evaluation necessarily involves examining both process and product behaviors of the students. Although process and product behaviors are usually intertwined, we will first address them separately in order to highlight the information that each can provide.

Process behaviors are important because they reveal the path the student followed to reach the destination, or product. Process evaluation captures the behaviors of the children as they actually engage in communication systems—reading, writing, drawing, singing—and thinking processes. Does the student revise for meaning during the reading of a piece of literature? Does he integrate the use of color, line, and form when expressing understanding of concepts and generalizations? Does she draw conclusions after engaging in several scientific investigations? Observing children in the act of doing provides valuable information to help answer such questions.

Two types of ongoing observations of process behavior are possible: casual and focused (Anthony et al. 1991; Herrell 1992; Goodman 1989). Both types allow the teacher to listen for the "sounds of children thinking" (Paley 1986, 122). Casual observations are unplanned; they are fortuitous moments that happen as teachers monitor students engaged in the thematic activities. Goodman (1989) refers to this monitoring as "kidwatching" and defines these unplanned observations as examining what students are doing as the teacher stands on the sidelines.

In contrast, focused observations are planned, and an agenda is set in advance. The teacher has a specific behavior or process in mind when observing the student or group of students. Planned observations, however, are still conducted while the students participate in authentic activities from the thematic unit and are grounded in instructional goals. In planned observations, particular communication and thinking processes (see Table 5.1) focus the teacher's attention. Keeping in mind the activity and the students involved, the teacher selects the appropriate process(es) that students may encounter during the lesson and then looks for the use of the process(es). Figure 8.1 is an example of how this might look. At the end of the lesson plan for an activity used with the theme Getting to Know About You, Me, and Others/*Tú, Yo, y Otros* are two suggestions teachers may select to observe for evaluative purposes. (The worksheet referred to in the lesson plan is included as Appendix 8.1.)

Another example of a focused observation comes from a fourth-grade unit on plants and seeds. The teacher observed students as they engaged in an "into" activity (see Table 6.1) focused on comparing and contrasting. (The students had been asked to bring in some seeds from fruits and vegetables they had at home.) Students first shared their seeds within their cooperative group, compared and contrasted the seeds, and identified categories. Then each group reporter shared the group's results with the whole class. To avoid redundancy, the reporter only shared information about seeds not previously mentioned by another group. Once everyone had access to all of the information, the categories were revisited to reach consensus. The final step was to graph the results.

As students worked in their cooperative groups, the teacher conducted planned observations of specific students she had previously identified, noting how they went about making comparisons and contrasts. She had several questions in mind:

1. What attributes did students choose to compare or contrast?
2. Did they use their background knowledge when comparing and contrasting?
3. How did their comparisons and contrasts add to their knowledge about seeds?
4. Did the students' observations move from simple features to more complex ones?
5. How much descriptive language did the students use? How sophisticated was this language?
6. Did the students use English or Spanish?

As the teacher observed one group after another, she was also able to capitalize on a fortuitous moment. Luisa was asking her group if fruits and vegetables also

Name: I Seem to Be..., But Really Am...
Possible Generalizations: People are oftentimes more than they appear.
Possible Concepts: Appearance / Image, true self
Materials: *Big Al* by Andrew Clements
Earl's Too Cool for Me by Leah Komaiko
Arnie and the New Kid by Nancy Carlson
"I Seem to Be..., But Really Am..." worksheet

Into:
1. Allow the students a few minutes to review the three books.
2. As a class, students briefly review the main characters—Big Al, Earl, and Philip—and the major events in each of the three books. Students' ideas are written on the board, each idea under the appropriate book title.

Through:
1. Each student receives a copy of the worksheet "I Seem to Be..., But Really Am..." In heterogenous groups of four or five members, students are to identify how each main character—Big Al, Earl, and Philip—appear to others and how he really was. With the entire class, do several examples.
2. Once the students are in groups, allow approximately thirty minutes for group work. Teacher circulates from group to group evaluating the progress of each group.
3. After the group work, students come together and list their "appeared to be, but really was" ideas on the board. Rotate from group to group, giving each group the opportunity to share one example per rotation.
4. Discuss what Big Al, Earl, and Philip all had in common.

Beyond:
1. The students are asked if they have ever heard of the saying, "You can't judge a book by its cover." First in small groups students discuss how this saying relates to the three main characters. Then their ideas are shared with the whole class.
2. The opportunity is provided for students to share experiences in which they have misjudged someone or have been misjudged themselves.

Evaluation:
The following information will be available for a focused observation:

What	How
• Student knowledge of generalizations/concepts	• Teacher listens to group discussions and group sharing and looks at student worksheet
• Student ability to see the common experiences among the three characters	• Student reflects on own performance in journal
• Student ability to link the saying, "You can't judge a book by its cover" to the three main characters	OR
• Student ability to analyze, compare, synthesize various stories	• Group reflects on group's performance

FIGURE 8.1 Sample lesson plan for focused observation and evaluation.

immigrated from one country to another, like people. The teacher asked Luisa what made her think that, and she replied that Armando's family and hers ate some fruits that were either different or prepared differently from those eaten by Anthony's and Jessica's family and vice versa. Luisa wondered if that was because their families were from different countries before living in the United States. The teacher told her that those were very good questions and asked her to save them for later on in the lesson so that the whole class could participate in a discussion. Though Luisa was not one of the students that the teacher had targeted to "kidwatch" that day, she could not ignore Luisa's insightful questions.

Sideline observations alone will not always provide the necessary windows into student cognition. Therefore, it is important that teachers interact with the students as well, questioning, probing, and discussing with the children what they are doing and learning within the activity. Writing conferences, reader-response groups, oral reading, and other structured student-teacher interactions are some of the instructional avenues through which the teacher can more actively engage with students during evaluation.

Student products are another window into the learner. Examining these products informs the teacher about student cognition. How well does the student understand a particular piece of literature after it is read? How coherent is a finished piece of writing? What meaning and feelings are conveyed in the student's drawing, painting, or dance?

A primary goal of evaluation is to paint a rich portrait of each student's abilities. Such a portrait requires the teacher to look for patterns of student behavior. For such patterns to emerge, evaluation must be ongoing and multidimensional. Process and product information must be observed and gathered over space and time rather than in one sitting (Anthony et al. 1991; Dagostino & Carifio 1994; Glazer & Brown 1993; Herrell 1992). Students' ability to use the communication and thinking processes effectively is often context specific. That is, the content being communicated and thought about and the purpose for the communication and thinking have a direct impact on how well the students are able to communicate and think.

For culturally and linguistically diverse students evaluation across contexts is even more critical. These students may be able to control particular processes in their home language but demonstrate less proficiency when using English. Or because of a cultural—that is, background—discrepancy between the home and the school, they may appear to lack certain abilities when in fact it is the lack of or difference in prior experiences with the content that is causing the problem. Continual and ongoing evaluation provides the teacher with a more complete understanding of what the bilingual child can and cannot do across language and cultural contexts.

The participation of second language learners in the evaluation process will also help teachers ensure that the student has indeed understood the learning task or that the teacher has interpreted the student's work appropriately. Murphy

(1994), drawing upon the work of Gumperz (1982a, 1982b), asserts that miscommunication on the part of the student or the teacher can result in unnecessary negative evaluations. The issue(s) can be clarified face to face and thus lead to a better understanding of the sociocultural factors that affect student performance. Furthermore, second language learners, even more than mainstream students, will benefit from explicit evaluation criteria. Culturally diverse students are often less testwise than their mainstream counterparts and therefore are less likely to be successful at guessing the evaluator's expectations.

A recent experience of a Chapter I teacher we know shows the importance of ongoing, multidimensional evaluation. She had been working with a small group of students on reasoning skills as part of a pull-out program. The students looked at a picture of a fan on a desk; the fan was blowing papers all over the room as a woman sitting in the background looked on. They then told what was happening in the picture, why they thought it was happening, and what they thought the woman in the picture would do next. As the students engaged in the discussion, Ging, a Hmong student, was quiet. After a while she asked the teacher what the round object in the picture was. She could tell that somehow it was making the papers fly away, but she did not know what this "wind maker" was.

The Chapter I teacher was reminded that she could not assume that all students have similar experiences with what the majority may consider common, everyday items. She was also reminded that she could not interpret any single observation as an absolute indicator of a student's ability. Had Ging not asked her question and if the teacher had been set on evaluating Ging on her contribution to the day's discussion, the assessment of the student's reasoning abilities would have been inaccurate.

Although ongoing and multidimensional evaluation across different contexts is important when evaluating all students, it is crucial for limited-English-proficient students, particularly when these students experience context-reduced instruction within the classroom curriculum or are segmented by pull-out programs that further decontextualize learning.

As teachers observe students working within various contexts, it is important that both group and individual student behaviors be noted. We believe that learning first develops on the social plane through interactions with more capable others. With time and experience, the child's learning becomes internalized and represents an independent ability. The teacher will want to know which processes the student can use effectively when working with others and which processes the student can control individually.

Ongoing evaluation allows for the unfolding of a dynamic rather than a static curriculum. Information gained through evaluation allows the teacher to reflect on the responsiveness of the curriculum to the needs and interests of the students and to make modifications. Revising curricular goals, materials, and activities in light of ongoing evaluation ensures that teachers as well as students are held accountable for classroom learning.

• • • • • • • • • • •

How Is Evaluation Information Collected, Recorded, and Interpreted?

Perhaps the biggest challenge faced by teachers as they attempt to implement an ongoing program of process and product evaluation within the thematic curriculum is capturing and making sense of student behavior. Many teachers use tests and other product-oriented evaluations not so much because they believe the instruments are valid but because they are "neat and tidy." Tests in particular allow teachers to collect, record, and interpret student behavior easily. However, such evaluation procedures are extremely limited and often yield invalid information.

Anecdotal records and portfolios are two of the most effective means by which to evaluate student behavior within a thematic curriculum. Anecdotal records are particularly effective at capturing process behavior, while portfolios typically represent the products of the students' work. However, as with process and product information, anecdotal records and portfolios are often intertwined and should not be viewed as distinct forms of assessment. Take for instance the casual observation of Luisa's ability to link the current activity on seeds with a previous unit on immigration. It became an anecdotal record that was later added to Luisa's portfolio.

Also, remember that the frameworks we share here for collecting, recording, and evaluating student behavior are just a beginning point. Teachers modify them or construct new ones according to their needs.

Using Anecdotal Records to Capture Process Behaviors

Anecdotal records are information about student behavior that the teacher jots down at the moment of observation. Because the classroom is a dynamic setting, record-keeping devices must be efficient and easy to maintain. And because many observable moments emerge suddenly, teachers must be prepared to capture them instantly. There are a number of ways in which observable moments can be recorded. Personal teaching and record-keeping styles tend to predispose teachers to particular formats. The kind of record-keeping system used is not important. What is important is that it be a framework for kidwatching—for observing and understanding the sounds of children thinking.

A first-grade teacher we know finds that the most efficient procedure for her is to record observations of student behavior on Post-it notes or gummed labels that she carries around the room on a clipboard, then paste these notes in a notebook containing blank sheets of paper with the students' names on them. As

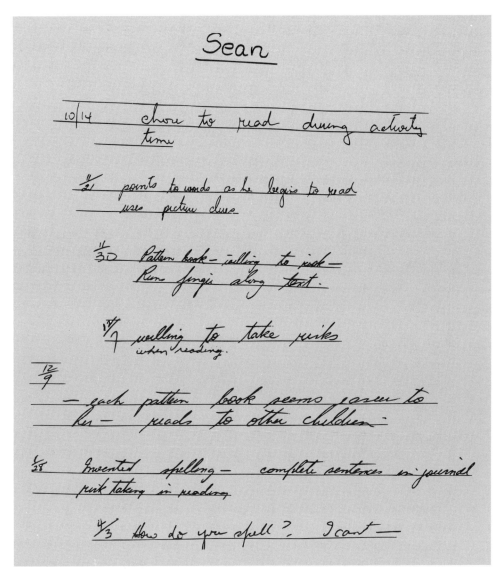

FIGURE 8.2 Sample anecdotal records in a first-grade classroom.

she observes significant student behavior throughout the day, she records her observations on the labels along with the child's name and the date. At the end of each day, she attaches each evaluation label to the appropriate sheet of paper in the notebook. (Figure 8.2 is a page from her notebook.) This running record of observations allowed this teacher to monitor each child's growth throughout the theme.

For some teachers, this procedure is too open-ended; they want an instrument that explicitly highlights what is valued within the curriculum. Such explicit instruments can be helpful because they serve to frame or guide teacher observations. The evaluation instruments in Appendices 8.2–8.7 highlight the communication processes involved in reading, writing, mathematics, music, movement, and art. Similarly, Appendices 8.8–8.10 reflect the thinking processes involved in literature, the social sciences, and the natural sciences. As the teacher observes the students' interactions with various activities within the thematic curriculum, instances in which a student does or does not effectively use various processes can be noted with a check under the appropriate column. "Yes" indicates that the student consistently and effectively engaged with the process during the observation; "somewhat" indicates that the process was used but not always effectively; and "no" indicates that the student did not use the process or was ineffective in its use.

For second language learners, codes can indicate which language was used by the student during the observation. An *S* can be placed in the appropriate column if the language was Spanish, an *E* if the language was English, and so forth. This type of coding can give the teacher insights into what processes are and are not used effectively by the students across language contexts. Another way some teachers have modified the form is by using a single column for the evaluation rather than three. When evaluations are recorded, a *Y* is used for yes, an *S* for somewhat, and an *N* for no. The only limitation with this modification is that it is more difficult to see the emergence of a pattern or profile of effective and ineffective process use by simply glancing at the form.

A problem some teachers find with this particular format is that a separate form must be kept for each student. This can make the procedure somewhat cumbersome, thereby limiting the extent to which the teacher is able to evaluate and record student behavior as it occurs. Some teachers solve this problem by noting student behavior or recording process numbers on scrap paper or Post-its during the lesson and then later transferring this information to the student forms.

Another way to capture the context of the lesson is to use an instructional activities summary sheet (see Appendix 8.11). The summary sheet is simply a numbered running account of all classroom activities that were used to evaluate student process behavior. In most cases, the summary sheet contains all taught activities, although not every student may experience or be evaluated on every activity. Then, as process behaviors are evaluated, rather than putting a check in the appropriate column, the number of the lesson is used instead. This procedure provides additional information and insight regarding contexts in which students can and cannot use particular processes effectively.

Some teachers prefer to have in mind the specific process or processes that are to be evaluated before a lesson is taught. To assist in the collection of data for this type of focused observation, teachers may choose to develop instruments like the one in Appendix 8.12. This form provides room for detailed, descriptive notes yet still keeps the focus on a particular process. After observations are recorded, the sections may be cut apart and attached to a running list of observations for each student in a class notebook. A modified version of Appendix 8.12 omits the specific process to be observed and can be used to record any and all anecdotal information.

Using Portfolios to Capture Product Behaviors

Samples of student products are another source of information about student performance. Portfolios are not, however, just a collection of student work. Rather, they are a selection of student accomplishments. Student work can be represented by stories, essays, art, photographs, tape recordings, learning logs, even anecdotal records. Although organized to demonstrate student development, portfolios may also include summary sheets or profiles documenting such growth. These profiles are written statements explaining the selections and incorporating patterns gathered from actual samples and anecdotal records (Anthony et al. 1991).

Developing portfolios involves selecting and excluding. The portfolio must be representative of the teaching and learning taking place in the classroom, but it should not include every artifact the students produce nor every observation of the students' engagement with various processes. Therefore, it is important that criteria be developed for selecting artifacts for the portfolio and that all the stakeholders—teachers, students, parents—take part in the selection process. Extending the process beyond selecting favorite or "best" work, teachers, students, and parents will want to consider samples that demonstrate risk taking or the development of processes previously not used by the student. Incorporating different types of products, establishing regular intervals for selection, and involving students and parents as well as the teacher ensures a continuous and multi-dimensional picture of student development.

When selecting products for the portfolio, we want to be aware of the type of activity that generated them. Activities whose products are most valuable to assessment are those that are conceptually linked to the thematic unit and that foster divergent, high-level thinking. Products that stem from activities that properly draw from student background knowledge to create meaning through a range of communication systems and thinking processes provide valuable information for the portfolio. Since each product in the portfolio is analyzed or interpreted in conjunction with the others included, it may also be worthwhile for the teacher, student, or parents to note on the product the circumstances under which it was generated as well as the rationale for selecting it.

A second-grade teacher we know has her students store all their thematic work in a personal folder kept in a box on the back counter. Toward the end of a marking period, the students go through their personal folders and select two or three items for their portfolio. As they select the items, students complete a short form for each one that includes their name, the date completed, the unit or activity the item represents, and their reason for selecting it. A portfolio conference is then held, and student and teacher share, discuss, and decide which additional items from the personal folder will become part of the portfolio.

One of her students, Andrés, selected two items for his portfolio. The information he included in his form contextualized his selections.

One was a copy of a page in a class book produced as a culminating activity for a unit on the water cycle. At the beginning of the water cycle unit, the teacher had asked the students to identify which question in their KWL chart they were most interested in researching. The students were then grouped by self-identified areas of interest. Each small group of students gathered information for their inquiry and wrote about and illustrated their findings. These pages were laminated and became part of a class book. Andrés wanted his group's page in his portfolio because it showed how well they had worked together to gather the information they needed.

His second selection was a story he had written about a family vacation. He had chosen the topic himself and had focused on making this story descriptive, because description was a goal he had identified in a teacher/student writing conference. Andrés felt that this story demonstrated how he was progressing in that area. Both pieces were included in his portfolio along with others the teacher had selected.

In evaluating portfolios, the teacher once again returns to the communication processes, thinking processes, and concepts and generalizations that framed the thematic unit. Products are assessed in terms of what they demonstrate about student ability with these processes and student knowledge of thematic content. Many teachers use the processes listed in Appendices 8.2–8.10 to guide their evaluations of student work. Although each piece of work in the portfolio is assessed, the goal is to discover patterns of student behavior rather than isolated instances of particular kinds of behavior.

Students can also contribute to the identification of these patterns in student-teacher portfolio conferences. At various times during the evaluation cycle, each student meets with the teacher to review the portfolio's contents. Students may add to or remove samples from their portfolio during the conferences as long as a reason is provided. The conference also provides opportunities for the students to receive feedback on their performance, reflect on their progress, and identify personal goals. Similarly, parents can also analyze their child's portfolio and contribute their insights and understanding of their child's abilities.

Inasmuch as there has been regular participation in the selection process by students and parents, the teacher can be more confident of the evaluation, since the interpretations can be corroborated from the different perspectives and across various data sources. At the end of the evaluation cycle (for example, at the end of the thematic unit or marking period), the teacher writes an evaluative summary. However, before doing so, it is desirable to have one last student-teacher portfolio conference. This will provide the student with the opportunity to engage in self-reflection and address any points of discord or confirm the teacher's interpretations. Parents could be given a similar opportunity by having them complete a form or provide verbal feedback on what they have observed at home. When working with second language learners, who often represent cultures and socio-economic class statuses different from that of the school, it is important to find ways to bring parents into the educational process. Asking for their input and insights about their child's growth and development can demonstrate to parents that they are a valued stakeholder in the education of their children. These parents' insights may provide perspectives of which the teacher is unaware.

The evaluative summary becomes the focus of the parent-student-teacher conference at the end of the evaluation cycle. If all the stakeholders have had the opportunity to contribute to the summary, it can serve as a tool to share their findings. If they haven't, this would be a good opportunity for all stakeholders to prepare a summary of their own before the conference. At the conference everyone offers their perspectives, and the teacher then makes any necessary adjustments and provides a copy of the final summary to all participants. This final conference is also an excellent opportunity for everyone to set goals for the next evaluation cycle.

● ● ● ● ● ● ● ● ● ● ●

A Look Back

At this point in the development of the thematic curriculum, after selecting a framework for assessing thematic instruction, the teacher, with student collaboration has:

1. Identified a significant thematic topic,
2. Gathered a variety of thematic materials,
3. Identified a set of potential generalizations and corresponding concepts on which the thematic curriculum can begin to be built,
4. Considered the characteristics of the activities to be generated from the thematic materials,
5. Grouped materials by generalizations,
6. Brainstormed "into," "through," and "beyond" activities for all significant materials,
7. Selected activities to include in the curriculum,
8. Arranged activities into a tentative order,
9. Identified the stakeholders in the evaluation process, and
10. Identified a framework to collect, record, and interpret students' process and product behaviors within a thematic curriculum.

Appendix of Forms

1. What did I learn from reading this story?

2. What did I feel as I was reading this story?

3. Why did the author write this story? What was the author trying to teach me?

4. What did I like? What were my favorite parts? What did I dislike?

5. Does this story remind me of something else I have read?

6. What would I change in the story if I had written it? What could the author have changed or done to make the story better?

7. Were there things I did not understand or words I did not know? How can I figure these things out? (Use the reading strategy wall chart as a guide.)

APPENDIX 2.1 Reader-response questions.

Name: _____ Date: _____

Title: _____

Things that we like about the piece:

Things that we think would improve the piece:

APPENDIX 2.2 Writer-response conference form.

What do you think time is?	What does Phyllis McGinley think time is?	What does William Shakespeare think time is?

APPENDIX 5.1 Writing about time.

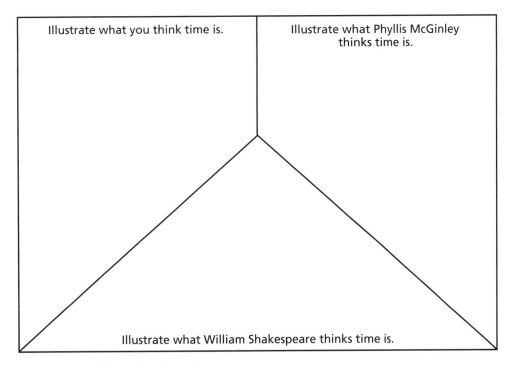

APPENDIX 5.2 Illustrating time.

A phrase that I am unclear about is:

My interpretation is:

Another possible interpretation is:

Another possible interpretation is:

Another possible interpretation is:

APPENDIX 5.3 Interpreting Shakespeare.

Characteristics of Salamanders	Characteristics of Frogs	Characteristics of Toads	Common Characteristics

APPENDIX 5.4 What is an amphibian?

Guiding Questions

Information Source	Q1	Q2	Q3	Q4	Q5	New Questions
Summary						

APPENDIX 5.5 Inquiry chart.

Libro / Book: _____

¿Cuál es el objetivo o propósito del personaje principal? / What is the goal of the main character?	¿Qué problema tiene el personaje principal? / What problem does the main character encounter?
¿Cómo se resuelve el problema? / How is the problem resolved?	¿Cómo te hace sentir el cuento? / How did the story make you feel?

APPENDIX 5.6 Book analysis.

¿En qué se parecen los libros? How are the books similar?

- Coloca un círculo alrededor de los libros que leíste o discutiste. / Circle the book read and the books discussed.
- ¿En qué se parecen todos estos libros? Haz una lista. / List all the ways in which the books are similar.

Amazing Grace	The Carrot Seed/ La Semilla de Zanahoria	The Gold Cadillac	William's Doll	Oliver Button Is a Sissy/ Oliver Button es una Nena

APPENDIX 5.7 Book similarities.

Materials
Big Al (Clements)
Big Al is a nice fish. But he is big. And scary-looking. He is a fish with no friends. Then one day Big Al proves what a truly terrific fish he is—and finds a whole school of new friends!

1

Materials
Earl's Too Cool for Me (Komaiko)
Earl's the coolest kid in town. He lunches with movie stars and keeps monster eyes in jelly jars. Why would he ever want to play with a regular kid? Maybe Earl isn't too cool for true friendship.

2

Materials
Arnie and the New Kid (Carlson)
Arnie teases Philip because he is confined to a wheelchair. Yet, when Arnie falls down the school steps and breaks a leg, twists a wrist, and sprains a tail, he begins to see life from a different perspective.

3

Into
Students share experiences in which they have been judged as "different." How did it make them feel?

4

Into
Students share experiences in which others misjudged them. How did it make them feel?

5

Into
Students share experiences in which they have misjudged someone.

6

Into
Ask students if they have ever heard of the saying, "You can't judge a book by it's cover." Discuss what it means to them.

7

Into
Students write poems in which each line is constructed, "I seem to be..., but really am..." Student poems are shared and the class guesses which student belongs to which poem.

8

Into
In pairs, students trace each other's head profile. Students cut out their profiles and make a collage on each side. One side illustrates "I seem to be"; the other side illustrates "I really am." Student silhouettes are shared and the class guesses which silhouette belongs to which student.

9

APPENDIX 7.1 Selecting activities and ordering the curriculum: sample activity cards.

Into
Read the book *Angel Child, Dragon Child* by Michelle Maria Surat. Children brainstorm the two sides of the story's main character.

10

Into
Through visual arts or movement, students depict the feelings they have experienced when they have been judged as being different.

11

Into
Students predict what the book will be about from looking at the pictures.

12

Through
Students read to the point in the book where the protagonist's problem is identified. Students write a solution.

13

Through
Throughout the reading of the book, stop occasionally and have students predict what will happen next. Read on to see how accurate the predictions were.

14

Through
As students read the book, they consider the question, Why was the protagonist misunderstood?

15

Through
Students read the book in pairs, discussing the ideas and helping each other through the "rough spots."

16

Through
As the book is read, students think about how the saying "You can't judge a book by its cover" applies to the characters in their book.

17

Through
On an I-chart, students keep a list of how the main character appears to be and how he really is.

18

APPENDIX 7.1 *(cont.)*

Through Students monitor their predictions of story content based on having looked at the pictures 19	**Beyond** Students compare their predictions of story content with what actually happened in the book. 20	**Beyond** Students share how the main character appeared to be and really was. 21
Beyond Students compare and contrast the three books, noting how each character was misjudged. 22	**Beyond** Students discuss what the saying "You can't judge a book by its cover" means to them now. 23	**Beyond** Discuss how the experiences of the main character in *Angel Child, Dragon Child* (Surat) were similar to the main characters in the three books. 24
Beyond In a learning log, students write what "People are often more than they appear" means to them. 25	**Beyond** Using a Venn diagram, illustrate the similarities and differences among the three books. 26	**Beyond** In book groups, students discuss the story from the point of view of various characters. 27

APPENDIX 7.1 *(cont.)*

Beyond
For one of the main characters in one of the books, students make a silhouette collage similar to what they made for themselves as an "into" activity. Students compare and contrast their own silhouette collage with the main character's.

28

Beyond
In book groups, students make a storyboard (a graphic depiction of the major events in a story). Each group decides which events are the most important and sketch six to eight scenes in sequence on a storyboard. Groups share their storyboard with the class. Students who read the same book may form smaller groups, make storyboards, and then compare/contrast storyboards for the same story.

29

Beyond
Students share their I-charts of how the main character appeared to be and how he really was.

30

Beyond
Students discuss why the protagonist was misunderstood.

31

APPENDIX 7.1 *(cont.)*

Name: _____

	Appeared to Be	But Really Was
Big Al		
Philip		
Earl		

APPENDIX 8.1 "I Seem to Be..., But Really Am..." worksheet.

Student's Name: _____

Reading Processes	Yes	Somewhat	No
1. Generates and organizes major ideas or concepts.			
2. Develops and supports major ideas or concepts with details and particulars.			
3. Integrates meaning into a logical and coherent whole.			
4. Uses a variety of linguistic cues: textual, semantic, graphophonic.			
5. Uses a variety of text aids: pictures, charts, graphs, subheadings, etc.			
6. Uses relevant conceptual and linguistic background knowledge.			
7. Makes meaningful predictions based on what has been previously read.			
8. Revises—rereads, reads on, or rethinks—when meaning is lost or when purposes/intentions or the needs of the audience are not met.			
9. Generates inferences or goes beyond the information given.			
10. Reflects on, and responds and reacts to, what is being read.			
11. Uses reading for various purposes or functions: instrumental, regulatory, interactional, personal, heuristic, imaginative, informative, diversionary, perpetuating.			
12. Varies the manner in which texts are read based on different purposes, intentions, and audiences.			
13. Takes risks.			
14. Sentences are meaningful as read.			

APPENDIX 8.2 Evaluation of reading processes.

Student's Name: _____

Writing Processes	Yes	Somewhat	No
1. Generates and organizes major ideas and concepts.			
2. Expands, extends, and elaborates on major ideas and concepts.			
3. Integrates meaning into a logical and coherent whole.			
4. Uses a variety of linguistic cues: textual, semantic, syntactic, graphophonic.			
5. Uses a variety of text aids: pictures, charts, graphs, subheadings, etc.			
6. Uses relevant conceptual and linguistic background knowledge.			
7. Predicts/plans future meanings based on what has been written.			
8. Revises when meaning is lost or when purposes and needs of the audience are not met.			
9. Uses writing to explore ideas and to discover new meanings.			
10. Reflects on and responds to what is being written.			
11. Uses writing for various purposes or functions: instrumental, regulatory, interactional, personal, heuristic, imaginative, informative, diversionary, perpetuating.			
12. Varies the manner in which texts are written based on different purposes and audiences.			
13. Takes risks.			
14. Sentences are meaningful as written.			
15. Revises conventions—spelling, punctuation, capitalization, penmanship—after meaning and purpose are met.			

APPENDIX 8.3 Evaluation of writing processes.

Student's Name: _____

Mathematical Processes	Yes	Somewhat	No
1. Uses various mathematical functions—adding, subtracting, multiplying, dividing—to solve problems and to investigate the world.			
2. Estimates to solve problems and to investigate the world.			
3. Uses mathematical knowledge to explain events.			
4. Interprets events using mathematical knowledge.			
5. Summarizes mathematical information.			
6. Predicts events using mathematical knowledge.			
7. Integrates and connects mathematical functions and information to solve problems and to investigate the world.			
8. Organizes mathematical information to solve problems and to investigate the world.			
9. Draws conclusions using mathematical knowledge.			
10. Categorizes information using mathematical knowledge.			
11. Seeks and forms patterns using mathematical knowledge.			

APPENDIX 8.4 Evaluation of mathematical processes.

Student's Name: _____

Movement Processes	Yes	Somewhat	No
1. Uses body parts for various actions—jumping, skipping, tumbling, stretching, clapping—to express ideas and feelings.			
2. Varies how actions are done—quickly, smoothly, slowly, lightly—to express ideas and feelings.			
3. Varies actions in space—up, down, forward, sideways, to the left, to the right—to express ideas and feelings.			
4. Varies the actions in relationship to a partner, group, or object to express ideas and feelings.			
5. Uses going and stopping contrasts—running and stopping, bouncing and crouching—to express ideas and feelings.			
6. Uses body-part contrasts—hands clap/feet jump/arms swing/feet stamp/feet slide—to express ideas and feelings.			
7. Uses qualitative contrasts—glide/explode/ rush/pounce—to express ideas and feelings.			
8. Uses spatial contrasts—traveling movements (leaping, rolling) with in-place movements (rising, sinking)—to express ideas and feelings.			
9. Integrates various elements of movement to form a coordinated whole and to express ideas and feelings.			
10. Reflects on and responds to the movement of others using knowledge of various elements of movements.			
11. Evaluates the quality or value of the movements of others.			

APPENDIX 8.5 Evaluation of movement processes.

Student's Name: _____

Art Processes	Yes	Somewhat	No
1. Uses elements of design—color, line, value, shape, form, texture, mass, space, volume—to express ideas and feelings.			
2. Uses principles of design—balance, symmetry, asymmetry, contrast, dominance, repetition, rhythm, theme, variation, and unity—to express ideas and feelings.			
3. Integrates design elements and principles to form a coordinated whole and to express ideas and feelings.			
4. Reflects on and responds to the artistic expression of others using knowledge of design elements and principles.			
5. Evaluates the quality or value of the artistic expression of others.			

APPENDIX 8.6 Evaluation of art processes.

Student's Name: _____

Musical Processes	Yes	Somewhat	No
1. Uses pitch—high, low, melody, scale—to express ideas and feelings.			
2. Uses rhythm—meter, tone—to express ideas and feelings.			
3. Uses harmony—tones, chords—to express ideas and feelings.			
4. Uses form—repetition, variation, patterns—to express ideas and feelings.			
5. Uses texture—thick, thin, opaque, transparent, legato, staccato—to express ideas and feelings.			
6. Uses tempo—speed, variation—to express ideas and feelings.			
7. Uses dynamics—volume, variation—to express ideas and feelings.			
8. Uses timbre—tonal qualities—to express ideas and feelings.			
9. Integrates various elements of music—pitch, rhythm, harmony, form, texture, tempo, dynamics, timbre—to form a coordinated whole and to express ideas and feelings.			
10. Reflects on and responds to the music of others using knowledge of various musical elements—pitch, rhythm, harmony, form, texture, tempo, dynamics, timbre.			
11. Evaluates the quality or value of the musical expression of others.			

APPENDIX 8.7 Evaluation of musical processes.

Student's Name: _____

Literary Processes	Yes	Somewhat	No
1. Analyzes information.			
2. Interprets.			
3. Establishes interpretations supported by textual information and background knowledge.			
4. Makes associations between and among texts.			
5. Forms mental images.			
6. Engages in vicarious experiences.			
7. Fantasizes.			
8. Adopts an efferent or aesthetic stance.			
9. Reflects on and responds to the meanings being generated.			
10. Evaluates the quality or value of the text.			
11. Develops concepts and generalizations.			

APPENDIX 8.8 Evaluation of literary processes.

Student's Name: _____

Social Science Processes	Yes	Somewhat	No
1. Analyzes information.			
2. Generates hypotheses.			
3. Formulates decisions.			
4. Formulates values.			
5. Compares and contrasts.			
6. Offers alternatives.			
7. Observes.			
8. Describes.			
9. Differentiates.			
10. Explains.			
11. Develops concepts and generalizations.			

APPENDIX 8.9 **Evaluation of social science processes.**

Student's Name: _____

Science Processes	Yes	Somewhat	No
1. Observes and gathers data.			
2. Generates hypotheses or predictions.			
3. Tests hypotheses.			
4. Modifies hypotheses.			
5. Compares and contrasts.			
6. Orders and classifies.			
7. Measures.			
8. Describes.			
9. Infers and draws conclusions.			
10. Develops concepts and generalizations.			

APPENDIX 8.10 Evaluation of science processes.

Activity	Date

APPENDIX 8.11 Instructional activities summary sheet.

Date:_____ Theme Topic: _____

Activity: _____

Process: _____

Student	Anecdotal Record

APPENDIX 8.12 Focused observation form.

Bibliography of Theme Topics, Generalizations, Concepts, and Materials

The following theme topics, generalizations, concepts, and materials are intended to demonstrate the range of issues and resources that are possible in thematic teaching and learning. Although certainly not exclusive in any sense, the topics and materials listed span the sciences, social sciences, and literature, clearly demonstrating that the thematic curriculum is not the domain of any one discipline. We encourage teachers to add to the bibliography, to develop their own, and to use our list of topics, generalizations, concepts, and materials as a beginning rather than as an ending point. Additionally, the generalizations and concepts listed for each topic only represent those that we have discovered with our children, university students, and classroom teachers in using the materials. As we have noted throughout the book, other generalizations and concepts are possible and we encourage teachers in collaboration with their students to be open to other possibilities.

Because we believe in the integration of all students into the curriculum, the bibliography is bilingual in the sense that materials written in both Spanish and English are included. Keeping in mind the range of abilities found in most classrooms, the materials in each theme also represent a range of reading and thinking abilities so as to ensure that all students will have access to the ideas being presented in the curriculum.

The following thematic topics are developed in the bibliography:

1. Be True to Yourself*
2. Continuity and Change
3. Culture: Human Diversity in Action
4. Dare to Be Different
5. Environment
6. Establishing Your Own Space*
7. Exploration and Discovery
8. Families and Family Relationships
9. Farmers, Their Lives, and Their Animals

10. Feelings and Emotions
11. Flights of Fancy: Me and My Imagination
12. Friendships and Community: People Need People
13. Getting to Know About You, Me and Others
14. The Grass Is Always Greener on the Other Side of the Fence or Things Aren't Always as They Appear
15. Growing and Using Plants and Seeds
16. Handicaps: Challenges to the Human Condition
17. Humankind: The Laughing Animal
18. Immigration: Strangers in a Strange Land
19. I'm O.K.; You're O.K.
20. It's Not Fair*
21. A Lot Can Be Said About "Little"**
22. Me, Myself, and I
23. People Are More Than They Appear
24. People Working Together Can Make a Difference*
25. Reptiles and Amphibians
26. Survival
27. Things That Go Bump in the Night: Getting to Understand Fears
28. With Freedom and Justice for All
29. Who Is a Hero?*

* Theme topics and initial materials from Galaxy Institute of Education. 1993. *Galaxy Classroom Thematic Bibliography.* Los Angeles: Galaxy Institute for Education.

** Theme topic and initial materials from Rhodes, L. 1983. In "Organizing the Elementary Classroom for Effective Language Learning." U. Hardt ed. *Teaching Reading with the Other Language Arts.* Newark, DE: International Reading Association.

Note: The Spanish titles in this bibliography may be located through the following distributors:

Bilingual Educational Services, California State Department of Education, 2514 S. Grand Avenue, Los Angeles, CA 90007

The Booksource, 4127 Forest Park Avenue, St. Louis, MO 63108

Hispanic Book Distributors, Inc., 1665 W. Grant, Tucson, AZ 85745

Lectorum Publications, 137 W. 14th Street, New York, NY 10011

Mariuccia Iaconi Books Imports, Inc., 970 Tennessee Street, San Francisco, CA 90029

1. THEME TOPIC: BE TRUE TO YOURSELF

Possible Generalizations:

• It is important to know what you want.

- It is not always easy to follow your dreams.
- Being true to ourselves many times involves making choices.

Possible Concepts:

self-awareness, self-identity, freedom, choices, consequences

Possible Materials:

Balzola, Asun. *Santino el Pastelero.*
Bauer, Marion. 1987. *On My Honor / Te Lo Prometo.* New York: Dell.
Blos, Joan. 1990. *Old Henry.* Illus. Stephen Gammell. New York: Morrow.
Burch, Robert. 1990. *Ida Early Comes Over the Mountain.* New York: Puffin.
Burningham, John. 1982. *Trubloff, el Ratón Que Quería Tocar la Balalaica.* New York: Yarrow Press.
Clement, Claude. 1990. *Painter and the Wild Swans.* New York: Dial.
Cooney, Barbara. 1985. *Miss Rumphius.* Illustrated. New York: Puffin.
de Paola, Tomie. 1979. *Oliver Button Is a Sissy / Oliver Button es un Nena.* Illus. by author. San Diego: Harcourt Brace.
Fern, Eugene. [1960] 1991. *Pepito's Story.* Illus. by author. New York: Yarrow Press.
Higginsen, Vy, and Tonya Bolden. 1992. *Mama, I Want to Sing.* New York: Scholastic.
Hoffman, Mary. 1991. *Amazing Grace.* New York: Dial.
Leaf, Munro. 1988. *El Cuento de Ferdinando: The Story of Ferdinand.* Trans. Pura Belpre. Illus. Robert Lawson. New York: Puffin.
Locker, Thomas. 1989. *The Young Artist.* Illustrated. New York: Dial.
Perera, Hilda. *Rana Ranita.*
Say, Allen. 1990. *El Chino.* Illus. by author. Boston: Houghton Mifflin.
Taylor, Theodore. 1989. *Trouble With Tuck.* New York: Doubleday.
Turín, Adela. *Arturo y Clementina.*
————. *Nuncajamas.*
Turín, Adela and Nella Bosnia. *Cajas de Cristal.*
Vigna, Judith. 1992. *Black Like Kyra, White Like Me.* Illus. by author, ed. Kathleen Tucker. Morton Grove, IL: Whitman.
Yarbrough, Camille. 1990. *The Shimmershine Queens.* New York: Knopf.
Zatón, Jesús. *Elefante Poff No Quiere Ser Payaso.*

2. THEME TOPIC: CONTINUITY AND CHANGE

Possible Generalizations:

- Change is a part of life.
- Living life involves accepting and adapting to the fact that some things change and others stay the same.
- Changes can cause fear and anxiety as well as provide opportunities for growth.
- Continuity can produce feelings of security as well as boredom.

Possible Concepts:

change, acceptance, adaptation, fear, anxiety, growth, security, boredom, continuity

Possible Materials:

Alexander, Lloyd. 1980. *Taran Wanderer*. New York: Dell.

Baker, Olaf. 1989. *Where the Buffaloes Begin*. Illus. Stephen Gammell. New York: Viking.

Balzola, Asun. *Los Zapatos de Munia*.

Barrett, Judith. 1982. *Cloudy With a Chance of Meatballs*. Illustrated. New York: Macmillan.

Blocksma, Mary. 1986. *¡Manzano, Manzano! Apple Tree! Apple Tree!* Chicago: Childrens Press.

Brenner, Barbara. 1984. *Wagon Wheels*. Illus. Don Bolognese. New York: HarperCollins.

Bulla, Clyde R. 1989. *Shoeshine Girl*. Illus. Leigh Grant. New York: HarperCollins.

Carle, Eric. 1991. *The Very Hungry Caterpillar / La Oruga Muy Hambrienta*. New York: Putnam.

Carlson, Nancy. 1992. *Arnie and the New Kid*. Illustrated. New York: Puffin.

Carpenter, Frances. 1972. *Tales of a Korean Grandmother*. Illustrated. Boston: C. E. Tuttle.

Cleary, Beverly. 1990. *Ramona and Her Father / Ramona y Su Padre*. New York: Avon.

———. 1992. *Dear Mr. Henshaw / Querido Señor Henshaw*. Illus. Paul O. Zelinsky. New York: Dell.

Clever, Vera and Bill. *Donde Florecen los Lirios*.

Dalgliesh, Alice. [1954] 1991. *The Courage of Sarah Noble / El Valor de Sarah Noble*. Illus. Leonard Weisgard. New York: Macmillan.

de Paola, Tomie. 1978. *Nana Upstairs and Nana Downstairs*. Illus. by author. New York: Puffin.

Estes, Eleanor. 1974. *The Hundred Dresses*. Illus. Louis Slobodkin. San Diego: Harcourt Brace.

Fox, Paula. 1991. *Slave Dancer / Que Bailen Los Esclavos*. New York: Dell.

Gates, Doris. 1976. *Blue Willow*. Illus. Paul Lantz. New York: Puffin.

Gipson, Fred. 1990. *Old Yeller*. New York: HarperCollins.

Greene, Bette. 1984. *Summer of My German Soldier*. New York: Bantam.

Greenfield, Eloise. 1987. *Sister*. Illus. Moneta Barnett. New York: HarperCollins.

———. 1988. *La Cara de Abuelito*. New York: Philomel Books.

Hall, Donald. 1983. *Ox-Cart Man*. Illus. Barbara Cooney. New York: Puffin.

Hamilton, Virginia. 1993. *Zeely*. Ed. Whitney Malone. Illustrated. New York: Macmillan.

Hoban, Russell. 1976. *Baby Sister for Frances*. Illus. Lillian Hoban. New York: HarperCollins.

Holman, Felice. 1986. *Slake's Limbo*. New York: Macmillan.

Hongo, Florence and Miyo Burton, ed. 1985. *Japanese-American Journey: The Story of a People*. Japanese American Curriculum Project, Inc. Staff.

Jukes, Mavis. 1987. *Like Jake and Me*. Illus. Lloyd Bloom. New York: Knopf.

Levert, Claude. *Pedro y su Roble*.

Levitin, Sonia. 1986. *Journey to America*. Illus. Charles Robinson. New York: Macmillan.

Livingston, Myra C. 1982. *A Circle of Seasons*. New York: Holiday.

Lord, Bette. 1986. *In the Year of the Boar and Jackie Robinson*. New York: HarperCollins.

Lowry, Lois. 1984. *Anastasia Krupnik*. New York: Bantam.

MacDonald, Golden. 1990. *Little Island*. Illus. Leonard Weisgard. New York: Scholastic.

Manes, Stephen. 1987. *Be a Perfect Person in Just Three Days!* New York: Bantam.

Mathers, Petra. 1993. *Maria Theresa*. Illus. by author. New York: HarperCollins.

Miles, Miska. 1972. *Annie and the Old One*. Boston: Little, Brown.

Miller, Marilyn. 1984. *The Bridge at Selma*. Illustrated. Morristown, NJ: Silver Burdett Press.

O'Dell, Scott. 1976. *Zia*. Illus. Ted Lewin. Boston: Houghton Mifflin.

———. 1990. *Island of the Blue Dolphins / Isla de los Delfines Azules*. Illus. Ted Lewin. Boston: Houghton Mifflin.

Orlev, Uri. 1984. *Island on Bird Street*. Trans. Hillel Halkin. Boston: Houghton Mifflin.

Osorio, Marta. *Mariposa Dorada*.

Paterson, Katherine. 1987. *Bridge to Terabithia / Puente Hasta Terabithia*. Illus. Donna Diamond. New York: HarperCollins.

Perera, Hilda. *Pericopín*.

Reiss, Johanna. 1987. *The Journey Back*. New York: HarperCollins.

Saller, Carol. 1991. *The Bridge Dancers*. Illus. Gerald Talifero. Minneapolis: Carolrhoda Books.

Steptoe, John. 1986. *Stevie*. Illus. by author. New York: HarperCollins.

Surat, Michele M. 1983. *Angel Child, Dragon Child*. Illus. Mai Vo-Dinh. New York: Scholastic.

Tsutsui, Yoriko. 1989. *Anna's Secret Friend*. Illus. Akiko Hayashi. New York: Puffin.

Uribe, Maria de la Luz. *Señorita Amelia*.

Wilheim, Hans. *Yo Siempre te Querré*.

Yashima, Taro. 1976. *Crow Boy*. Illus. by author. New York: Puffin.

Zatón, Jesús. *Hato Viejo y Triste*.

Zendrera, C. *Yaci y su Muñeca*.

3. THEME TOPIC: CULTURE: HUMAN DIVERSITY IN ACTION

Possible Generalizations:

- People use rituals to express who and what they are.
- Rituals of various cultures are both similar and different.
- Cultures "mark" significant human events.
- Cultures are both similar and different.

Possible Concepts:

rituals, identity, culture, similar, different, mark, significant events

Possible Materials:

Adoff, Arnold. 1982. *All the Colors of the Race*. Illus. John Steptoe. New York: Lothrop.

Araki, Nancy K., and Jane Horii. 1985. *Matsuri Festival! Japanese American Celebrations and Activities*. Torrance, CA: Heian International.

Baylor, Byrd. 1987. *And It Is Still That Way*. Santa Fe, NM: Trails West Publishing.

———. 1989. *Amigo*. Illus. Garth Williams. New York: Macmillan.

Behrens, June. 1982. *Gung Hay Fat Choy*. Chicago: Childrens Press.

Brown, Tricia. 1987. *Chinese New Year*. Photos by Fran Ortiz. New York: Henry Holt.

———. 1992. *Hello, Amigos!*. Photos by Fran Ortiz. New York: Henry Holt.

Caen, Herb. 1986. *The Cable Car and the Dragon*. Illus. Barbara Byfield. San Francisco: Chronicle Books.

Carpenter, Frances. 1972. *Tales of a Korean Grandmother*. Illustrated. Boston: C. E. Tuttle.

Charlip, Remy and Mary Beth Miller. 1987. *Handtalk: An ABC of Finger Spelling and Sign Language*. Illus. George Ancona. New York: Macmillan.

Chin, Steven A. 1992. *Dragon Parade: A Chinese New Year Story*. Madison, NJ: Raintree/Steck-Vaughn.

Ching, Emily, et al, ed. 1992. *Celebrating New Year*. Trans. Wonder Kids Publications Group Staff. Cerritos, CA: Wonder Kids.

Delacre, Lulu. *Vejigante Masquerader*.

de Paola, Tomie. 1980. *The Lady of Guadalupe*. Illus. by author. New York: Holiday.

Enright, Elizabeth. 1987. *Thimble Summer*. New York: Dell.

Handforth, Thomas. 1955. *Mei Li*. Illus. by author. New York: Doubleday.

Henry, Marguerite. 1991. *King of the Wind*. Illus. Wesley Dennis. New York: Macmillan.

Kalman, Bobbie. 1985. *We Celebrate New Year*. New York: Crabtree.

Lomas Garza, Carmen, and Harriet Tohmer. 1990. *Cuadros de Familia*. Emeryville, CA: Children's Book Press.

Lord, Bette. 1986. *In the Year of the Boar and Jackie Robinson*. New York: HarperCollins.

Mathers, Petra. 1993. *Maria Theresa*. Illus. by author. New York: HarperCollins.

Miller, Marilyn. 1984. *The Bridge at Selma*. Illustrated. Morristown, NJ: Silver Burdett Press.

Pfeffer, Susan B. 1989. *Turning Thirteen*. New York: Scholastic.

Pinkwater, Manus. 1992. *Wingman*. New York: Bantam.

Politi, Leo. 1973. *The Nicest Gift*. New York: Macmillan

Provensen, Alice. 1981. *A Peaceable Kingdom: The Shaker Abecedarius*. Illus. Martin Provensen. New York: Puffin.

Roland, Donna. 1984. *Grandfather's Stories from Cambodia*. San Diego: Open My World.

Speare, Elizabeth G. 1984. *The Sign of the Beaver / Signo del Casto*. New York: Dell.

Surat, Michele M. 1983. *Angel Child, Dragon Child*. Illus. Mai Vo-Dinh. New York: Scholastic.

Taylor, Mildred D. 1991. *Roll of Thunder, Hear My Cry*. New York: Puffin.

Taylor, Sydney. [1951] 1988. *All-of-a-Kind Family*. Illus. Helen John. New York: Taylor Productions.

Tran, Kim-Lan. 1993. *Tet: The New Year*. Illus. Mai Vo-Dinh. New York: Simon & Schuster.

Uchida, Yoshiko. 1985. *Journey to Topaz*. Illus. Donald Carrick. Berkeley, CA: Creative Arts Books.

———. [1978] 1992. *Journey Home*. Illus. Charles Robinson. New York: Macmillan.

Wallace, Ian. 1984. *Chin Chiang and The Dragon's Dance*. New York: Macmillan.

Waters, Kate, and Madeline Slovenz-Low. 1990. *Lion Dancer: Ernie Wan's Chinese New Year*. Photos by Martha Cooper. New York: Scholastic.

Yarbrough, Camille. 1992. *Cornrows*. Illus. Carole Byard. New York: Putnam.

Yen, Clara. 1991. *Why Rat Comes First: The Story of the Chinese Zodiac*. Emeryville, CA: Children's Book Press.

Yep, Laurence. 1990. *Child of the Owl*. New York: HarperCollins.

4. THEME TOPIC: DARE TO BE DIFFERENT

Possible Generalizations:

- Differences add spice to life.
- You can be who you want to be if you work at it.
- Being different can have its ups and downs.
- Following your own desires can lead to greater fulfillment than following the desires of others.
- Being true to yourself can involve taking risks and breaking the mold.
- Differences can be strengths.
- Our self-esteem may be affected by those who surround us.
- People may fear others who are different from themselves.

Possible Concepts:

difference, similarity, desires, fulfillment, acceptance, risks, growth

Possible Materials:

Adoff, Arnold. 1992. *Black Is Brown Is Tan*. Illus. Emily A. McCully. New York: HarperCollins.

Bulla, Clyde R. 1989. *Shoeshine Girl*. Illus. Leigh Grant. New York: HarperCollins.

Byars, Betsy. 1981. *Summer of the Swans / Verano de los Cisnes*. Illus. Ted CoConis. New York: Puffin.

Carrasco, Marta. *Club de los Diferentes*.

Clements, Andrew. 1991. *Big Al*. Illus. Yoshi. New York: Scholastic.

Cole, Babette. *Princesa Listilla*.

de Paola, Tomie. 1979. *Oliver Button Is a Sissy / Oliver Button es un Nena*. Illus. by author. San Diego: Harcourt Brace.

Escudié, René. *Paul and Sebastian*. Trans. Roderick Townley. Illus. Ulises Wensell. Brooklyn, NY: Kane-Miller.

Fern, Eugene. [1960] 1991. *Pepito's Story*. Illus. by author. New York: Yarrow Press.

Fuschgruber, Annegert. *Toribio y el Sombrero Mágico*.

Goytisolo, José A. and Juan Ballesta. *Lobito Bueno*.

Jusayu, Miguel A. 1984. *Ni Era Vaca Ni Era Caballo*. Illus. Monika Doppert. Caracas, Spain: Ekare-Banco del Libro.

Leaf, Munro. 1962. *Ferdinand the Bull*. New York: Penguin.

————. 1987. *Ferdinando el Toro*.

Lepscky, Ibi. 1985. *Pablito*. Illus. Paolo Cardoni.

Maury, Inez. 1976. *My Mother the Mail Carrier / Mi Madre la Cartera*. Trans. Norah Alemany. Illus. Lady McCrady. New York: Feminist Press.

Rico de Alba, Lolo. 1975. *Angelita, la Ballena Pequeñita*.

Thomas, Marlo and Friends. 1972. "Free To Be You and Me." New York: Arista Records and Tapes.

Turín, Adela. *Nuncajamas*.

————. *Rosa Caramelo*.

Vannini, Marisa. *Cuatro Gatitos*.

Wendell, Paloma y Ulises. *Valentín Nos Gustas Así*.

Wilkon, Piotr. *Gata Rosalinda*.

Zolotow, Charlotte. 1985. *William's Doll*. Illus. William Pene Du Bois. New York: HarperCollins.

5. THEME TOPIC: ENVIRONMENT

Possible Generalizations:

- All organisms have specific requirements for survival.
- Altering the environment affects all life forms and the interrelationship among them.
- Organisms adapt to change.
- Quality of life depends on how human beings maintain a balance with nature.
- Effective citizen involvement in environmental decision making involves a careful study of all sides.
- Everyone is responsible for practicing conservation.

Possible Concepts:

habitat, ecology, pollution, recycling, energy, conservation, environment, renewable resources, nonrenewable resources, interdependency

Possible Materials:

Allen, Marjorie N. and Shelly Rotner. 1991. *Changes*. Photos by Shelly Rotner. New York: Macmillan.

Arguenta, Manlio, et al. 1990. *Magic Dogs of the Volcanoes / Los Perros Mágicos de los Volcanes*. Illus. Elly Simmons. Emeryville, CA: Children's Book Press.

Baker, Lucy. *Selvas*.

Baker, Susan. 1991. *First Look at Using Energy*. Milwaukee, WI: Gareth Stevens.

Bauman, Kurt. *Joachim, el Barrendero*.

Cabal, Graciela B. *S.O.S. Planeta en Peligro*.

————. *Cuidemos la Tierra*.

————. *La vida de las plantas*.

————. *La vida de los animales*.

Cherry, Lynne. 1990. *Great Kapok Tree: A Tale of the Amazon Rain Forest*. San Diego: Harcourt Brace.

————. 1992. *A River Ran Wild*. San Diego: Harcourt Brace.

Chinery, Michael. *Mi primer libro de ecologia*.

Chow, Octavio, and Morris Vidaura. 1987. *Invisible Hunters / Los Cazadores Invisibles.* Illus. Joe Sam. Emeryville, CA: Children's Book Press.

Cole, Joanna. 1986. *The Magic Schoolbus at the Waterworks / El Autobús Mágico Viaja por el Agua.* Illus. Bruce Degen. New York: Scholastic.

———. 1987. *The Magic Schoolbus Inside the Earth / El Autobús Mágico en el Interior de la Tierra.* Illus. Bruce Degen. New York: Scholastic.

———. 1992. *The Magic Schoolbus on the Ocean Floor / El Autobús Mágico en el Fondo del Mar.* New York: Scholastic.

Cosgrove, Stephen. 1980. *Serendipity.* Los Angeles: Price Stern.

Cowcher, Helen. 1992. *El Bosque Tropical: Rain Forest.* New York: Farrar, Straus & Giroux.

Earth Works Project Staff. 1990. *Fifty Simple Things You Can Do to Save the Earth/50 Cosas que los Niños Pueden Hacer para Salvar la Tierra.* Pasadena, CA: Greenleaf Press.

EarthWorks Group Staff. *Salvar la Tierra.*

Edelson, Edward. 1992. *Clean Air.* New York: Chelsea House.

Ehlert Lois. 1992. *Planting a Rainbow.* San Diego: Harcourt Brace.

Elkington, John, and Julia Hailes. *Guía del Joven Consumidor Verde.*

Escrivá, Viví. *Niño y el Arbol.*

Gantschev, Ivan. *Oso Ota.*

George, Jean Craighead. *Día en el Desierto.*

Hare, Tony. *La Polución de los Mares.*

———. *La Contaminación del Aire.*

Hasler, Eveline. *Pipistrelli.*

Ingpen, Robert, and Margaret Dunkle. 1991. *Conservación.*

Jané, Jordi. *Cigüeña Guita.*

Jeffers, Susan. 1991. *Brother Eagle, Sister Sky.* Illus. by author. New York: Dial.

Krafft, Frederico. *El Día que los Pájaros Cayeron del Cielo.*

Leedy, Loreen. 1991. *Cura el Mal de la Basura.* New York: Scholastic.

Marcus, Elizabeth. *Vida de las Plantas.*

Martinez Gil, Fernando. *Río de los Castores.*

Marzot, Livio. *Liebres Blancas.*

McNulty, Faith. 1987. *The Lady and the Spider.* Illus. Bob Marstall. New York: HarperCollins.

Nussbaum, Hedda. 1977. *Plants Do Amazing Things.* Illus. Joe Mathieu. New York: Random House.

O'Neill, Mary. 1991. *Nature In Danger.* Illus. John Bindon. Mahwah, NJ: Troll.

Parramón, Josep M., et al. 1985. *Air / El Aire.* New York: Barron.

Patent, Dorothy. 1990. *Yellowstone Fires: Flames and Rebirth.* Illus. William Munoz et al. New York: Holiday.

Peters, Lisa W. 1991. *Water's Way.* Illus. Ted Rand. New York: Arcade Publishers.

Puncel, María. *Prado del Tio Pedro.*

Remolina, Tere. *En Busca de la Lluvia.*

Rius, María, and Josep M. Parramon. 1987. *The Mountains / La Montaña.* New York: Barron.

———. 1988. *Green Kingdom.* New York: Barron.

Roettger, Doris. *Seeds and Plants.*

Satchwell, John. *Como Funciona la Energia.*

Savan, Beth. 1992. *Earthwatch: Earth Cycles and Ecosystems*. Illus. Pat Cupples. Boston: Addison-Wesley.

Scholes, Katherine. 1990. *Peace Begins with You*. Illus. Robert Ingpen. San Francisco: Sierra.

Schwartz, Linda. 1990. *Earth Book for Kids: Activities to Help Heal the Environment*. Illus. Beverly Armstrong. Santa Barbara, CA: Learning Works.

Seuss, Dr. 1971. *The Lorax*. Illus. by author. New York: Random House.

Silverstein, Alvin. 1990. *Life in a Tidal Pool*. Boston: Little, Brown.

Silverstein, Alvin, et al. 1992. *Recycling: Meeting the Challenge of the Trash Crisis*. New York: Putnam.

Simonds, Christopher. 1990. *Samuel Slater's Mill and the Industrial Revolution*. Morristown, NJ: Silver Burdett Press.

Taylor, Theodore. 1991. *Weirdo*. San Diego: Harcourt Brace.

Turín, Adela. *Planeta Mary Año 35*.

Van Allsburg, Chris. 1990. *Just a Dream*. Illus. by author. Boston: Houghton Mifflin.

Willow, Diane. 1991. *At Home in the Rain Forest*. Illustrated. Watertown, MA: Charlesbridge.

Willow, Diane, and Laura Jacques. 1993. *Dentro de la Selva Tropical*. Illustrated. Watertown, MA: Charlesbridge.

Wright, Alexandra. 1993. *Les Echaremos de Menos? Especies en Peligro de Extinción*. Watertown, MA: Charlesbridge.

Yeh, Phoebe, and Nancy E. Krulik. 1992. *Preservar las Selvas Tropicales*. New York: Scholastic.

Zak, Monica. *Salven mi Selva*.

Zavrel, Stepan. *Último Árbol*.

6. THEME TOPIC: ESTABLISHING YOUR OWN SPACE

Possible Generalizations:

• There are many different kinds of "space."
• Different people need different kinds and different amounts of space.

Possible Concepts:

public space, private space, needs, wants

Possible Materials:

Baumann, Kurt. *Joachim*.

Baylor, Byrd. 1991. *Your Own Best Secret Place*. Illustrated. New York: Macmillan.

Bunting, Eve. 1991. *Fly Away Home*. Ed. James Giblin. Illus. Ronald Himler. Boston: Houghton Mifflin.

Byars, Betsy. 1987. *Cartoonist*. Illus. Richard Cuffari. New York: Puffin.

Frank, Anne. 1967. *Anne Frank: The Diary of a Young Girl / Diario de Ana Frank*. Trans. B. M. Mooyaart. New York: Doubleday.

Hill, Elizabeth S. 1993. *Evan's Corner*. Illus. Sandra Speidel. New York: Puffin.

Pinkwater, Daniel M. [1972] 1992. *Big Orange Splot*. Illustrated. New York: Hastings House.

Smith, Robert Kimmel. 1984. *The War With Grandpa*. Illus. Richard Lauter. New York: Dell.

Torrents, Mercedes. *Derechos del Niño*.

Turín, Adela. *Arturo y Clementina*.

Turín, Adela, and Sylvie Selig. *Cañones y Manzanas*.

Wheatley, Nadia. 1992. *My Place*. Illus. Donna Rawlins. Brooklyn, NY: Kane-Miller.

7. THEME TOPIC: EXPLORATION AND DISCOVERY

Possible Generalizations:

• Exploration can involve both danger and excitement.
• Discoveries frequently involve time and effort.

Possible Concepts:

exploration, danger, excitement, time, effort, discovery

Possible Materials:

Chambers, Catherine. 1984. *Frontier Dream: Life on the Great Plains*. Mahwah, NJ: Troll.

Crofford, Emily. 1991. *Frontier Surgeons: A Story About the Mayo Brothers*. Minneapolis: Carolrhoda Books.

Fleischman, Sid. 1988. *By the Great Horn Spoon*. New York: Little, Brown.

Haber, Louis. 1992. *Black Pioneers of Science and Invention* San Diego: Harcourt Brace.

Krensky, Stephan. 1991. *Who Really Discovered America?* Mamaroneck, NY: Hastings.

Lepscky, Ibi. 1992. *Albert Einstein*. Illus. Paolo Cardoni. Hauppauge, NY: Barron.

———. 1993. *Marie Curie*. Illus. Paolo Cardoni. Hauppage, NY: Barron.

Mitchell, Barbara. 1992. *The Wizard of Sound: A Story About Thomas Edison*. Illus. Hetty Mitchell. Minneapolis: Carolrhoda Books.

O'Dell, Scott. 1976. *Zia*. Illus. Ted Lewin. Boston: Houghton Mifflin.

———. 1977. *Carlota*. Illus. by author. Boston: Houghton Mifflin.

———. 1990. *Island of the Blue Dolphins / Isla de los Delfines Azules*. Illus. Ted Lewin. Boston: Houghton Mifflin.

Shore, Nancy. 1987. *Amelia Earhart*. Matina Horner. New York: Chelsea House.

8. THEME TOPIC: FAMILIES AND FAMILY RELATIONSHIPS

Possible Generalizations:

• Families should provide support, love, and care for all of their members.
• Families can be a source of joy and sadness.
• Family members may not always see things the same way.
• Families come in many shapes and sizes.

Possible Concepts:

family, support, love, care, joy, sadness, perspectives

Possible Materials:

Ackerman, Karen. 1992. *Song and Dance Man*. Illus. Stephen Gammell. New York: Knopf.

Adoff, Arnold. 1992. *Black Is Brown Is Tan*. Illus. Emily A. McCully. New York: HarperCollins.

Ames, Mildred. 1990. *Grandpa Jake and the Grand Christmas*. New York: Macmillan.

Anaya, Rudolfo A. 1987. *The Farolitos of Christmas: A New Mexican Christmas Story*. Illus. Richard Sandoval. Santa Fe, NM: New Mexico Magazine.

Asch, Frank. 1984. *Just Like Daddy*. Illustrated. New York: Simon & Schuster.

Balzola, Asun. *Munia y la Señora Piltronera*.

Banks, Lynne R. 1985. *The Indian in the Cupboard*. Illus. Brock Cole. New York: Doubleday.

Baylor, Byrd. 1989. *Amigo*. Illus. Garth Williams. New York: Macmillan.

Blume, Judy. 1992. *The One In the Middle Is the Green Kangaroo*. Illus. Irene Trivas. New York: Dell.

Bogart, Jo Ellen. 1992. *Daniel's Dog*. Illus. Janet Wilson. New York: Scholastic.

Borack, Barbara. 1967. *Grandpa*. Illus. B. Shecter. New York: HarperCollins.

Boyd, Candy D. 1984. *Circle of Gold*. New York: Scholastic.

Bröger, Achim. *Mi Abuela y Yo*.

Bunting, Eve. 1989. *The Wednesday Surprise*. Illus. Donald Garrick. Boston: Houghton Mifflin.

Burch, Robert. 1987. *Queenie Peavy*. New York: Puffin.

Burningham, John. 1985. *Granpa*. Illus. by author. New York: Crown Books.

Butterworth Nick. 1992a. *My Grandpa is Amazing*. Illus. by author. Cambridge, MA: Candlewick Press.

———. 1992b. *My Grandma is Wonderful*. Illus. by author. Cambridge, MA: Candlewick Press.

Byars, Betsy. 1981. *Summer of the Swans / Verano de los Cisnes*. Illus. Ted CoConis. New York: Puffin.

———. 1987. *The Pinballs*. New York: HarperCollins.

———. *Casa de las Alas*.

Carlstrom, Nancy W. 1990. *Grandpappy*. Illus. Laurel Molk. Boston: Little, Brown.

Carpenter, Frances. 1972. *Tales of a Korean Grandmother*. Illustrated. Boston: C. E. Tuttle.

Carson, Jo. 1992. *You Hold Me and I'll Hold You*. Illus. Annie Cannon. New York: Orchard Books.

Cleary, Beverly. 1990. *Ramona and Her Father / Ramona y Su Padre*. New York: Avon.

———. 1992. *Dear Mr. Henshaw / Querido Señor Henshaw*. Illus. Paul O. Zelinsky. New York: Dell.

Coerr, Eleanor. 1979. *Sadako and the Thousand Paper Cranes*. Illus. Ronald Himler. New York: Dell.

Danziger, Paula. 1980. *Can You Sue Your Parents for Malpractice?* New York: Dell.

de Paola, Tomie. 1978. *Nana Upstairs and Nana Downstairs*. Illus. by author. New York: Puffin.

———. 1992. *Now One Foot, Now the Other / Un Pasito . . . Y Otro Pasito*. Illus. by author. New York: Putnam.

Dorros, Arthur. 1991. *Abuela*. Illus. Elisa Kleven. New York: Dutton.

Estes, Eleanor. 1989. *The Moffats*. New York: Dell.

Felipe, Nersys. *Cuentos de Guane*.

Fleischman, Sid. 1988. *Humbug Mountain*. Illus. Eric Von Schmidt. Boston: Little, Brown.

Friedman, Ina R. 1987. *How My Parents Learned to Eat*. Illus. Allen Say. Boston: Houghton Mifflin.

Garaway, Margaret. K. 1989. *Ashkii and His Grandfather*. Illus. Harry Warren. Tucson: Treasure Chest Publications.

Garcia, Richard. 1987. *My Aunt Otilia's Spirits / Espiritus de Mi Tia Otilia*. Trans. Jesus G. Rea. Illus. Robin Cherin and Roger I. Reyes. Emeryville, CA: Children's Book Press.

Gates, Doris. 1976. *Blue Willow*. Illus. Paul Lantz. New York: Puffin.

Greene, Bette. 1984. *Summer of My German Soldier*. New York: Bantam.

Greenfield, Eloise. 1981. *La Cara de Abuelito*. New York: Philomel Books.

———. 1987. *Sister*. Illus. Moneta Barnett. New York: HarperCollins.

———. 1991. *Grandpa's Face*. Illus. Floyd Cooper. New York: Putnam.

———. 1993. *Talk About a Family*. Illustrated. New York: HarperCollins.

Grifalconi, Ann. 1986. *Village of Round and Square Houses*. Illus. by author. Boston: Little, Brown.

Guillén, Nicolás. 1934. *Balada de los Abuelos*.

Guthrie, Donna W. 1986. *Grandpa Doesn't Know It's Me: A Family Adjusts to Alzheimer's Disease*. Illus. Katy Arnsteen. New York: Human Sciences Press.

Hague, Kathleen. 1988. *The Man Who Kept House*. Illus. Michael Hague. San Diego: Harcourt Brace.

Hamilton, Virginia. 1990. *Cousins*. New York: Putnam.

Haskins, Francine. 1992. *Things I Like About Grandma*. Emeryville, CA: Children's Book Press.

Hautzig, Esther A. 1992. *Gift For Mama*. Magnolia, MA: Peter Smith.

Hazel, Beth, and Jerome Harste. 1984. *My Icky Picky Sister*. Illustrated. St. Petersburg, FL: Willowisp Press.

Hermes, Patricia. 1985. *You Shouldn't Have to Say Good-bye*. New York: Scholastic.

Hines, Anna G. 1990. *Grandma Gets Grumpy*. Boston: Houghton Mifflin.

Hirsh, Marilyn. 1987. *Could Anything Be Worse?* Illus. by author. New York: Holiday.

Hoban, Russell. 1976. *Baby Sister for Frances*. Illus. Lillian Hoban. New York: HarperCollins.

———. 1986. *Bread and Jam for Frances*. Illus. Lillian Hoban. New York: HarperCollins.

Hudson, Wade. 1985. *I Love My Family*. Illus. Tony Tallerico. New York: Putnam.

Irwin, Hadley. 1991. *What About Grandma?* New York: Avon.

Janeczko, Paul. 1984. *Strings: A Gathering of Family Poems*. New York: Macmillan.

Johnson, Angela. 1990. *When I Am Old With You*. Illus. David Soman. New York: Orchard Books.

———. 1992. *Tell Me a Story, Mama*. Illus. David Soman. New York: Orchard Books.

Johnston, Tony. 1991. *Grandpa's Song*. Illus. Brad Sneed. New York: Dial.

Jukes, Mavis. 1987. *Like Jake and Me*. Illus. Lloyd Bloom. New York: Knopf.

Karkowsky, Nancy. 1984. *Grandma's Soup*. Illus. Shelly O. Haas. Rockville, MD: Kar Ben.

Kibbey, Marsha. 1991. *My Grammy: A Book About Alzheimers Disease*. Minneapolis: Carolrhoda Books.

Konigsburg, E. L. 1987. *From the Mixed-Up Files of Mrs. Basil E. Frankweiler.* New York: Macmillan.

Krauss, Robert. 1987. *Leo the Late Bloomer.* Illus. Jose Aruego. New York: Simon & Schuster.

Kuklin, Susan. 1992. *How My Family Lives in America.* Illus. by author. New York: Macmillan.

L'Engle, Madeleine. 1976. *A Wrinkle In Time / Arruga en el Tiempo.* New York: Dell.

Leonard, Marcia, and Karen Schmidt. *Conejo y su Hermana.*

Lindgren, Astrid. *Yo También Quiero Tener Hermanos.*

Llimona, Mercedes. *Del Tiempo de la Abuela.*

Lobel, Arnold. 1984. *Tio Elefante.* Illus. Pablo Lizcano.

Lomas Garza, Carmen, and Harriet Tohmer. 1990. *Cuadros de Familia.* Emeryville, CA: Children's Book Press.

Lööf, Jan. *Mi Abuelo es Pirata*

Lowry, Lois. 1984a. *Anastasia Krupnik.* New York: Bantam.

———. 1984b. *Summer to Die.* New York: Bantam.

MacLachlan, Patricia. 1987. *Sarah, Plain and Tall / Sarah, Sencilla y Alta.* New York: HarperCollins.

Martin, Bill, Jr., and John Archambault. 1987. *Knots On a Counting Rope.* Illus. Ted Rand. New York: Henry Holt.

Mathis, Sharon B. 1986. *The Hundred-Penny Box.* Illus. Leo and Diane Dillon. New York: Puffin.

Maury, Inez. 1976. *My Mother the Mail Carrier / Mi Madre la Cartera.* Trans. Norah Alemany. Illus. Lady McCrady. New York: Feminist Press.

McKissack, Patricia, *¿Quien es Quien?*

Miles, Miska. 1972. *Annie and the Old One.* Boston: Little, Brown.

Mora, Pat. 1992. *A Birthday Basket for Tia.* Illus. Cecily Lang. New York: Macmillan.

Munsch, Robert. 1986. *Love You Forever / Siempre Te Querre.* Illus. Sheila Mcgraw. Buffalo, NY: Firefly Books.

Neasi, Barbara. 1988. *Igual que Yo.* Illus. Lois Axelman. Chicago: Childrens Press.

Nodar, Carmen S. 1992. *Abuelita's Paradise / Paraíso de Abuelita.* Morton Grove, IL: Albert Whitman.

Orr, Katherine. 1990. *My Grandpa and the Sea.* Illus. by author. Minneapolis: Carolrhoda Books.

Oxenbury, Helen. *En Casa de los Abuelos.*

Parramón, Josep. M., and Rius, María. *Abuelos.*

Paterson, Katherine A. 1987. *The Great Gilly Hopkins / La Gran Gilly Hopkins.* New York: HarperCollins.

———. 1990. *Jacob Have I Loved / Ame a Jacob.* New York: HarperCollins.

Pellegrini, Nina. 1991. *Families Are Different.* Illus. by author. New York: Holiday.

Politi, Leo. *Mieko.*

Polushkin, Maria. 1988. *Mother, Mother, I Want Another.* Illus. Diane Dawson. New York: Crown Books.

Puncel, Maria. 1985. *Abuelita Opalina.*

Red Hawk, Richard. 1987. *Grandmother's Christmas Story: A True Tale of the Quechan Indians.* Sacramento, CA: Sierra Oaks.

Rock, Gail. 1985. *The House Without a Christmas Tree*. New York: Dell.

Rodgers, Mary. 1973. *Freaky Friday / Viernes Embrujado*. New York: HarperCollins.

Roe, Eileen. 1992. *Con Mi Hermano / With My Brother*. Illus. Robert Casilla. New York: Scholastic.

Ruckman, Ivy. 1986. *Night of the Twisters*. New York: HarperCollins.

Rugeles, E. F. *El Cantico del Verano*.

Rylant, Cynthia. 1985. *When I Was Young in the Mountains*. Illustrated. New York: Dutton.

Sachs, Marilyn. 1989. *The Bears' House*. New York: Avon.

Sakai, Kimiko. 1990. *Sachiko Means Happiness*. Illus. Tomie Arai. Emeryville, CA: Children's Book Press.

Sariola, Eulalia. *Reloj de mi Barrio*.

Shyer, Marlene F. 1988. *Welcome Home, Jellybean*. New York: Macmillan.

Smith, Robert K. 1984. *War With Grandpa*. New York: Dell.

Sonneborn, Ruth A. 1987. *Friday Night Is Papa Night*. Illus. Emily A. McCully. New York: Puffin.

Stanek, Muriel. 1989. *I Speak English For My Mom*. Ed. Kathleen Tucker. Illus. Judith Friedman. Morton Grove, IL: Albert Whitman.

Super, Gretchen. 1991. *What Kind of Family Do You Have?* Illus. Kees De Keefte. New York: Twenty First Century Books.

Surat, Michele M. 1983. *Angel Child, Dragon Child*. Illus. Mai Vo-Dinh. New York: Scholastic.

Tafuri, Nancy. 1991. *Have You Seen My Duckling?* Illustrated. New York: Morrow.

Taylor, Sydney. [1951] 1988. *All-of-a-Kind Family*. Illus. Helen John. New York: Taylor Productions.

Thomas, Jane R. 1990. *Saying Good-bye to Grandma*. Illus. Marcia Sewall. Boston: Houghton Mifflin.

Thomas, Marlo, et al. 1990. (Book and record) *Free to Be. . . A Family*. Illustrated. New York: Bantam.

Turín, Adela, and Nella Bosnia. *Una Feliz Catástrofe*.

Udry, Janice M. 1991. *What Mary Jo Shared*. Illus. Eleanor Mill. New York: Scholastic.

Ungerer, Tomi. *Ningún Beso Para Mamá*.

Van Allsburg, Chris. 1981. *Jumanji*. Illus. by author. Boston: Houghton Mifflin.

Van Leeuwen, Jean. 1979. *Tales of Oliver Pig*. Illus. Arnold Lobel. New York: Dial.

Vannini, Marisa. *Cuatro Gatitos*.

Vigna, Judith. 1984. *Grandma Without Me*. Ed. Kathleen Tucker. Illus. by author. New York: A. Whitman.

Viorst, Judith. 1987. *The Tenth Good Thing About Barney*. Illus. Eric Blegvad. New York: Macmillan.

———. 1993. *Sunday Morning*. Ed. Whitney Malone. Illus. Hilary Knight. New York: Macmillan.

Waber, Bernard. 1987. *Ira Sleeps Over / Quique Duerme Fuera De Casa*. Illus. by author. Boston: Houghton Mifflin.

Wells, Rosemary. *Julieta, Estate Quieta*.

Wilson, Johnniece M. 1989. *Oh, Brother*. New York: Scholastic.

———. 1992. *Robin On His Own*. New York: Scholastic.

Zavrel, Stepán. *Abuelo Tomás.*

Zolotow, Charlotte. 1982. *The Quarreling Book.* Illus. Arnold Lobel. New York: HarperCollins.

———. 1985. *My Grandson Lew.* Illus. William Pene Du Bois. New York: HarperCollins.

———. 1987. *I Know a Lady / Mi Amiga la Señora Mayor.* Illus. James Stevenson. New York: Bantam.

9. THEME TOPIC: FARMERS, THEIR LIVES, AND THEIR ANIMALS

Possible Generalizations:

- Most of what we eat originates on farms.
- Most of what we wear originates on farms.
- Farm life and farming practices have changed greatly over the last one hundred years.

Possible Concepts:

farms, originates, farming practices

Possible Materials:

Demuth, Patricia. 1982. *Joel: Growing Up a Farm Man.* New York: Putnam.

Dunn, Judy. 1976. *The Little Duck.* Photos by Phoebe Dunn. New York: Random House.

Duvoisin, Roger. 1962. *Petunia.* Illus. by author. New York: Knopf.

Enright, Elizabeth. 1987. *Thimble Summer.* New York: Dell.

Ginsburg, Mirra. 1988. *The Chick and the Duckling.* Illus. Jose Aruego and Ariane Dewey. New York: Macmillan.

Greene, Bette. 1975. *Philip Hall Likes Me, I Reckon Maybe.* Illus. Charles Lilly. New York: Dell.

Hamilton, Virginia. 1993. *Zeely.* Ed. Whitney Malone. Illustrated. New York: Macmillan.

Heller, Ruth. 1982. *Animals Born Alive and Well.* Illus. by author. New York: Putnam.

———. 1992. *Chickens Aren't the Only Ones / Los Pollos No Son los Únicos.* Illus. by author. New York: Putnam.

Hutchins, Pat. 1992. *Rosie's Walk.* New York: Scholastic.

Imershein, Betsy. 1990. *Farmer.* Ed. Jane Steltenpohl. Illustrated. New York: Simon & Schuster.

James, Robin. 1992. *Baby Farm Animals.* Los Angeles: Price Stern.

Lauber, Patricia. 1991. *What's Hatching Out of That Egg?* Illustrated. New York: Crown Books.

Locker, Thomas. 1988. *Family Farm.* Illus. by author. New York: Dial.

Parramón, Josep. M. *A la Granja.*

Pinkwater, Daniel M. 1988. *The Wuggie Norple Story.* Illus. Tomie de Paola. New York: Macmillan.

Pomerantz, Charlotte. 1984. *One Duck, Another Duck.* Illus. Jose Areugo and Ariane Dewey. New York: Greenwillow.

Rius, María, and Josep M. Parramón. 1987. *El Campo.* Hauppauge, NY: Barron.

Royston, Angela. *Oveja.*

Sanchez, Isidro, and Carmen Peris. 1991. *Farm*. Illustrated. Hauppauge, NY: Barron.

Smith, E. Boyd. 1990. *Farm Book*. Illus. by author. Boston: Houghton Mifflin.

Solano Flores, Guillermo. 1986. *El Campo*. Illus. Silvia Luz Alvarado.

10. THEME TOPIC: FEELINGS AND EMOTIONS

Possible Generalizations:

- We should acknowledge and accept our feelings and emotions.
- We should acknowledge and accept the feelings and emotions of others.
- Humans experience a range of emotions throughout their lives.

Possible Concepts:

feelings, emotions, acknowledge, acceptance, experience

Possible Materials:

Alexander, Lloyd. 1980. *Taran Wanderer*. New York: Dell.

Andersen, Hans Christian. 1992. *The Ugly Duckling*. Illus. Robin Officer. Kansas City, MO: Andrews & McMeel.

Avery, Charles. 1992. *Everybody Has Feelings / Todos Tenemos Sentimientos: The Moods of Children as Photographed by Charles E. Avery*. Trans. Sandra Marulanda. Seattle, WA: Open Hand.

Baylor, Byrd. 1989. *Amigo*. Illus. Garth Williams. New York: Macmillan.

Bemelmans, Ludwig. 1977. *Madeline*. Illus. by author. New York: Puffin.

Blanco, Cruz. *Kalamito Quiere Otra Familia*.

Blume, Judy. 1985. *The Pain and the Great One*. Illus. Irene Trivas. New York: Dell.

Bollinger, Max. *Cuento de Enanos*.

Bulla, Clyde R. 1989. *Shoeshine Girl*. Illus. Leigh Grant. New York: HarperCollins.

Burch, Robert. 1987. *Queenie Peavy*. New York: Puffin.

Byars, Betsy. 1981. *Summer of the Swans / Verano de los Cisnes*. Illus. Ted CoConis. New York: Puffin.

Carle, Eric. 1986. *The Grouchy Ladybug*. Illustrated. New York: HarperCollins.

Carlson, Nancy. 1992. *Arnie and the New Kid*. Illustrated. New York: Puffin.

Charlip, Remy, and Supree Burton. 1993. *Mother, Mother, I Feel Sick, Send for the Doctor Quick, Quick, Quick*. Illustrated. Cutchogue, NY: Buccaneer Books.

Cleary, Beverly. 1990. *Ramona and Her Father / Ramona y Su Padre*. New York: Avon.

Clements, Andrew. 1991. *Big Al*. Illus. Yoshi. New York: Scholastic.

Dalgliesh, Alice. [1954] 1991. *The Courage of Sarah Noble / El Valor de Sarah Noble*. Illus. Leonard Weisgard. New York: Macmillan.

de Paola, Tomie. 1978. *Nana Upstairs and Nana Downstairs*. Illus. by author. New York: Puffin.

———. 1979. *Oliver Button Is a Sissy / Oliver Button es un Nena*. Illus. by author. San Diego: Harcourt Brace.

Ende, Michael. *Norberto Nucagorda*.

Estes, Eleanor. 1974. *The Hundred Dresses*. Illus. Louis Slobodkin. San Diego: Harcourt Brace.

Fitzhugh, Louise. 1990. *Harriet the Spy*. Illus. by author. New York: HarperCollins.

Fox, Paula. 1985. *One-Eyed Cat*. New York: Dell.

Gates, Doris. 1976. *Blue Willow*. Illus. Paul Lantz. New York: Puffin.

Gipson, Fred. 1990. *Old Yeller*. New York: HarperCollins.

Goble, Paul. 1986. *The Girl Who Loved Wild Horses*. Ed. Julia Silbert. Illus. by author. New York: Macmillan.

Greene, Bette. 1975. *Philip Hall Likes Me, I Reckon Maybe*. Illus. Charles Lilly. New York: Dell.

———. 1984. *Summer of My German Soldier*. New York: Bantam.

Greenfield, Eloise. 1987. *Sister*. Illus. Moneta Barnett. New York: HarperCollins.

Grip, Maria. *"Auténtico" Elvis*.

Hazel, Beth, and Jerome Harste. 1984. *My Icky Picky Sister*. Illustrated. St. Petersburg, FL: Willowisp Press.

Hien. *Doi Song Moi/Tren Dat Moi: A New Life in a New Land*.

Heine, Helme. *Perla*.

Hoban, Russell. 1976. *Baby Sister for Frances*. Illus. Lillian Hoban. New York: HarperCollins.

Holman, Felice. 1986. *Slake's Limbo*. New York: Macmillan.

Komaiko, Leah. 1990. *Earl's Too Cool For Me*. Illus. Laura Cornell. New York: HarperCollins.

Konigsburg, E. L. 1985. *Jennifer, Hecate, Macbeth, William McKinley, and Me, Elizabeth*. New York: Dell.

———. 1987. *From the Mixed-Up Files of Mrs. Basil E. Frankweiler*. New York: Macmillan.

Krauss, Robert. 1987. *Leo the Late Bloomer*. Illus. Jose Aruego. New York: Simon & Schuster.

Lopes de Almeida, Fernanda. *Margarita Friolenta*.

Lowry, Lois. 1984. *Anastasia Krupnik*. New York: Bantam.

Martínez, Antonio. *Fosco*.

Martínez I Vendrell, María. 1984. *Yo las Quería*. Illus. Carme Sole Vendrell.

Mathers, Petra. 1993. *Maria Theresa*. Illus. by author. New York: HarperCollins.

Maury, Inez. 1976. *My Mother the Mail Carrier / Mi Madre la Cartera*. Trans. Norah Alemany. Illus. Lady McCrady. New York: Feminist Press.

Mayer, Mercer. 1985. *There's a Nightmare In My Closet / Hay Una Pesadilla en mi Armario*. Illus. by author. New York: Dial.

Miles, Miska. 1972. *Annie and the Old One*. Boston: Little, Brown.

Paterson, Katherine A. 1987a. *Bridge to Terabithia / Puente Hasta Terabithia*. Illus. Donna Diamond. New York: HarperCollins.

———. 1987b. *The Great Gilly Hopkins / La Gran Gilly Hopkins*. New York: HarperCollins.

Pinkwater, Manus. 1992. *Wingman*. New York: Bantam.

Politi, Leo. *Mieko*.

———. 1973. *The Nicest Gift*. New York: Macmillan

Polushkin, Maria. 1988. *Mother, Mother, I Want Another*. Illus. Diane Dawson. New York: Crown Books.

Preston, Edna, and Rainy Bennett. 1976. *The Temper Tantrum Book*. Illustrated. New York: Puffin.

Raskin, Ellen. 1988. *Spectacles*. Illus. by author. New York: Macmillan.

Rodgers, Mary. 1973. *Freaky Friday / Viernes Embrujado*. New York: HarperCollins.

Saller, Carol. 1991. *The Bridge Dancers*. Illus. Gerald Talifero. Minneapolis: Carolrhoda Books.

Sendak, Maurice. 1988. *Where the Wild Things Are*. Illus. by author. New York: HarperCollins.

Silverstein, Shel. 1964. *The Giving Tree / Árbol Generoso*. New York: Harper Row.

Sonneborn, Ruth A. 1987. *Friday Night Is Papa Night*. Illus. Emily A. McCully. New York: Puffin.

Sperry, Armstrong. 1990. *Call It Courage*. New York: Macmillan.

Steptoe, John. 1986. *Stevie*. Illus. by author. New York: HarperCollins.

Surat, Michele M. 1983. *Angel Child, Dragon Child*. Illus. Mai Vo-Dinh. New York: Scholastic.

Thomas, Marlo, and Friends. 1972. *Free to be You and Me* (Cassette Recording). New York: Arista Records and Tapes.

Uchida, Yoshiko. [1978] 1992. *Journey Home*. Illus. Charles Robinson. New York: Macmillan.

Viorst, Judith. 1987. *The Tenth Good Thing About Barney*. Illus. Eric Blegvad. New York: Macmillan.

———. [1974] 1988. *Rosie and Michael*. Illus. Lorna Tomei. New York: Macmillan.

———. 1989. *Alexander and the Terrible, Horrible, No Good, Very Bad Day / Alexander Y el Día Terrible, Horrible, Espantoso, Horroroso*. Trans. Alma F. Ada. Illus. Ray Cruz. New York: Macmillan.

Wells, Rosemary. *Carlos el Tímido*.

———. *Timoteo Va a la Escuela*.

Williams, Margery. 1991. *The Velveteen Rabbit*. Illus. William Nicholson. New York: Doubleday.

Yashima, Taro. 1976. *Crow Boy*. Illus. by author. New York: Puffin.

Yep, Laurence. 1990. *Child of the Owl*. New York: HarperCollins.

Zatón, Jesús. *Elefante Poff No Quiere Ser Payaso*.

Zemach, Margot. 1990. *It Could Always Be Worse*. New York: Farrar, Straus & Giroux.

Zolotow, Charlotte. 1985. *William's Doll*. Illus. William Pene Du Bois. New York: HarperCollins.

11. THEME TOPIC: FLIGHTS OF FANCY: ME AND MY IMAGINATION

Possible Generalizations:

- Our imagination can take us to new and different worlds.
- Our imagination can help us cope with difficult situations.
- Our imagination can be used to avoid dealing with difficult situations.
- Our imagination can lead to creativity.

Possible Concepts:

imagination, reality, coping, avoidance, creativity

Possible Materials:

Ballesta, Juan. *Tommy y el Elefante.*

Bodecker, N. M. 1976. *Hurry, Hurry, Mary Dear!* Illustrated. New York: Macmillan.

Brewton, Sara, et al., ed. 1989. *My Tang's Tungled and Other Ridiculous Situations.* Illus. Graham Booth. New York: HarperCollins.

Cooney, Barbara. 1985. *Miss Rumphius.* Illustrated. New York: Puffin.

Coville, Bruce, and Katherine Coville. 1985. *Sarah's Unicorn.* Illus. by authors. New York: HarperCollins.

Dahl, Roald. [1961] 1990. *James and the Giant Peach / James y el Melocotón Gigante.* Cutchogue, New York: Buccaneer Books.

de Paola, Tomie. 1992. *Strega Nona.* New York: Scholastic.

de Saint-Exupery, Antoine. 1982. *Little Prince / Principito.* Illus. Katherine Woods. San Diego: Harcourt Brace.

Fitzgerald, John. 1985. *Great Brain.* Illus. Mercer Mayer. New York: Dial.

Fraire, Isabel. *Aventura Inesperada.* Illus. Felip de la Fuente.

Grahame, Kenneth. 1992. *Wind In the Willows.* Mahwah, NJ: Troll.

Grimm, Jacob, and Wilhem K. Grimm. 1983. *Devil With the Three Golden Hairs.* Illus. Nonny Hogrogian. New York: Knopf.

———. 1992. *The Shoemaker and the Elves.* Illus. Barbara J. Roman. Kansas City, MO: Andrews & McMeel.

Hamilton, Virginia. 1993. *Zeely.* Ed. Whitney Malone. Illustrated. New York: Macmillan.

Hiriart, Hugo. *Vuelo de Apolodoro.* Illus. by author.

Jarrell, Randall. 1985. *Animal Family.* Illus. Maurice Sendak. New York: Pantheon.

Keats, Ezra J. 1987. *John Henry: An American Legend.* Ed. Anne Schwartz. New York: Knopf.

Kellogg, Steven. 1984. *Paul Bunyan.* Adapt. and illus. by author. New York: Morrow.

Lionni, Leo. 1987. *Frederick.* Illus. by author. New York: Knopf.

Louie, Al-Ling. 1990. *Yeh Shen: A Cinderella Story From China.* Illus. Ed Young. New York: Putnam.

Mathers, Petra. 1993. *Maria Theresa.* Illus. by author. New York: HarperCollins.

Mayer, Marianna. 1984. *Beauty and the Beast.* Illus. by author. New York: Macmillan.

McPhail, David. *Baño de Andrés.*

Munter, Anke. *Gafas Maravillosas.*

Ness, Evaline. 1966. *Sam, Bangs, and Moonshine.* New York: Henry Holt.

Norton, Mary. *The Borrowers.* 1989. Illus. Beth and Joe Krush. San Diego: Harcourt Brace.

Pausewang, Gudrun. *Escuela de Los Niños Felices.*

Pierini, Fabio. *Niño Que Quería Volar.*

Rico de Alba, Lolo. *Angelita, la Ballena Pequeñita.*

———. *Mausito.*

Ruano, Moisés. *El Caballo Fantástico.* Illus. Alfonso Ruano.

Sendak, Maurice. 1988. *Where the Wild Things Are.* Illus. by author. New York: HarperCollins.

Sennell, Joles. *Guía Fantástica.*

Seuss Dr. [1937] 1989. *And To Think I Saw It On Mulberry Street.* Illus. by author. New York: Random House.

Stoutenburg, Adrien. 1976. *American Tall Tales.* Illus. Richard Powers. New York: Puffin.

Turín, Adela. *Ovillo Blanco.*

Vendrell, Carme S. *Luna de Juan.*

Viorst, Judith. 1989. *Alexander and the Terrible, Horrible, No Good, Very Bad Day / Alexander Y el Día Terrible, Horrible, Espantoso, Horroroso.* Trans. Alma F. Ada. Illus. Ray Cruz. New York: Macmillan.

Wild, Margaret. 1987. *There's a Sea in My Bedroom.* St. Petersburg, FL: Willowisp Press.

Williams, Jay. 1984. *Everyone Knows What a Dragon Looks Like.* Illus. Mercer Mayer. New York: Macmillan.

Williams, Leslie. 1985. *¿Qué Hay Detraz del Árbol?* Trans. Facrici Calvano. Illus. Carme S. Vendrell.

Williams, Margery. 1991. *The Velveteen Rabbit.* Illus. William Nicholson. New York: Doubleday.

Yagawa, Sumiko. 1992. *Crane Wife.* Trans. Katherine Paterson. Illus. Suekichi Akaba. Magnolia, MA: Peter Smith.

Yashima, Taro. 1977. *Umbrella.* Illus. by author. New York: Puffin.

Zatón, Jesús. *Mi Papá Y Yo Somos Piratas.*

12. THEME TOPIC: FRIENDSHIPS AND COMMUNITY: PEOPLE NEED PEOPLE

Possible Generalizations:

- Friendship requires both giving and receiving.
- People working together can make a difference.

Possible Concepts:

friendship, giving, receiving

Possible Materials:

Ada, Alma Flor. *Amigos.*

Adorjan, Carol. 1990. *That's What Friends Are For.* New York: Scholastic.

Alcantara Sgarb, Ricardo. *Bruja que Quizo Matar el Sol.*

Andersen, Hans Christian. 1992a. *Nightingale.* Illus. Catherine Huerta. Kansas City, MO: Andrews & McMeel.

———. 1992b. *The Ugly Duckling.* Illus. Robin Officer. Kansas City, MO: Andrews & McMeel.

Bemelmans, Ludwig. 1977. *Madeline.* Illus. by author. New York: Puffin.

Bollinger, Max. *Enanos y Gigantes.*

Bröger, Achim. *Buenos Díaz, Querida Ballena.*

Bunting, Eve. 1989. *The Wednesday Surprise.* Illus. Donald Garrick. Boston: Houghton Mifflin.

———. 1992. *Summer Wheels.* San Diego: Harcourt Brace.

Byars, Betsy. 1987. *The Pinballs.* New York: HarperCollins.

Carle, Eric. 1987. *Do You Want To Be My Friend?* Illus. by author. New York: HarperCollins.

Carlson, Nancy. 1992. *Arnie and the New Kid.* Illustrated. New York: Puffin.

Cleary, Beverly. 1992. *Dear Mr. Henshaw / Querido Señor Henshaw.* Illus. Paul O. Zelinsky. New York: Dell.

Clements, Andrew. 1991. *Big Al.* Illus. Yoshi. New York: Scholastic.

Cohen, Barbara. 1989. *Thank You, Jackie Robinson.* New York: Scholastic.

De Jong, Meindert. 1972. *Wheel on the School / Una Rueda en la Escuela.* Illus. Maurice Sendak. New York: HarperCollins.

de la Fontaine, Jean. 1988. *León y el Ratón.* Chicago: Childrens Press.

de Paola, Tomie. 1992. *Now One Foot, Now the Other / Un pasito...Y otro pasito.* Illus. by author. New York: Putnam.

Escrivá, Viví. *Niño y el Árbol.*

Estes, Eleanor. 1974. *The Hundred Dresses.* Illus. Louis Slobodkin. San Diego: Harcourt Brace.

Fox, Mem. 1989. *Wilfrid Gordon McDonald Partridge / Guillermo Jorge Manual Jose.* Illus. Julie Vivas. Brooklyn, NY: Kane-Miller.

Gates, Doris. 1976. *Blue Willow.* Illus. Paul Lantz. New York: Puffin.

Grimm, Jacob, and Wilhelm K. Grimm. 1992. *The Shoemaker and the Elves.* Illus. Barbara J. Roman. Kansas City, MO: Andrews & McMeel.

Hayes, Geoffrey. 1988. *Patrick and Ted Ride the Train.* Illus. by author. New York: Random House.

Holman, Felice. 1986. *Slake's Limbo.* New York: Macmillan.

Hunter, Edith F. 1963. *Child of the Silent Night: The Story of Laura Bridgman.* Illus. Bea Holmes. Boston: Houghton Mifflin.

Kantrowitz, Mildred. [1970] 1980. Maxie. Illus. Emily A. McCully. New York: Macmillan.

Komaiko, Leah. 1990. *Earl's Too Cool For Me.* Illus. Laura Cornell. New York: HarperCollins.

Konigsburg, E. L. 1985. *Jennifer, Hecate, Macbeth, William McKinley, and Me, Elizabeth.* New York: Dell.

Lobel, Arnold. 1985. *Frog and Toad Are Friends.* Illus. by author. New York: HarperCollins.

MacLachlan, Patricia. 1987. *Sarah, Plain and Tall / Sarah, Sencilla y Alta.* New York: HarperCollins.

Madenski, Melissa. 1991. *Some of the Pieces.* Illus. Debra K. Ray. Boston: Little, Brown.

Marshall, James. 1987. *George and Martha.* Illus. by author. Boston: Houghton Mifflin.

Martin, Bill Jr., and John Archambault. 1987. *Knots On a Counting Rope.* Illus. Ted Rand. New York: Henry Holt.

McGovern, Ann. 1986. *Stone Soup.* Illus. Winslow P. Pels. New York: Scholastic.

McLerran, Alice. 1991. *The Mountain That Loved a Bird.* Illus. Eric Carle. New York: Picture Book Studio.

Mills, Lauren. 1991. *Rag Coat.* Illustrated. Boston: Little, Brown.

Monjo, F. N. 1983. *The Drinking Gourd.* Illus. Fred Brenner. New York: HarperCollins.

O'Brien, Robert C. 1986. *Mrs. Frisby and the Rats of NIMH.* New York: Macmillan.

Osofsky, Audrey. 1992. *My Buddy.* Illus. Ted Rand. New York: Henry Holt.

Paterson, Katherine A. 1987b. *Bridge to Terabithia / Puente Hasta Terabithia*. Illus. Donna Diamond. New York: HarperCollins.

———. 1987a. *The Great Gilly Hopkins / La Gran Gilly Hopkins*. New York: HarperCollins.

Polacco, Patricia. 1992. *Mrs. Katz and Tush*. New York: Bantam.

Politi, Leo. 1973. *The Nicest Gift*. New York: Macmillan

Puncel, Maria. *Abuelita Opalina*.

———. *Hatillo de Cerezas*. Illus. Vivi Escriva.

———. *Hombre de Lluvia*.

———. *Prado del Tio Pedro*.

Reiss, Johanna. 1990. *The Upstairs Room / Habitaciones de Arriba*. New York: HarperCollins.

Sachs, Marilyn. 1989. *The Bears' House*. New York: Avon.

Spinelli, Eileen. 1992. *Somebody Loves You, Mr. Hatch*. Illus. Paul Yalowitz. New York: Macmillan.

Steadman, Ralph. *Puente*.

Steptoe, John. 1986. *Stevie*. Illus. by author. New York: HarperCollins.

Taha, Karen. 1991. *Gift for Tia Rosa*. New York: Bantam.

Taylor, Sydney. [1951] 1988. *All-of-a-Kind Family*. Illus. Helen John. New York: Taylor Productions.

Turín, Adela, and Nella Bosnia. *Una Feliz Catástrofe*.

Walter, Mildred P. 1990. *Justin and the Best Biscuits in the World*. Illus. Catherine Stock. New York: Knopf.

Wells, Rosemary. *Timoteo Va a la Escuela*.

White, E. B. 1974. *Charlotte's Web / Las Telarañas de Carlota*. New York: HarperCollins.

Yashima, Taro. 1976. *Crow Boy*. Illus. by author. New York: Puffin.

13. THEME TOPIC: GETTING TO KNOW ABOUT YOU, ME, AND OTHERS

Possible Generalizations:

- People are oftentimes more than they appear.
- People are both similar and unique.
- People need to accept and respect themselves as well as others for who and what they are.
- Cooperation is a key element in any community—family, neighborhood, classroom, etc.
- Walking a mile in another's shoes can lead to understanding.
- All people have their strengths and weaknesses.
- People may fear the unknown or what they do not understand.
- People may fear those who are different than themselves.
- Being true to yourself may have negative as well as positive consequences.
- Self-esteem may be affected by those around us.

Possible Concepts:

similar, unique, acceptance, respect, cooperation, community, understanding, experience, strength, weakness, risktaking, conflict, resolution, feelings, apperance/image, true self, self-esteem

Possible Materials:

Ashley, Bernard. 1992. *Cleversticks*. Illus. Derek Brazell. New York: Crown Books.

Bollinger, Max. *Pájaro de Colores*.

Bonsall, Crosby. 1985. *Who's Afraid of the Dark?* Illus. by author. New York: HarperCollins.

Brown, Tricia. 1992. *Hello, Amigos!* Photos by Fran Ortiz. New York: Henry Holt.

Carlson, Nancy. 1992. *Arnie and the New Kid*. Illustrated. New York: Puffin.

Clements, Andrew. 1991. *Big Al*. Illus. Yoshi. New York: Scholastic.

de Paola, Tomie. 1979. *Oliver Button Is a Sissy / Oliver Button es un Nena*. Illus. by author. San Diego: Harcourt Brace.

Eco, Humberto. *Tres Cosmonautas*.

Estes, Eleanor. 1974. *The Hundred Dresses*. Illus. Louis Slobodkin. San Diego: Harcourt Brace.

Fox, Paula. *Lugar Aparte*.

Goss, Janet, and Jerome Harste. 1985. *It Didn't Frighten Me*. Illus. Steve Rommey. St. Petersburg, FL: Willowisp Press.

Graves, Robert. *Dos Niños Sabios*.

Gray, Nigel. 1991. *A Country Far Away*. Illustrated. New York: Orchard Books.

Grip, Maria. *"Auténtico" Elvis*.

Hayes, Geoffrey. 1988. *Patrick and Ted Ride the Train*. Illus. by author. New York: Random House.

Hazel, Beth, and Jerome Harste. 1984. *My Icky Picky Sister*. Illustrated. St. Petersburg, FL: Willowisp Press.

Hazen, Barbara S. 1983. *Tight Times*. Illus. Tina S. Hyman. New York: Puffin.

Henkes, Kevin. 1990. *Jessica*. Illustrated. New York: Puffin.

Kantrowitz, Mildred. [1970] 1980. *Maxie*. Illus. Emily A. McCully. New York: Macmillan.

Kates, Bobby J. 1992. *We're Different, We're The Same*. Illus. Joc Mathieu. New York: Random House.

Komaiko, Leah. 1990. *Earl's Too Cool For Me*. Illus. Laura Cornell. New York: HarperCollins.

Krauss, Robert. 1987. *Leo the Late Bloomer*. Illus. Jose Aruego. New York: Simon & Schuster.

Lepscky, Ibi. 1992. *Albert Einstein*. Illus. Paolo Cardoni. Hauppauge, NY: Barron.

Marshall, James. 1987. *George and Martha*. Illus. by author. Boston: Houghton Mifflin.

Mateos, Pilar. *Zapatones*.

Mathers, Petra. 1993. *Maria Theresa*. Illus. by author. New York: HarperCollins.

Mayer, Mercer. 1985. *When I Get Bigger*. Illus. by author. Racine, WI: Western Publishing Group.

Milios, Rita. 1990. *Yo Soy*. Illus. Clovis Martin. Chicago: Childrens Press.

Munsch, Robert. 1986. *Love You Forever / Siempre Te Querre*. Illus. Sheila Mcgraw. Buffalo, NY: Firefly Books.

Murphy, Joanne B. 1985. *Feelings*. Illustrated. Buffalo, NY: Firefly Books.

Quinlan, Patricia. 1987. *My Dad Takes Care of Me*. Illus. Vlasta Van Kampen. Buffalo, NY: Firefly Books.

Sachs, Marilyn. 1989. *The Bears' House*. New York: Avon.

Sendak, Maurice. 1988. *Where the Wild Things Are*. Illus. by author. New York: HarperCollins.

Surat, Michele M. 1983. *Angel Child, Dragon Child*. Illus. Mai Vo-Dinh. New York: Scholastic.

Thomas, Marlo, and Friends. 1972. (Cassette). *Free to be You and Me*. New York: Arista Records and Tapes.

———. 1990. (Book and record) *Free to Be. . . A Family*. Illustrated. New York: Bantam.

Van Kempen, Corrigan. 1984. *Emily Umily*. Illustrated. Buffalo, NY: Firefly Books.

Viorst, Judith. 1987. *My Mama Says There Aren't Any Zombies, Ghosts, Vampires, Creatures, Demons, Monsters, Fiends, Goblins, or Things*. Illus. Kay Chorao. New York: Macmillan.

———. 1989. *Alexander and the Terrible, Horrible, No Good, Very Bad Day / Alexander Y el Día Terrible, Horrible, Espantoso, Horroroso*. Trans. Alma F. Ada. Illus. Ray Cruz. New York: Macmillan.

Waber, Bernard. 1987. *Ira Sleeps Over / Quique Duerme Fuera De Casa*. Illus. by author. Boston: Houghton Mifflin.

Williams, Vera B. 1988. *Chair For My Mother*. Illus. by author. New York: Morrow.

Yashima, Taro. 1976. *Crow Boy*. Illus. by author. New York: Puffin.

Zolotow, Charlotte. 1985. *William's Doll*. Illus. William Pene Du Bois. New York: HarperCollins.

———. 1988a. *When I Have a Little Boy*. Illus. Hilary Knight. New York: HarperCollins.

———. 1988b. *When I Have a Little Girl*. Illus. Hilary Knight. New York: HarperCollins.

14. THEME TOPIC: THE GRASS IS ALWAYS GREENER ON THE OTHER SIDE OF THE FENCE OR THINGS AREN'T ALWAYS AS THEY APPEAR

Possible Generalizations:

- We often do not appreciate what we have.
- What we want may not be so appealing once we have it.
- You cannot always judge a book by its cover.

Possible Concepts:

apperance, reality, appreciation, appeal

Possible Materials:

Allard, Harry, and James Marshall. 1987. *Miss Nelson Is Missing!* Illus. James Marshall. Boston: Houghton Mifflin.

Bofill, Francese. *Guisantes Maravillosos*.

Bollinger, Max. *Canción Más Bonita*.

Damjan, Mischa and Hans de Beer. *El bosque de las mil sombras*.

Elena, Horacio. *Majo el Rinoceronte*.

Forero, Maria Teresa. *Magolasko Amigo*.

França, Mary, and Eliardo França. *Rabo de Gato.*

Gates, Doris. 1976. *Blue Willow.* Illus. Paul Lantz. New York: Puffin.

Hague, Kathleen. 1988. *The Man Who Kept House.* Illus. Michael Hague. San Diego: Harcourt Brace.

Hirsh, Marilyn. 1987. *Could Anything Be Worse?* Illus. by author. New York: Holiday.

Janosch. *Qué Bonita es Panamá.*

Komaiko, Leah. 1990. *Earl's Too Cool For Me.* Illus. Laura Cornell. New York: HarperCollins.

Perera, Hilda. 1981. *Rana Ranita.*

Pierini, Fabio. 1979. *Niño Que Quería Volar.*

Rodgers, Mary. 1973. *Freaky Friday / Viernes Embrujado.* New York: HarperCollins.

San Souci, Robert D. 1994. *Song of Sedna.* New York: Bantam Doubleday Dell.

Solé Vendrell, Carmen. *Juana, la Princesa de Sal.*

Wendell, Paloma y Ulises. *Valentín Nos Gustas Así.*

15. THEME TOPIC: GROWING AND USING PLANTS AND SEEDS

Possible Generalizations:

- Plants and seeds can be started and grown in various ways.
- A region's vegetation can influence the local culture and its folklore.
- All plants and seeds have common needs.
- The use of pesticides can have negative as well as positive consequences.
- Plants and seeds "travel" in various ways with the help of "others."

Possible Concepts:

germination, environment, responsibility, needs, fruits, vegetables, seeds, roots, cuttings, growth requirements, organic/inorganic, pesticides

Possible Materials:

Aliki. 1987. *Story of Johnny Appleseed.* Illus. by author. New York: Prentice-Hall.

Alonso, Fernando. *Gallina Paulina y el Grano de Trigo.*

Burnie, David. 1989. *Plant.* Illus. Dave King, et al. New York: Knopf.

Carle, Eric. 1991. *Tiny Seed.* Illus. by author. New York: Picture Book Studio.

Cooney, Barbara. 1985. *Miss Rumphius.* Illustrated. New York: Puffin.

de Paola, Tomie. 1978. *Popcorn Book.* Illustrated. New York: Holiday.

———. 1983. *Legend of the Bluebonnet: An Old Tale of Texas.* Retold and illus. by author. New York: Putnam.

Haley, Gail. 1986. *Jack and the Bean Tree.* New York: Crown Books.

Heller, Ruth. 1992a. *Plants That Never Ever Bloom.* Illus. by author. New York: Putnam.

———. 1992b. *The Reason for a Flower.* Illus. by author. New York: Putnam.

Jennings, Terry. 1988. *Seeds.* Illus. David Anstey. New York: Watts.

Jordan, Helene J. 1992. *How a Seed Grows.* Illus. Joseph Low. New York: HarperCollins.

Julivert, M. Angels. 1994. *Life of Plants.* Illustrated. New York: Chelsea House.

Kellogg, Steven. 1991. *Jack and the Beanstalk.* Retold and illus. by author. New York: Morrow.

Krauss, Ruth. 1990. *The Carrot Seed / La Semilla de Zanahoria*. Illus. Crockett Johnson. New York: HarperCollins.

Kuchalla, Susan. 1982. *All About Seeds*. Illus. Jane McBee. Mahweh, NJ: Troll.

Lauber, Patricia. 1991. *Seeds: Pop! Stick! Glide!* Photos by Jerome Wexler. New York: Crown Books.

Lobel, Arnold. 1993. *The Rose in My Garden*. Illus. Anita Lobel. New York: Morrow.

Marcus, Elizabeth. *Vida de las plantas*.

Nussbaum, Hedda. 1977. *Plants Do Amazing Things*. Illus. Joe Mathieu. New York: Random House.

Olavarria, Agustin. *Nace una Sandia*.

Overbeck, Cynthia. 1982a. *Carnivorous Plants*. Minneapolis: Lerner Publications.

———. 1982b. *How Seeds Travel*. Minneapolis: Lerner Publications.

Rahn, Joan E. 1981. *Plants Up Close*. Boston: Houghton Mifflin.

Sabin, Louis. 1985. *Plants, Seeds and Flowers*. Illus. Holly Moylan. Mahwah, NJ: Troll.

Sánchez, Isidro. *Huerto*.

———. *Jardín*.

Saunders, Susan. 1986. *Attack of the Monster Plants*. New York: Bantam.

Silverstein, Shel. 1964. *Giving Tree / Árbol Generoso*. New York: Harper Row.

Suzuki, David. 1992. *Looking at Plants*. New York: John Wiley.

Torres, Gregorio. *Mirada a las Flores*.

———. *Mirada a las Hojas*.

———. *Mirada a los Arboles*.

Wyler, Rose. 1986. *Science Fun With Peanuts and Popcorn*. Illus. Pat Stewart. New York: Simon & Schuster.

York, Carol B. 1980. *Johnny Appleseed*. Mahwah, NJ: Troll.

Zendrera, C. *Yaci y su Muñeca*.

16. THEME TOPIC: HANDICAPS: CHALLENGES TO THE HUMAN CONDITION

Possible Generalizations:

- Most humans have some type of "handicap."
- Some handicaps are more visible than others.
- Handicaps provide us with both challenges and opportunities.
- A handicap in one situation may be a strength in another situation.
- Handicaps come in many different forms.
- Sometimes people can make something into a handicap that is not a handicap.

Possible Concepts:

handicaps, challenge, opportunity, coping

Possible Materials:

Blume, Judy. 1991. *Deenie*. New York: Dell.

Bode, Janet. 1991. *Beating the Odds: Stories of Unexpected Achievers*. New York: Watts.

Byars, Betsy. 1981. *Summer of the Swans / Verano de los Cisnes*. Illus. Ted CoConis. New York: Puffin.

Carlson, Nancy. 1992. *Arnie and the New Kid*. Illustrated. New York: Puffin.

Caudill, Rebecca. 1987. *A Certain Small Shepherd*. New York: Dell.

Charlip, Remy, and Mary Beth Miller. 1987. *Handtalk: An ABC of Finger Spelling and Sign Language*. Illus. George Ancona. New York: Macmillan.

———. 1991. *Handtalk Birthday: A Number and Storybook in Sign Language*. Illus. George Ancona. New York: Macmillan.

Corcoran, Barbara. *Hija de la Mañana*.

Estes, Eleanor. 1974. *The Hundred Dresses*. Illus. Louis Slobodkin. San Diego: Harcourt Brace.

———. 1989. *The Moffats*. New York: Dell.

Fleming, Virginia. 1993. *Be Good to Eddie Lee*. New York: Philomel Books.

Fox, Paula. 1985. *One-Eyed Cat*. New York: Dell.

Garfield, James B. 1987. *Follow My Leader*. Illus. Robert Greiner. New York: Scholastic.

Gates, Doris. 1976. *Blue Willow*. Illus. Paul Lantz. New York: Puffin.

Gilson, Jamie. 1980. *Do Bananas Chew Gum?* New York: Lothrop.

Hiriart, Bertha. *Aventuras de Polo y Jacinta*.

Hunter, Edith F. 1963. *Child of the Silent Night: The Story of Laura Bridgman*. Illus. Bea Holmes. Boston: Houghton Mifflin.

Little, Jean. 1991. *Little by Little: A Writer's Education*. Illustrated. New York: Puffin.

Martin, Bill, Jr., and John Archambault. 1987. *Knots On a Counting Rope*. Illus. Ted Rand. New York: Henry Holt.

Munter, Anke. *Gafas Maravillosas*.

Paterson, Katherine A. 1987. *The Great Gilly Hopkins / La Gran Gilly Hopkins*. New York: HarperCollins.

Rolfe, John. 1991. *Jim Abbott: Sports Illustrated Kids*. Boston: Little, Brown.

Rosenberg, Maxine B. 1983. *My Friend Leslie: The Story of a Handicapped Child*. Photos by George Ancona. New York: Lothrop.

Shyer, Marlene F. 1988. *Welcome Home, Jellybean*. New York: Macmillan.

Taylor, Theodore. 1989. *Trouble With Tuck*. New York: Doubleday.

Ungerer, Tomi. *Sombrero*.

Wilkie, Katherine. 1986. *Hellen Keller: From Tragedy to Triumph*. Illus. Robert Doremus. New York: Macmillan.

17. THEME TOPIC: HUMANKIND: THE LAUGHING ANIMAL

Possible Generalizations:

- Many characteristics of humor are universal.
- The effects of humor may include both a sense of belonging or group membership as well as a sense of rejection or exclusion.
- Humor may be used to diffuse negative feelings such as fear, jealousy, inequality, inadequacy, and boredom.

Possible Concepts:

universal characteristics, humor, belonging, exclusion, negative, feelings

Possible Materials:

Armijo, Consuela. *Risas, Poesia y Chirigotas.*

Catling, Patrick S. [1952] 1979. *The Chocolate Touch.* Illus. Margot Apple. New York: Morrow.

de Paola, Tomie. 1992. *Strega Nona.* New York: Scholastic.

Kellogg, Steven. 1984. *Paul Bunyan.* Adapt. and illus. by author. New York: Morrow.

Luz Uribe, María de la. *Cuenta Que Te Cuento.*

Prelutsky, Jack. 1984. *The New Kid on the Block.* Illus. James Stevenson. New York: Greenwillow.

Rodgers, Mary. 1973. *Freaky Friday / Viernes Embrujado.* New York: HarperCollins.

Silverstein, Shel. 1974. *Where the Sidewalk Ends: Poems and Drawings.* Illus. by author. New York: HarperCollins.

Smith, Robert K. 1992. *Chocolate Fever.* New York: Dell.

Thayer, Ernest L. 1992. *Casey at the Bat.* Illus. Patricia Polacco. New York: Putnam.

Tripp, Wallace. 1974. *A Great Big Ugly Man Came Up and Tied His Horse to Me: A Book of Nonsense Verse.* Illustrated. Boston: Little, Brown.

18. THEME TOPIC: IMMIGRATION: STRANGERS IN A STRANGE LAND

Possible Generalizations:

- There are many reasons why people immigrate from one place to another.
- Immigrant groups have made significant contributions to society in the United States.
- To a large extent, the United States is a land of immigrants.

Possible Concepts:

immigration, migration, economics, religion, demographics, ethnicity, culture, acculturation, assimilation, prejudice, contributions

Possible Materials:

Ashley, Bernard. 1992. *Cleversticks.* Illus. Derek Brazell. New York: Crown Books.

Balzola, Asun. *Santino el Pastelero.* Illus. by author.

Beatty, Patricia. 1992. *Lupita Manana.* New York: Morrow.

Bode, Janet. 1991. *New Kids in Town: Oral Histories of Immigrant Teens.* New York: Scholastic.

Brown, Tricia. 1992. *Hello, Amigos!* Photos by Fran Ortiz. New York: Henry Holt.

Bunting, Eve. 1990. *How Many Days to America? A Thanksgiving Story.* Illus. by author. Boston: Houghton Mifflin.

Chetin, Helen. 1982. *Angel Island Prisoner.* Trans. Catherine Harvey. Illus. Jan Lee. Berkeley, CA: New Seed.

Cohen, Barbara. 1990. *Molly's Pilgrim.* Illus. Michael R. Deraney. New York: Bantam.

Crofford, Emily. 1991. *Born in the Year of Courage.* Minneapolis: Carolrhoda Books.

Fassler, David. 1992. *Coming to America: The Kids' Book About Immigration.* Illustrated. Burlington, VT: Waterfront Books.

Friedman, Ina R. 1987. *How My Parents Learned to Eat.* Illus. Allen Say. Boston: Houghton Mifflin.

Gilson, Jamie, and John Wallner. 1991. *Hello, My Name is Scrambled Eggs*. Illus. by author. New York: Pocket Books.

Graff, Nancy P. 1993. *Where the River Runs: A Portrait of a Refugee Family*. Photos by Richard Howard. Boston: Little, Brown.

Greenwald, Sheila. 1985. *Rosy Cole Discovers America!* Boston: Little, Brown.

Hartmann, Edward. 1979. *American Immigration*. Illustrated. Minneapolis: Lerner Publications.

Heller, Linda. 1990. *The Castle on Hester Street*. Illus. by author. Philadelphia: Jewish Publication Society.

Hewett, Joan. 1990. *Hector Lives in the United State Now: The Story of a Mexican-American Child*. Illus. Richard R. Hewett. New York: HarperCollins.

Jin, Sarunna. 1990. *My First American Friend*. Illustrated. Madison, NJ: Raintree/Steck-Vaughn.

Kidd, Diana. 1991. *Onion Tears*. Illus. Lucy Montgomery. New York: Watts.

Krensky, Stephan. 1991. *Who Really Discovered America?* Mamaroneck, NY: Hastings.

Kuklin, Susan. 1992. *How My Family Lives in America*. Illus. by author. New York: Macmillan.

Larsen, Ronald J. 1991. *Puerto Ricans in America*. Illustrated. Minneapolis: Lerner Publications.

Levine, Ellen. 1989. *I Hate English!* New York: Scholastic.

———. 1993. *If Your Name Was Changed at Ellis Island*. New York: Scholastic.

Levinson, Riki. 1985. *Watch the Stars Come Out*. New York: Dutton.

Levitin, Sonia. 1986. *Journey to America*. Illus. Charles Robinson. New York: Macmillan.

Los Angeles Teachers' Committee on Central America, ed. 1986. "Wilfredo: The Story of a Boy from El Salvador." United Teachers of Los Angeles. Los Angeles, CA.

Namioka, Lensey. 1992. *Yang the Youngest and His Terrible Ear*. Boston: Little, Brown.

Paek, Min. 1988. *Aekyung's Dream*. Illus. by author. Emeryville, CA: Children's Book Press.

Pellegrini, Nina. 1991. *Families Are Different*. Illus. by author. New York: Holiday.

Perera, Hilda. *Kike*.

———. *Mai*.

———. *Rana Ranita*.

Pettit, Jayne. 1992. *My Name is San Ho*. New York: Scholastic.

Rosenberg, Maxine. 1986. *Making a New Home in America*. New York: Lothrop.

Sandoval, Dinorah. "Of Secret Wars and Roses." 1988. Ed. Los Angeles Teachers' Committee on Central America. United Teachers of Los Angeles. Los Angeles, CA.

Sennell, Joles. *Yuyo, el Niño que no Podía Llorar*.

Stanek, Muriel. 1989. *I Speak English For My Mom*. Ed. Kathleen Tucker. Illus. Judith Friedman. Morton Grove, IL: A. Whitman.

Stelzer, Ulli. 1988. *New Americans*. Intro. Peter Marin. Troutdale, OR: NewSage Press.

Tierney, Hanne. *Asi Vivimos en Nueva York*.

Trân-Khánh-Tuyêt. 1987. *Little Weaver of Thái-Yên Village*. Emeryville, CA: Children's Book Press.

Yee, Paul. 1992. *Roses Sing on New Snow: A Delicious Tale*. Illus. Harcey Chan. New York: Macmillan.

19. THEME TOPIC: I'M O.K.; YOU'RE O.K.

Possible Generalizations:

- How we feel about ourselves will influence how we feel about others.
- Our actions usually say something about how we feel about ourselves.
- There is good in all of us.
- You are worth feeling good about.
- Our self-esteem may be affected by the opinions of those who surround us.
- Differences can be strengths.

Possible Concepts:

self-awareness, self-acceptance, feelings, behavior

Possible Materials:

Andersen, Hans Christian. 1992. *The Ugly Duckling*. Illus. Robin Officer. Kansas City, MO: Andrews & McMeel.

Balzola, Asun. *Historia de un Erizo*.

Bulla, Clyde R. 1989. *Shoeshine Girl*. Illus. Leigh Grant. New York: HarperCollins.

Burch, Robert. 1987. *Queenie Peavy*. New York: Puffin.

Cantieni, Benita. *Elefantito y Gran Ratón*.

Cleary, Beverly. 1992. *Dear Mr. Henshaw / Querido Señor Henshaw*. Illus. Paul O. Zelinsky. New York: Dell.

Clements, Andrew. 1991. *Big Al*. Illus. Yoshi. New York: Scholastic.

de la Fontaine, Jean. *Zorra y la Cigüeña*.

Elena, Horacio. *Majo el Rinoceronte*.

Estes, Eleanor. 1974. *The Hundred Dresses*. Illus. Louis Slobodkin. San Diego: Harcourt Brace.

Fitzhugh, Louise. 1990. *Harriet the Spy*. Illus. by author. New York: HarperCollins.

Fox, Paula. 1985. *One-Eyed Cat*. New York: Dell.

Garcia, María. 1987. *Aventuras de Connie y Diego*. Emeryville, CA: Children's Book Press.

Garcia Sanchez, José Luís. *Niña Invisible*.

Holman, Felice. 1986. *Slake's Limbo*. New York: Macmillan.

Komaiko, Leah. 1990. *Earl's Too Cool For Me*. Illus. Laura Cornell. New York: HarperCollins.

Krauss, Robert. 1987. *Leo the Late Bloomer*. Illus. Jose Aruego. New York: Simon & Schuster.

Lewis, C. S. 1988a. *The Lion, the Witch, and the Wardrobe*. New York: Macmillan.

——. 1988b. *El Leion, la Bruja y el Armario*. New York: Santilla.

Mateos, Pilar. *Zapatones*.

Mathers, Petra. 1993. *Maria Theresa*. Illus. by author. New York: HarperCollins.

Mazer, Norma. 1981. *Mrs. Fish, Ape, and Me, the Dump Queen*. New York: Avon.

Paterson, Katherine. 1987a. *Bridge to Terabithia / Puente Hasta Terabithia*. Illus. Donna Diamond. New York: HarperCollins.

——. 1987b. *The Great Gilly Hopkins / La Gran Gilly Hopkins*. New York: HarperCollins.

Perera, Hilda. 1981. *Rana Ranita*.

Rico de Alba, Lolo. 1975. *Angelita, la Ballena Pequeñita*.

———. *Mausito*.

Solotareff, Grégoire. *No Volváis a Llamarme "Conejito Mío"*.

Surat, Michele M. 1983. *Angel Child, Dragon Child*. Illus. Mai Vo-Dinh. New York: Scholastic.

Uribe, Kurusa. *Cocuyo y la Mora*.

Vannini, Marisa. *Cuatro Gatitos*.

Wendell, Paloma y Ulises. *Valentín Nos Gustas Así*.

Yashima, Taro. 1976. *Crow Boy*. Illus. by author. New York: Puffin.

20. THEME TOPIC: IT'S NOT FAIR

Possible Generalizations:

* Sometimes what is and is not fair is a matter of perspective.
* Different people may be treated differently because of who and what they are.

Possible Concepts:

fairness/justice, perspective, independence

Possible Materials:

Aaseng, Nathan. 1991. *Peace Seekers: The Nobel Peace Prize*. Minneapolis: Lerner Publcations.

Ada, Alma Flor. *Amigos*.

Blume, Judy. 1985. *Pain and the Great One*. New York: Dell.

Felipe, Nersys. *Cuentos de Guane*.

Gaes, Jason. 1991. *My Book For Kids With Cansur: A Child's Autobiography of Hope*. Illus. Adam and Tim Gaes. Pierre, SD: Melius Pub.

Gallaz, Christopher, and Roberto Innocenti. *Rosa Blanche*.

Golenbock, Peter. 1992. *Teammates*. San Diego: Harcourt Brace.

Hazen, Barbara S. 1983. *Tight Times*. Illus. Tina S. Hyman. New York: Puffin.

Maruki, Toshi. 1982. *Hiroshima No Pika / El Destello de Hiroshima*. New York: Lothrop.

Miller, Marilyn. 1984. *The Bridge at Selma*. Illustrated. Morristown, NJ: Silver Burdett Press.

Naylor, Phyllis R. 1991. *Shiloh*. New York: Macmillan.

Perera, Hilda. *Mumu*.

Rock, Gall. 1985. *The House Without a Christmas Tree*. New York: Dell.

Scieszka, Jon. 1992. *True Story of the Three Little Pigs / La Verdadera Historia de los Tres Cerditos*. Illus. Lane Smith. New York: Viking.

Smith, Doris B. 1988. *Taste of Blackberries*. New York: HarperCollins.

Steadman, Ralph. *Puente*.

Taylor, Mildred D. 1975. *Song of the Trees*. Illus. Jeny Pinkney. New York: Dial.

———. 1987. *Gold Cadillac*. Illus. Michael Hays. New York: Dial.

———. 1992. *Mississippi Bridge*. Illus. Max Ginsberg. New York: Bantam.

Tsuchiya, Yukio. 1988. *Faithful Elephants*. Trans. Tomoko T. Dykes. Illus. Ted Lewin. Boston: Houghton Mifflin.

Turín, Adela. *Rosa Caramelo*.

Turner, Ann. 1987. *Nettie's Trip South*. Illus. Ronald Himler. New York: Macmillan.

Tusquests, Ester. 1980. *Conejita Marcela*.

Viorst, Judith. 1989. *Alexander and the Terrible, Horrible, No Good, Very Bad Day / Alexander Y el Día Terrible, Horrible, Espantoso, Horroroso*. Trans. Alma F. Ada. Illus. Ray Cruz. New York: Macmillan.

Zolotow, Charlotte. 1976. *It's Not Fair*. Illus. William Pene Du Bois. New York: HarperCollins.

21. THEME TOPIC: A LOT CAN BE SAID ABOUT "LITTLE"

Possible Generalizations:

- Little fellows can make a big difference.
- Little things can be the beginning of something much bigger or something new and different.
- Biggest isn't always best.
- Sometimes you have to make the best of being little.

Possible Concepts:

little, big, best, difference

Possible Materials:

Andersen, Hans Christian. 1992. *Thumbelina*. Illus. Robyn Officer. Kansas City, MO: Andrews & McMeel.

Bemelmans, Ludwig. 1977. *Madeline*. Illus. by author. New York: Puffin.

Bennett, Jill. 1986. *Teeny Tiny*. Illus. Tomie de Paola. New York: Putnam.

Brown, Margaret W. 1990. *The Important Book*. Illus. Leonard Weisgard. New York: HarperCollins.

———. 1991. *The Runaway Bunny*. Illus. Clement Hurd. New York: HarperCollins.

Buffett, Jimmy, and Savannah Buffett. *Trouble Dolls*. Intro. Bonnie V. Ingber. Illus. Lambert Davis. San Diego: Harcourt Brace.

Cantieni, Benita. *Elefantito y Gran Ratón*.

Carle, Eric. 1991. *The Very Hungry Caterpillar / La Oruga Muy Hambrienta*. New York: Putnam.

de Paola, Tomie. 1978. *Popcorn Book*. New York: Holiday.

Galdone, Paul. 1987. *Little Red Hen / La Gallinita Roja*. Boston: Houghton Mifflin.

Garcia Sánchez, José Luis. *Niño Gigante*.

Grimm, Jacob, and Wilhelm K. Grimm. 1981. *Little Red Riding Hood*. Illustrated. Kansas City, MO: Andrews & McMeel.

Greene, Graham. *Pequeña Apisonadora*.

Howe, James. 1987. *I Wish I Were a Butterfly*. Illus. Ed Young. San Diego: Harcourt Brace.

Krauss, Ruth. 1990. *The Carrot Seed / La Semilla de Zanahoria*. Illus. Crockett Johnson. New York: HarperCollins.

Kuklin, Susan. 1986. *Thinking Big: The Story of a Young Dwarf*. Illustrated. New York: Lothrop.

Lionni, Leo. 1987. *Swimmy / Nadarín*. Illustrated. New York: Knopf.

Martin, Bill Jr., and John Archambault. 1989. *Here Are My Hands*. Illus. Ted Rand. New York: Henry Holt.

Mayer, Mercer. [1976] 1980. *Liza Lou and the Yeller Belly Swamp*. Illus. by author. New York: Macmillan.

McCloskey, Robert. 1978. *Lentil*. New York: Puffin.

McGovern, Ann. 1986. *Stone Soup*. Illus. Winslow P. Pels. New York: Scholastic.

Mosel, Ariene. 1992. *Tikki Tikki Tembo*. Illus. Blair Lent. New York: Henry Holt.

Nazoa, Aquiles. *Fábula de la Ratoncita Presumida*.

Norton, Mary. *Incursores*.

Okawa, Essei. 1985. *The Adventures of the One Inch Boy: Issun Boshi*. Trans. D.T. Ooka. Illus. Teruyo Endo. Union City, CA: Heian International.

Peet, Bill. 1982. *Big Bad Bruce*. Illus. by author. Boston: Houghton Mifflin.

Piper, Watty. 1991. *The Little Engine That Could / La Pequeña Locomotora Que si Pudo*. New York: Putnam.

Rico de Alba, Lolo. *Angelita, la Ballena Pequeñita*.

Stinson, Kathy. *Soy Grande, Soy Pequeño*.

Tazewell, Charles. [1946] 1991. *Littlest Angel*. Illus. Paul Micich. Nashville, TN: Ideals Publishing.

Uchida, Yoshiko. 1987. "Tiny God." *Magic Listening Cap: More Folktales From Japan*. Illus. by author. Berkely, CA: Creative Arts Books.

Van Lann, Nancy. 1993. *Tiny, Tiny Boy and the Big, Big, Cow*. Illus. Marjorie Priceman. New York: Knopf.

Vuong, Lynnette and Mai Vo-Dinh. 1992. "Little finger of the watermelon patch." *The Brocaded Slipper and Other Vietnamese Tales*. Illus. Mai Vo-Dinh. New York: HarperCollins.

Watson, Richard J. 1989. *Tom Thumb*. Illustrated. San Diego: Harcourt Brace.

Wood, Don. 1990. *Quick as a Cricket*. Clarkston, MI: Childs Play.

22. THEME TOPIC: ME, MYSELF, AND I

Possible Generalizations:

- Getting to know yourself will help you to understand others as well.
- Everyone is a star in something.
- Accept yourself for who and what you are.

Possible Concepts:

self-awareness, self-acceptance, abilities

Possible Materials:

Alexander, Lloyd. 1980. *Taran Wanderer*. New York: Dell.

Baylor, Byrd. 1989. *Amigo*. Illus. Garth Williams. New York: Macmillan.

Bojunga, Lygia. *Bolso Amarillo*.

Bulla, Clyde R. 1989. *Shoeshine Girl*. Illus. Leigh Grant. New York: HarperCollins.

Burch, Robert. 1987. *Queenie Peavy*. New York: Puffin.

Byars, Betsy. 1981. *Summer of the Swans / Verano de los Cisnes*. Illus. Ted CoConis. New York: Puffin.

Carrasco, Marta. *Club de los Diferentes*.

Cleary, Beverly. 1992. *Dear Mr. Henshaw / Querido Señor Henshaw*. Illus. Paul O. Zelinsky. New York: Dell.

del Canizo, José A. *Pintor de Recuerdos*.

Elena, Horacio. 1979. *Majo el Rinoceronte*.

Fernández, Laura. *Luís y su Genio*.

Fitzhugh, Louise. 1990. *Harriet the Spy*. Illus. by author. New York: HarperCollins.

Fox, Paula. 1985. *One-Eyed Cat*. New York: Dell.

Goble, Paul. 1986. *The Girl Who Loved Wild Horses*. Ed. Julia Silbert. Illus. by author. New York: Macmillan.

Graves, Robert. *Dos Niños Sabios*.

Grip, Maria. *"Auténtico" Elvis*.

Juster, Norton. 1993. *The Phantom Tollbooth*. Illus. Jules Feiffer. New York: Knopf.

Komaiko, Leah. 1990. *Earl's Too Cool For Me*. Illus. Laura Cornell. New York: HarperCollins.

Krauss, Robert. 1987. *Leo the Late Bloomer*. Illus. Jose Aruego. New York: Simon & Schuster.

Krumgold, Joseph. 1987. *And Now Miguel*. Illus. Jean Charlot. New York: HarperCollins.

Lepscky, Ibi. *Pablito*. Illus. Paolo Cardoni.

Mathers, Petra. 1992. *Maria Theresa*. Illus. by author. New York: HarperCollins.

Mendez, Phil. 1991. *The Black Snowman*. Illus. Carole Byard. New York: Scholastic.

Nazoa, Aquiles. *Fábula de la Ratoncita Presumida*.

Piper, Watty. 1991. *The Little Engine That Could / La Pequeña Locomotora Que si Pudo*. New York: Putnam.

Politi, Leo. 1973. *The Nicest Gift*. New York: Macmillan

Rico de Alba, Lolo. 1975. *Angelita, la Ballena Pequeñita*.

———. *Llorón, Hijo de Dragón*.

Rodgers, Mary. 1973. *Freaky Friday / Viernes Embrujado*. New York: HarperCollins.

Steig, William. 1985. *Abel's Island*. Illus. by author. New York: Farrar, Straus & Giroux.

Surat, Michele M. 1983. *Angel Child, Dragon Child*. Illus. Mai Vo-Dinh. New York: Scholastic.

Viorst, Judith. 1989. *Alexander and the Terrible, Horrible, No Good, Very Bad Day / Alexander Y el Día Terrible, Horrible, Espantoso, Horroroso*. Trans. Alma F. Ada. Illus. Ray Cruz. New York: Macmillan.

Waber, Bernard. 1987. *Ira Sleeps Over / Quique Duerme Fuera De Casa*. Illus. by author. Boston: Houghton Mifflin.

Wilson, Johnniece M. 1992. *Poor Girl, Rich Girl*. New York: Scholastic.

Yashima, Taro. 1976. *Crow Boy*. Illus. by author. New York: Puffin.

23. THEME TOPIC: PEOPLE ARE MORE THAN THEY APPEAR

Possible Generalizations:

- People are oftentimes more than they appear.
- First impressions oftentimes are misleading.
- People are multidimensional in nature.

Possible Concepts:

appearance, identity

Possible Materials:

Balzola, Asun. 1978. *Historia de un Erizo.*

Carlson, Nancy. 1992. *Arnie and the New Kid.* Illustrated. New York: Puffin.

Clements, Andrew. 1991. *Big Al.* Illus. Yoshi. New York: Scholastic.

Cohen, Barbara. 1990. *Molly's Pilgrim.* Illus. Michael R. Deraney. New York: Bantam.

Estes, Eleanor. 1974. *The Hundred Dresses.* Illus. Louis Slobodkin. San Diego: Harcourt Brace.

Kidd, Diana. 1991. *Onion Tears.* Illus. Lucy Montgomery. New York: Watts.

Komaiko, Leah. 1990. *Earl's Too Cool For Me.* Illus. Laura Cornell. New York: HarperCollins.

Lepscky, Ibi. 1992. *Albert Einstein.* Illus. Paolo Cardoni. Hauppauge, NY: Barron.

Maynes, William. 1986. *Corbie.* New York: Prentice Hall.

Mohr, Nicholasa. 1979. *Felita.* Illus. Ray Cruz. New York: Dial.

Scieszka, Jon. 1992. *True Story of the Three Little Pigs / La Verdadera Historia de los Tres Cerditos.* Illus. Lane Smith. New York: Viking.

Sperry, Armstrong. 1990. *Call It Courage.* New York: Macmillan.

Surat, Michele M. 1983. *Angel Child, Dragon Child.* Illus. Mai Vo-Dinh. New York: Scholastic.

Yashima, Taro. 1976. *Crow Boy.* Illus. by author. New York: Puffin.

24. THEME TOPIC: PEOPLE WORKING TOGETHER CAN MAKE A DIFFERENCE

Possible Generalizations:

- Two heads are better than one.
- Many hands working together lighten the load.

Possible Concepts:

cooperation, independence, interdependence

Possible Materials:

Ackerman, Karen. 1991. *The Leaves in October.* New York: Macmillan.

Browne, Anthony. 1990. *Piggybook.* Illus. by author. New York: Knopf.

Burnford, Sheila Every. 1990. *The Incredible Journey.* Illus. Carl Burger. New York: Bantam.

Cherry, Lynne. 1990. *Great Kapok Tree: A Tale of the Amazon Rain Forest.* San Diego: Harcourt Brace.

DiSalvo-Ryan, Dyanne. 1991. *Uncle Willie and the Soup Kitchen*. Illus. by author. New York: Morrow.

Kurusa. *La Calle es Libre*.

Lionni, Leo. 1987. *Swimmy / Nadarín*. Illustrated. New York: Knopf.

Locker, Thomas. 1988. *Family Farm*. Illus. by author. New York: Dial.

Lowry, Lois. *¿Quién Cuenta las Estrellas?*

McGovern, Ann. 1986. *Stone Soup*. Illus. Winslow P. Pels. New York: Scholastic.

Polacco, Patricia. 1992. *Chicken Sunday*. Illus. by author. New York: Putnam.

Rand, Gloria. 1992. *Prince William*. Illus. Ted Rand. New York: Henry. Holt.

Winter, Jeanette. 1992. *Follow the Drinking Gourd*. Illustrated. New York: Knopf.

Zavrel, Stepan. *Último Árbol*.

25. THEME TOPIC: REPTILES AND AMPHIBIANS

Possible Generalizations:

- Reptiles and amphibians are both similar and different.
- Reptiles and amphibians have been on the earth in various forms for thousands and thousands of years.
- Reptiles and amphibians are "friends" of humankind.
- Certain reptiles and amphibians from the past continue to fascinate and intrigue humankind.

Possible Concepts:

amphibians, reptiles, similarity, difference, various forms, contribution, fascination, "friends," cold-blooded, skin, life-cycle, hibernation

Possible Materials:

Aliki. 1990. *Dinosaur Bones*. Illus. by author. New York: HarperCollins.

Barrett, Norman. 1992. *Dragons and Lizards*. New York: Watts.

Bröger, Achim. *Historia de Dragolina*.

Burns, Diane L. 1988. *Snakes Alive! Jokes about Snakes*. Illus. Joan Hanson. Minneapolis: Lerner Publications.

Caitlin, Stephen. 1990. *Discovering Reptiles and Amphibians*. Illus. Pamela Johnson. Mahwah, NJ: Troll.

Carrick, Carol. 1985. *Patrick's Dinosaurs*. Illus. by author. Boston: Houghton Mifflin.

———. 1988. *What Happened to Patrick's Dinosaurs?* Illus. by author. Boston: Houghton Mifflin.

Charbonnet, Gabrielle. 1991. *Snakes Are Nothing to Sneeze At*. Illus. Abby Carter. New York: Henry Holt.

Cole, Joanna. 1981. *A Snake's Body*. Photos by Jerome Wexler. New York: Morrow.

Curtis, Neil. 1990. *Discovering Snakes and Lizards*. New York: Watts.

Cutts, David. *Dinosaurios*.

Dauer, Rosamund. 1988a. *Bullfrog Builds a House*. New York: Dell

———. 1988b. *Bullfrog Grows Up*. New York: Dell

Gay, Tanner O. 1991. *Snakes and Other Reptiles in Action.* Illus. Jean Cassels. New York: Macmillan.

Hoff, Syd. 1985. *Danny and the Dinosaur.* Illus. by author. New York: HarperCollins.

———. 1994. *Danielito y el Dinosaurio.* Trans. Teresa Mawler. Illus. by author. New York: Lectorum Publications.

Holabird, Katharine. 1988. *Alexander and the Dragon.* Illus. Helen Craig. New York: Crown Books.

Jacob, Esther. *Tortugas De Mar.*

Johnson, Sylvia. 1986. *Snakes.* Photos by Modoki Masuda. Minneapolis: Lerner Publications.

Kalan, Robert. *Jump, Frog, Jump!* Illus. Byron Barton. New York: Scholastic.

Kroll, Steven. 1978. *The Tyronnasaurus Game.* Illus. Tomie de Paola. Ancramdale, New York: Holiday.

Lauber, Patricia. 1987. *Dinosaurs Walked Here and Other Stories Fossils Tell.* Illustrated. New York: Macmillan.

———. 1988. *Snakes Are Hunters.* Illus. Holly Keller. New York: HarperCollins.

———. 1989. *The News About Dinosaurs.* Illus. John Gurche, et al. New York: Macmillan.

Mayer, Mercer, and Marianna Mercer. 1985. *One Frog Too Many.* Illus. Mercer Mayer. New York: Dial.

Milton, Joyce. 1988. *Dinosaur Days.* Illus. Richard Roe. New York: Random House.

Most, Bernard. 1990. *Dinosaur Cousins?* San Diego: Harcourt Brace.

Noble, Trinka. 1987. *Jimmy's Boa Bounces Back.* Illus. Stephen Kellogg. New York: Dial.

Norman, David and Angela Milner. *Dinosaurios.*

O'Neill, Mary. 1989. *Dinosaur Mysteries.* Illus. John Bindon. Mahwah, NJ: Troll.

Parish, Peggy. 1983. *Dinosaur Time.* Illus. Arnold Lobel. New York: HarperCollins.

Petty, Kate. 1985. *Snakes.* Illus. Alan Baker. New York: Watts.

Rowe, Erna. 1973. *Dinosaurios Gigantes.* New York: Scholastic.

———. 1975. *Giant Dinosaurs.* Illus. Merle Smith. New York: Scholastic.

Sabin, Louis. 1985. *Reptiles and Amphibians.* Illus. Nancy Zink-White. Mahwah, NJ: Troll.

Shannon, George. 1992. *Lizard's Song.* Illus. Jose Aruego and Ariane Dewey. New York: Morrow.

Sharmat, Marjorie W. 1985. *Mitchell Is Moving.* Illus. Jose Aruego and Ariane Dewey. New York: Macmillan.

Stewart, Janet. 1989. *Snakes and Reptiles.* Illustrated. Niagra Falls, NY: Durkin Hayes.

Waber, Bernard. 1987. *Lyle, Lyle, Crocodile.* Boston: Houghton Mifflin.

West, Colin. 1986. *Have You Seen the Crocodile?* Illus. by author. New York: HarperCollins.

Wildsmith, Brian. 1991. *Python's Party.* Illustrated. New York: Oxford University Press.

Zallinger, Peter. 1981. *Prehistoric Animals.* Illus. by author. New York: Random House.

26. THEME TOPIC: SURVIVAL

Possible Generalizations:

• There is a universal need for all living things to survive.
• People need to interact with others and their environment in order to survive.

- One key to survival is evaluating the circumstances and adjusting your behavior.
- People need to be able to distinguish between what they want and what they need.
- A person's emotional/psychological and social survival cannot be separated.

Possible Concepts:

survival, interaction, adaptation, needs, desires, emotions

Possible Materials:

Alcántara, Ricardo. *Viaje de los Pájaros.*

Beatty, Patricia. 1992. *Lupita Manana.* New York: Morrow.

Brenner, Barbara. 1984. *Wagon Wheels.* Illus. Don Bolognese. New York: HarperCollins.

Bröger, Achim. *Historia de Dragolina.*

Burch, Robert. 1987. *Queenie Peavy.* New York: Puffin.

Childress, Alice. *When the Rattlesnake Sounds: A Play About Harriet Tubman.* New York: Coward-McCann.

Cleary, Beverly. 1990. *Ramona and Her Father / Ramona y Su Padre.* New York: Avon.

———. 1992. *Dear Mr. Henshaw / Querido Señor Henshaw.* Illus. Paul O. Zelinsky. New York: Dell.

Clements, Andrew. 1991. *Big Al.* Illus. Yoshi. New York: Scholastic.

Dalgliesh, Alice. [1954] 1991. *The Courage of Sarah Noble / El Valor de Sarah Noble.* Illus. Leonard Weisgard. New York: Macmillan.

Davis, Ossie. 1990. *Escape to Freedom: A Play About Young Frederick Douglass.* New York: Puffin.

Eco, Humberto. *Bomba y el General.*

Fox, Paula. 1991. *Slave Dancer / Que Bailen Los Esclavos.* New York: Dell.

Frank, Anne. 1967. *Anne Frank: The Diary of a Young Girl / Diario de Ana Frank.* Trans. B. M. Mooyaart. New York: Doubleday.

Galdone, Paul. 1984. *The Three Little Pigs.* Illus. by author. Boston: Houghton Mifflin.

Gates, Doris. 1976. *Blue Willow.* Illus. Paul Lantz. New York: Puffin.

Greene, Bette. 1984. *Summer of My German Soldier.* New York: Bantam.

Grifalconi, Ann. 1986. *Village of Round and Square Houses.* Illus. by author. Boston: Little, Brown.

Hall, Donald. 1983. *Ox-Cart Man.* Illus. Barbara Cooney. New York: Puffin.

Hill, Kirkpatrick. 1990. *Toughboy and Sister.* New York: Macmillan.

Holman, Felice. 1986. *Slake's Limbo.* New York: Macmillan.

Hunter, Edith F. 1963. *Child of the Silent Night: The Story of Laura Bridgman.* Illus. Bea Holmes. Boston: Houghton Mifflin.

Kroeber, Theodore. 1964. *Ishi: Last of His Tribe.* Illus. Ruth Robbins. Boston: Houghton Mifflin.

Lauber, Patricia. 1993. *Volcano: The Eruption and Healing of Mt. St. Helens.* Ed. Leslie Ward. New York: Macmillan.

Levitin, Sonia. 1987. *Journey to America.* Illus. Charles Robinson. New York: Macmillan.

Martínez, María. *Yo las Quería.*

Mathers, Petra. 1992. *Maria Theresa.* Illus. by author. New York: HarperCollins.

McCloskey, Robert. 1976. *Make Way for Ducklings.* Illus. by author. New York: Puffin.

Moeri, Louise. 1990. *Save Queen of Sheba*. New York: Avon.

O'Dell, Scott. 1976. *Zia*. Illus. Ted Lewin. Boston: Houghton Mifflin.

———. 1990. *Island of the Blue Dolphins / Isla de los Delfines Azules*. Illus. Ted Lewin. Boston: Houghton Mifflin.

Orlev, Uri. 1984. *Island on Bird Street*. Trans. Hillel Halkin. Boston: Houghton Mifflin.

Paterson, Katherine. 1987a. *Bridge to Terabithia / Puente Hasta Terabithia*. Illus. Donna Diamond. New York: HarperCollins.

Paterson, Katherine A. 1987b. *The Great Gilly Hopkins / La Gran Gilly Hopkins*. New York: HarperCollins.

Paulsen, Gary. 1988. *Hatchet / El Hacha*. New York: Puffin.

Pinkwater, Manus. 1992. *Wingman*. New York: Bantam.

Reiss, Johanna. 1990. *The Upstairs Room / Habitaciones de Arriba*. New York: HarperCollins.

Ruckman, Ivy. 1986. *Night of the Twisters*. New York: HarperCollins.

Saller, Carol. 1991. *The Bridge Dancers*. Illus. Gerald Talifero. Minneapolis: Carolrhoda Books.

Speare, Elizabeth G. 1984. *The Sign of the Beaver / Signo del Casto*. New York: Dell.

Sperry, Armstrong. 1990. *Call It Courage*. New York: Macmillan.

Stevens, Janet. 1990. *The Three Billy Goats Gruff*. Illus. by author. San Diego: Harcourt Brace.

Sweet, Muriel. 1976. *Common Edible and Useful Plants of the West*. Illustrated. Happy Camp, CA: Naturegraph.

Taylor, Mildred D. 1992. *Mississippi Bridge*. New York: Bantam.

Taylor, Theodore. 1987. *Cay*. New York: Doubleday.

Tejima, Keizaburo. 1990. *Fox's Dream*. Putnam.

Uchida, Yoshiko. 1985. *Journey to Topaz*. Illus. Donald Carrick. Berkeley, CA: Creative Arts Books.

———. [1978] 1992. *Journey Home*. Illus. Charles Robinson. New York: Macmillan.

Williams, Vera B. 1988. *Chair For My Mother*. Illus. by author. New York: Morrow.

27. THEME TOPIC: THINGS THAT GO BUMP IN THE NIGHT: GETTING TO UNDERSTAND FEAR

Possible Generalizations:

- Once you determine what is frightening you, you can face it, deal with it, and usually it will be less frightening.
- There is no need to be frightened by imaginary things because they cannot hurt you.
- People may fear the unknown or what they do not understand.
- People cope with their fears in different ways.
- Facing our fears can lead to personal growth.
- Most of us fear something.

Possible Concepts:

fear, confrontation, imagination, coping, growth, facing fears

Possible Materials:

Alcántara, Ricardo. *Viaje de los Pájaros*.

Bemelmans, Ludwig. 1977. *Madeline*. Illus. by author. New York: Puffin.

Bollinger, Max. *Montaña de los Osos*.

Bröger, Achim. *Historia de Dragolina*.

Carlson, Nancy. *Niña Bailarina*.

Clements, Andrew. 1991. *Big Al*. Illus. Yoshi. New York: Scholastic.

Company González, Mercé. *Nana Bunilda Come Pesadillas*.

———. *Que Viene El Coco*.

Dalgliesh, Alice. [1954] 1991. *The Courage of Sarah Noble / El Valor de Sarah Noble*. Illus. Leonard Weisgard. New York: Macmillan.

de la Luz Uribe, María. 1981. *Doña Piñones*.

de la Luz Uribe, María, and Fernando Krahn. 1983. *El Cururía*.

Ende, Michael. *Tragasueños*.

Estes, Eleanor. 1974. *The Hundred Dresses*. Illus. Louis Slobodkin. San Diego: Harcourt Brace.

Gackenback, Dick. 1984. *Harry and the Terrible Watzit / Harry y El Terrible Quiensabeque*. Illus. by author. Boston: Houghton Mifflin.

Goss, Janet, and Jerome Harste. 1985. *It Didn't Frighten Me*. Illus. Steve Rommey. St. Petersburg, FL: Willowisp Press.

Henderson, Kathy. 1992. *In the Middle of the Night*. Illus. Jennifer Eachus. New York: Macmillan.

Johnston, Tony. 1980. *Four Scary Stories*. Illustrated. New York: Putnam.

Mayer, Mercer. 1985. *There's a Nightmare In My Closet / Hay Una Pesadilla en mi Armario*. Illus. by author. New York: Dial.

———. 1987. *There's an Alligator Under My Bed*. Illustrated. New York: Dial.

Pank, Rachel. 1991. Sonia and Barnie and the Noise in the Night. New York: Scholastic.

Peck, Richard. 1987. *Ghost Belonged to Me*. New York: Dell.

Saller, Carol. 1991. *The Bridge Dancers*. Illus. Gerald Talifero. Minneapolis: Carolrhoda Books.

Sendak, Maurice. 1988. *Where the Wild Things Are*. Illus. by author. New York: HarperCollins.

Sperry, Armstrong. 1990. *Call It Courage*. New York: Macmillan.

Stevenson, James. 1990. *What's Under My Bed / ¿Qué Hay Debajo de Mi Cama?* New York: Morrow.

Tester, Sylvia. 1979. *Sometimes I'm Afraid*. Illus. Frances Hook. Mankato, MN: Childs World.

Tompert, Ann. 1992. *Will You Come Back For Me?* Morton Grove, IL: A. Whitman.

Waber, Bernard. 1987. *Ira Sleeps Over / Quique Duerme Fuera De Casa*. Illus. by author. Boston: Houghton Mifflin.

Wilhlm, Hans. 1990. *Un Chico Valiente Como Yo*.

28. THEME TOPIC: WITH FREEDOM AND JUSTICE FOR ALL

Possible Generalizations:

- Justice involves treating all people fairly, regardless of who or what they are.

Possible Concepts:

freedom, justice, peace, fairness, differences, similarities

Possible Materials:

Childress, Alice. 1976. *When the Rattlesnake Sounds: A Play About Harriet Tubman*. New York: Coward-McCann.

Clark, Margaret Goff. 1991. *Freedom Crossing*. New York: Scholastic.

Davis, Ossie. 1990. *Escape to Freedom: A Play About Young Frederick Douglass*. New York: Puffin.

Estes, Eleanor. 1974. *The Hundred Dresses*. Illus. Louis Slobodkin. San Diego: Harcourt Brace.

Fox, Paula. 1985. *One-Eyed Cat*. New York: Dell.

———. 1991. *Slave Dancer / Que Bailen Los Esclavos*. New York: Dell.

Franchere, Ruth. 1986. *Cesar Chavez*. Illus. Earl Thollander. New York: HarperCollins.

Goble, Paul. 1992. *Red Hawk's Account of Custer's Last Battle*. Illus. by author. Lincoln, NE: University of Nebraska Press.

Greene, Bette. 1984. *Summer of My German Soldier*. New York: Bantam.

Krensky, Stephan. 1991. *Who Really Discovered America?* Mamaroneck, NY: Hastings.

L'Engle, Madeleine. 1976. *A Wrinkle In Time / Arruga en el Tiempo*. New York: Dell.

Levitin, Sonia. 1987. *Journey to America*. Illus. Charles Robinson. New York: Macmillan.

Lewis, C. S. 1988a. *The Lion, the Witch, and the Wardrobe*. Illus. Pauline Baynes. New York: Macmillan.

———. 1988b. *El Leion, la Bruja Y el Armario*. New York: Santilla.

Mathers, Petra. 1992. *Maria Theresa*. Illus. by author. New York: HarperCollins.

Miller, Marilyn. 1984. *The Bridge at Selma*. Illustrated. Morristown, NJ: Silver Burdett Press.

Monjo, F. N. 1983. *The Drinking Gourd*. Illus. Fred Brenner. New York: HarperCollins.

Peet, Bill. 1982. *Big Bad Bruce*. Illus. by author. Boston: Houghton Mifflin.

Pinkwater, Manus. 1992. *Wingman*. New York: Bantam.

Reiss, Johanna. 1987. *The Journey Back*. New York: HarperCollins.

———. 1990. *The Upstairs Room / Habitaciones de Arriba*. New York: HarperCollins.

Schloredt, Valerie. 1990. *Martin Luther King, Jr.* Ridgefield, CT: Morehouse Publishing.

Taylor, Mildred D. 1991. *Roll of Thunder, Hear My Cry*. New York: Puffin.

———. 1992. *Mississippi Bridge*. New York: Bantam.

Tusquests, Ester. 1980. *Conejita Marcela*.

Uchida, Yoshiko. 1985. *Journey to Topaz*. Illus. Donald Carrick. Berkeley, CA: Creative Arts Books.

———. [1978] 1992. *Journey Home*. Illus. Charles Robinson. New York: Macmillan.

29. THEME TOPIC: WHO IS A HERO?

Possible Generalizations:

- There are positive as well as negative aspects to being a hero.
- Anyone can be a hero.

Possible Concepts:

hero, positive aspects, negative aspects

Possible Materials:

Adler, David A. 1989. *Picture Book of Martin Luther King Jr. / Un Libro Ilustrado Sobre Martin Luther King, Hijo.* Illus. Robert Casilla. New York: Holiday.

———. 1990. *Jackie Robinson, He Was the First.* Illus. Robert Casilla. New York: Holiday.

Bauer, Marion. 1987. *On My Honor / Te Lo Prometo.* New York: Dell.

Behrens, June. 1984. *Sally Ride, Astronaut: An American First.* Illustrated. Chicago: Childrens Press.

Blegvad, Lenore. *Ana Banana y Yo.*

Blos, Juan. 1990. *Old Henry.* New York: Morrow.

Burch, Robert. 1990. *Ida Early Comes Over the Mountain.* New York: Puffin.

Clement, Claude. 1990. *Painter and the Wild Swans.* New York: Dial.

Coerr, Eleanor. 1979. *Sadako and the Thousand Paper Cranes.* Illus. Ronald Himler. New York: Dell.

Cooney, Barbara. 1985. *Miss Rumphius.* Illustrated. New York: Puffin.

de Paola, Tomie. *Oliver Button Is a Hero / Oliver Button es un Heróe.*

Fern, Eugene. [1960] 1991. *Pepito's Story.* Illus. by author. New York: Yarrow Press.

Ferris, Jeri. 1989. *Go Free or Die: A Story about Harriet Tubman.* Illus. Karen Ritz. Minneapolis: Lerner Publications.

Gantschev, Ivan. *Tren de Navidad.*

Gardiner, John R. 1983. *Stone Fox.* Illus. Marcia Sewall. New York: HarperCollins.

Greene, Graham. *Pequeña Apisonadora.*

Hill, Kirkpatrick. 1990. *Toughboy and Sister.* New York: Macmillan.

Hoffman, Mary. 1991. *Amazing Grace.* New York: Dial.

Leaf, Munro. 1988. *El Cuento de Ferdinando: The Story of Ferdinand.* Trans. Pura Belpre. Illus. Robert Lawson. New York: Puffin.

Lobato, Arcadio. *Valle de la Niebla.*

Locker, Thomas. 1989. *The Young Artist.* Illustrated. New York: Dial.

Miller, Marilyn. 1984. *The Bridge at Selma.* Illustrated. Morristown, NJ: Silver Burdett Press.

Paulsen, Gary. 1988. *Hatchet / El Hacha.* New York: Puffin.

Rappaport, Doreen. 1991. *Living Dangerously: American Women Who Risked Their Lives for Adventure.* Illustrated. New York: HarperCollins.

Roberts, Naurice. 1986. *Cesar Chavez and La Causa.* Illustrated. Chicago: Childrens Press.

———. 1990. *Barbara Jordan: The Great Lady From Texas.* Chicago: Childrens Press.

Ruckman, Ivy. 1986. *Night of the Twisters.* New York: HarperCollins.

Saller, Carol. 1991. *The Bridge Dancers.* Illus. Gerald Talifero. Minneapolis: Carolrhoda Books.

Schlank, Carol H., and Metzger, Barbara. 1990. *Martin Luther King Jr., A Biography For Young Children.* Mt. Rainier, MD: Gryphon House.

Steig, William. 1988. *Brave Irene / Irene, la Valiente.* New York: Farrar, Straus & Giroux.

Taylor, Theodore. 1989. *Trouble With Tuck.* New York: Doubleday.

Vendrell, Carme Solé. *Luna de Juan.*

Vicarte and Chavarria. *Mujeres en la Independencia.*

Wetterer, Margaret K. 1990. *Kate Shelley and the Midnight Express.* Minneapolis: Carolrhoda Books.

Yarbrough, Camille. 1990. *The Shimmershine Queens.* New York: Knopf.

Zak, Monica. *Salven Mi Selva.*

References

Anthony, R. J., T. D. Johnson, N. I. Mickelson, and A. Preece. 1991. *Evaluating Literacy: A Perspective for Change*. Portsmouth, NH: Heinemann.

Armstrong, J. 1992. *Steal Away*. New York: Orchard.

Asimov, I. 1986. *Como Descubrimos los Dinosaurios*. Barcelona, España: Editorial Molino.

Atwell, N. 1987. *In the Middle: Writing, Reading, and Learning with Adolescents*. Portsmouth, NH: Heinemann-Boynton/Cook.

———, ed. 1990. *Coming to Know*. Portsmouth, NH: Heinemann.

Austin, R. G. 1984. *Brontosaurus Moves In*. New York: Archway.

Ballard, L. 1982. *Reptiles*. Chicago, IL: Childrens Press.

Banks, J. A. 1991. *Teaching Strategies for Ethnic Studies*. Boston, MA: Allyn & Bacon.

———. 1994. *An Introduction to Multicultural Education*. Boston, MA: Allyn & Bacon.

Berghoff, B. and K. Egawa. 1991. No more "rocks": Grouping to give students control of their learning. *The Reading Teacher* 44:536–41.

Bevans, M. H. 1956. *The Book of Reptiles and Amphibians*. Garden City, NY: Doubleday.

California Bilingual Education Department. 1986. *Beyond Language: Social and Cultural Factors in Schooling Language Minority Students*. Sacramento, CA: Evaluation, Dissemination and Assessment Center.

Calkins, L. M. 1986. *The Art of Teaching Writing*. Portsmouth, NH: Heinemann.

Carlson, N. 1990. *Arnie and the New Kid*. New York: Puffin.

Carrick, C. 1983. *Patrick's Dinosaurs*. New York: Houghton Miffiin.

Chetin, H. 1992. *Angel Island Prisoner, 1922*. Berkeley, CA: New Seed Press.

Claret, M. 1986. *Los Tres Osos*. Barcelona, España: Editorial Juventud.

Clements, A. 1988. *Big Al*. Illus. Yoshi. New York: Scholastic.

Corrigan, K. 1987. *Emily Umily,* Toronto: Annick.

Dagostino, L., and J. Carifio. 1994. *Evaluative Reading and Literacy: A Cognitive View*. Boston, MA: Allyn & Bacon

de Paola, T. 1978. *The Popcorn Book*. New York: Holiday.

———. 1979. *Oliver Button Is a Sissy*. San Diego, CA: Harcourt Brace.

———. 1982. *Oliver Button es una Nena*. Madrid, España: Susaeta.

Dewey, J. 1916. *Democracy and Education*. New York: Macmillan.

———. 1929. *My Pedagogic Creed*. Washington, DC: The Progressive Education Association.

———. 1938. *Experience and Education*. New York: Collier.

Edelsky, C., and K. Smith. 1984. Is that writing—or are those marks just a figment of your curriculum? *Language Arts* 61:24–32.

EdiNorma, Carvajal. n.d. *Juanito y las Habas.* Bogota, Colombia: Carvajal EdiNorma.

Eisner, E. 1982. *Cognition and Curriculum.* New York: Longman.

Estes, E. 1971. *The Hundred Dresses.* New York: Harcourt Brace.

Faltis, C. J. 1993. *Jointfostering.* New York: Macmillan.

Ferdman, B. 1990. Literacy and cultural identity. *Harvard Educational Review* 60:181–204.

Ferris, J. 1988. *Go Free or Die.* Minneapolis, MN: Carolrhoda.

Freeman, Y. S., and D. E. Freeman. 1992. *Whole Language for Second Language Learners.* Portsmouth, NH: Heinemann.

Freeman, D. E. and Y. S. Freeman. 1994. *Between Worlds: Access to Second Language Acquisition.* Portsmouth, NH: Heinemann.

Friedman, I. 1984. *How My Parents Learned to Eat.* Boston, MA: Houghton Miffiin.

Gee, J. 1990. *Social Linguistics and Literacies: Ideology and Discourses.* London: Falmer Press.

Gibbs, J. 1987. *Tribes: A Process for Social Development and Cooperative Learning.* Santa Rosa, CA: Center Source Publications.

———. 1994. *Tribes: A New Way of Learning Together.* Santa Rosa, CA: Center Source Publications.

Glazer, S. M., and C. S. Brown. 1993. *Portfolios and Beyond: Collaborative Assessment in Reading and Writing.* Norwood, MA: Christopher-Gordon.

Goodman, K. 1985. A linguistic study of cues and miscues. In *Theoretical Models and Processes of Reading,* ed. H. Singer and R. Ruddell. Newark, DE: International Reading Association.

Goodman, Y. 1989. Evaluation of students. In *The Whole Language Evaluation Book,* ed. K. A. Goodman, Y. M. Goodman, and W. J. Hood. Portsmouth, NH: Heinemann.

Goodman, K., Y. Goodman, and B. Flores. 1979. *Reading in the Bilingual Classroom: Literacy and Biliteracy.* Rosslyn, VA: National Clearinghouse for Bilingual Education.

Graves, D. 1983. *Writing: Teachers and Children at Work.* Portsmouth, NH: Heinemann.

Gumperz, J. 1982a. *Discourse Strategies.* Cambridge, England: Cambridge University Press.

———. 1982b. *Language and Social Identity.* Cambridge, England: Cambridge University Press.

Halliday, M. A. K. 1973. *Explorations in the Functions of Language.* London: Edward Arnold.

———. 1975. *Learning How to Mean.* London: Edward Arnold.

Hansen, J. F. 1979. *Sociocultural Perspective on Human Learning.* Prospect Heights, IL: Prentice-Hall.

Harste, J. 1993. Inquiry-based instruction. *Primary Voices K-6.* Premiere Issue, 2-5.

Harste, J., K. Short, and C. Burke. 1988. *Creating Classrooms for Authors.* Portsmouth, NH: Heinemann.

Harste, J., V. Woodward, and C. Burke. 1984. *Language Stories and Literacy Lessons.* Portsmouth, NH: Heinemann.

Hazen, B. 1983. *Tight Times.* New York: Puffin.

Heath, S. B. 1983. *Ways with Words.* Cambridge, England: Cambridge University Press.

Herman, J. L., P. R. Aschbacher, and L. Winters. 1992. *A Practical Guide to Alternative Assessment*. Alexandria, VA: Association for Supervision and Curriculum Development.

History-Social Science Curriculum Framework and Criteria Committee. 1987. *History-Social Science Framework*. Sacramento, CA: California State Department of Education.

Hoffman, J. 1992. Critical reading/thinking across the curriculum: Using I-charts to support learning. *Language Arts* 69:121–27.

Hoffman, M. 1991. *Amazing Grace*. New York: Dial.

Huntington, H. E. 1973. *Let's Look at Reptiles*. Garden City, NY: Doubleday.

Johnson, D. M. 1994. Grouping strategies for second language learners. In *Educating Second Language Children*, ed. F. Genesee. Cambridge, England: Cambridge University Press.

Joyce, W. 1988. *Dinosaur Bob*. New York: Harper & Row.

Kagan, S. 1986. Cooperative learning and sociocultural factors in schooling. In *Beyond Language: Social and Cultural Factors in Schooling Language Minority Students*, ed. California State Department of Education, 231–98. Los Angeles, CA: Evaluation, Dissemination and Assessment Center, California State University, Los Angeles.

———. 1992. *Cooperative Learning*. San Juan Capistrano, CA: Resources for Teachers.

Komaiko, L. 1988. *Earl's Too Cool for Me*. New York: Harper Trophy.

Krashen, S. D. 1981. Bilingual education and second language acquisition theory. In *Schooling and Language Minority Students: A Theoretical Framework*, ed. California State Department of Education, 51–79. Los Angeles, CA: Evaluation, Dissemination and Assessment Center, California State University, Los Angeles.

———. 1982. *Principles and Practice in Second Language Acquisition*. New York: Pargamon.

Kraus, R. 1945. *The Carrot Seed / Le Semilla de Zanahoria*. New York: Scholastic.

Kroll, S. 1976. *The Tyrannosaurus Game*. New York: Holiday House.

Kucer, S. B. 1991. Authenticity as the basis for instruction. *Language Arts* 68:532–40.

———. 1994. Real world literacy events for real world kids. *The California Reader* 27:3–10.

———. 1995. Guiding bilingual students "through" the literacy processes. *Language Arts* 72:20–29.

Leaf, M. 1977 *Ferdinand the Bull / Ferdinando el Toro*. New York: Puffin.

Levine, E. 1989. *I Hate English*. New York: Scholastic.

Macdonald Educational. 1977. *The Life of Plants*. London: Macdonald Educational.

McGinley, P. 1966. What is time? In *Wonderful Time*, ed P. McGinley. Philadelphia, PA: Lippencott.

McGovern, A. 1965. *Wanted Dead or Alive*. New York: Scholastic.

McKeon, D. 1994. Language culture, and schooling. In *Educating Second Language Children*, ed. F. Genesee. Cambridge, England: Cambridge University Press.

Martin, B. 1970. *Brown Bear, Brown Bear, What Do You See?* New York: Holt.

Mayer, M. 1968. *There's a Nightmare in My Closet / Hay una Pesadilla en Mi Armario*. New York: Dial.

———. 1976. *Ah-Choo*. New York: Dial.

———. 1988. *There's Something in My Attic*. New York: Dial.

Murphy, S. 1994. Writing portfolios in K–12 schools: Implications for linguistically diverse students. In *New Directions in Portfolio Assessment*, ed. D. Daiker, L. Black, J. Sommers, and G. Segall. Portsmouth, NH: Heinemann-Boyton Cook.

National Geographic Society. 1983. *What Is a Seed?* Washington, DC: National Geographic Society.
Nussbaum, H. 1977. *Plants Do Amazing Things*. New York: Random House.

Ogle, D. M. 1986. K-W-L: A teaching model that develops active reading of expository text. *The Reading Teacher* 39:564–70.
Oropeda, A. 1986. *Wilfredo: The Story of a Boy from El Salvador*. Los Angeles, CA: Teachers' Committee on Central America.

Paley, V. 1986. On listening to what the children say. *Harvard Educational Review* 56:122–31.
Pardo, L. S. and T. E. Raphael. 1991. Classroom organization for instruction in content areas. *The Reading Teacher* 44:556–65.
Paulson, T. 1992. *Jack and the Beanstalk*. New York: Carol.

Quinlan, P. 1987. *My Dad Takes Care of Me*. Toronto: Annick.

Rhodes, L. 1983. Organizing the elementary classroom for effective language learning. In *Teaching Reading with the Other Language Arts,* ed. U. Hardt. Newark, DE: International Reading Association.
Rhodes, L., and C. Dudley-Marling. 1988. *Readers and Writers with a Difference: A Wholistic Approach to Teaching Learning Disabled and Remedial Students*. Portsmouth, NH: Heinemann.
Rico, L. 1975. *Angelita, la Ballena Pequeñita*. Madrid, España: Susaeta.
Rigg, P., and V. Allen. 1989. *When They Don't All Speak English*. Urbana, IL: National Council of Teachers of English.
Rosenblatt, L. 1978. *The Reader, the Text, the Poem*. Carbondale, IL: Southern Illinois University Press.
Rumelhart, D. 1985. Toward an interactive model of reading. In *Theoretical Models and Processes of Reading,* ed. H. Singer and R. Ruddell. Newark, DE: International Reading Association.

Sabin, L. 1985. *Reptiles and Amphibians*. Mahwah, NJ: Troll.
Sholinsky, J. 1974. *Growing Plants from Fruits and Vegetables*. New York: Scholastic.
Short, K. G. and C. Burke. 1991. *Creating Curriculum*. Portsmouth, NH: Heinemann.
Short, K. G., and K. Pierce. 1990. *Talking About Books*. Portsmouth, NH: Heinemann.
Silva, C., and E. L. Delgado-Larocco. 1993. Facilitating learning through interconnections: A concept approach to core literature units. *Language Arts* 70:469–74.
Simon, S. B., L. W. Howe, and H. Kirschenbaum. 1972. *Values Clarification*. New York: Hart.
Smith, F. 1975. *Comprehension and Learning*. New York: Holt Rinehart & Winston.
———. 1977. The uses of language. *Language Arts* 54:638–44.
———. 1981. Demonstrations, engagement, and sensitivity: A revised approach to language learning. *Language Arts* 60:103–12.

————. 1988. *Understanding Reading*. Hillsdale, NJ: Lawrence Erlbaum.
Snow, M. A., M. Met, and F. Genesee. 1992. A conceptual framework for the integration of language and content instruction. In *The Multicultural Classroom*, ed. P. A. Richard-Amato and M. A. Snow. White Plains, NY: Longman.
Stanek, M. 1989. *I Speak English for My Mom*. Niles, IL: Albert Whitman.
Sterling, D. 1954. *Freedom Train*. New York: Scholastic.
Stevenson, J. 1983. *What's Under My Bed?* New York: Viking Penguin.
Suhor, C. 1984. Towards a semiotics-based curriculum. *Curriculum Studies* 16:247–57.
Surat, M. 1983. *Angel Child, Dragon Child*. New York: Scholastic.

Taba, H., M. C. Durkin, J. R. Fraenkel, and A. H. McNaughton. 1971. *A Teacher's Handbook to Elementary Social Studies*. Reading, MA: Addison-Wesley.
Tabors, P. O., and C. E. Snow. 1994. English as a second language in preschool programs. In *Educating Second Language Children*, ed. F. Genesee. Cambridge, England: Cambridge University Press.
Taylor, M. 1987. *The Gold Cadillac*. New York: Dial.
Tester, S. 1979. *Sometimes I'm Afraid*. Illus. Frances Hook. Mankato, MN: Childs World.
Thomas, Marlo, vocalist. 1972. *Free to Be You and Me*. New York: Arista Records.
Tolstoy, A. 1971. *The Great Big Enormous Turnip*. Glenview, IL: Scott Foresman.
Tompert, A. 1988. *Will You Come Back for Me?* Niles, IL: Whitman.
Turín, A., and N. Bosnia 1976. *Rosa Caramelo*. Barcelona, España: Editorial Lumen.
Tusa, T. 1984. *Libby's New Glasses*. New York: Holiday House.

Uribe, M. de la L., and F. Krahn. 1982. *El Cururía*. Venezuela: Ediciones Ekare-Banco del Libro.

Vygotsky, L. 1978. *Mind in Society*. Cambridge, MA: Harvard University Press.
————. 1986. *Thought and Language*. Cambridge, MA: MIT Press.

Waber, B. 1972. *Ira Sleeps Over*. New York: Scholastic.
Webber, I. 1944. *Travelers All*. New York: Scott.
Wertsch, J., ed. 1985. *Culture, Communication, and Cognition*. Cambridge, England: Cambridge University Press.
Wilder, L. I. 1953. *Little House on the Prairie*. New York: Harper.

Yashima, T. 1983. *Crow Boy*. New York: Puffin.
Yee, S., and L. Kokin. 1977. *Got Me a Story to Tell*. San Francisco, CA: St. John's Educational Threshold Center.

Zolotow, C. 1972. *William's Doll*. New York: Harper & Row.

Other books from Stenhouse that you will enjoy…

Literature Circles
Voice and Choice in the Student-Centered Classroom

Harvey Daniels

Drawing on stories from twenty-two classroom teachers who work with students from kindergarten through college, this unique model of literature circles delivers ample guidance and inspiration for teachers who want to implement literature circles for themselves. Daniels and his colleagues pay particular attention to the issues of management, preparation of students, and enacting the principles of group dynamics. Reproducible role sheets in English and Spanish are included.

1-57110-000-8   Paperback

If This Is Social Studies, Why Isn't It Boring?

Edited by Stephanie Steffey and Wendy J. Hood

Many books have been published about whole language, but few have dealt with the holistic teaching of social studies. In this contributed collection, twenty-three teachers explain their successful strategies for teaching the social studies disciplines in a whole language context. Teachers at elementary through middle school will find the holistic approach a refreshing departure and a source of new and practical ideas. The diversity of ideas and styles is as broad as the subject area!

1-57110-003-2   Paperback

Exploring the Multiage Classroom

Anne A. Bingham

Foreword by Charles Rathbone

If you are planning to move into multiage or have already made that transition from a conventional classroom, you will welcome the honest, practical advice that makes *Exploring the Multiage Classroom* a genuine handbook—comprehensive, realistic, and accessible. You will see what teachers find rewarding in multiage teaching and why it works so well for children who can learn from the models provided by the literacy and learning of other children around them.

1-57110-013-X   Paperback

Literature Study Circles in a Multicultural Classroom

Katharine Davies Samway and Gail Whang

This book is an in-depth look at one teacher's implementation of literature study circles in an inner-city, low-income school whose students are often non-native English speakers. Students select the books they will read and then meet with the teacher in small groups to discuss their book. Gail Whang's approach not only engaged and involved the students, but helped them develop their abilities to think and talk intelligently about issues and events in their lives.

1-57110-018-0   Paperback

A Room with a Different View

First Through Third Graders Build Community and Create Curriculum

Jill Ostrow

In *A Room with a Different View*, Jill Ostrow reveals how her class of six- to nine-year-old children physically transformed their classroom, created a community, and completed projects that grew out of the Island and involved everyone in real-world problem-solving. Jill presents a new and different approach to curriculum and a philosophy you may want to apply with your own students. Although this classroom will introduce you to some unusual features, it is still one in which traditional school subjects—math, writing, reading, art, and science—are thoroughly integrated in projects that center on the Island.

1-57110-009-1   Paperback

For information on all Stenhouse publications please write or call for a catalogue.

Stenhouse Publishers
P. O. Box 360
York, ME 03909
1-800-988-9812